SERIES

The Virtuosity Of Eddie Durham

VOLUME ONE

Topsy M. Durham

George T. Wein - Foreword

Albert Vollmer & Dan Weinstein - Editors

Charles B. Frazier - Cover Art, Illustrations/Logos

Swingin' The Blues! Durham Publishing

Self-Published

Electronic version: Latest update *August 28, 2021*

Copyright USA card#'s: Feb. 2018 *TXu2-085-336*

Aug. 2020 *VAu1-406-416*

ALL RIGHTS RESERVED

Music Licensing: A.S.C.A.P. - BMG-Gold

DURHAMJAZZ.com

Dedicated to All
Family, Friends & Mentors,

with Special Thanks to :

Michael "MURCH" Powers

The City of San Marcos, Texas:
"Eddie Durham Day" August 19th
The Eddie Durham Park & Pavilion

Johnnie Armstead's Calaboose African American Museum:
permanent ***Eddie Durham Exhibit***

Paul Ash - *Sam Ash Music Stores:*
Eddie Durham Commemorative Centennial Guitars

Barbara A. Jones, President
The Harlem Swing Dance Society

FOREWORD

"**EDDIE DURHAM**, born in San Marcos, Texas in the early 1900s, was a pioneer in the early transition to the swing beat that emerged in Kansas City. As a composer and arranger in addition to playing slide & valve trombone and acoustic & electric guitar, he covered the entire spectrum of this rhythmic development. His input into the amplification of the guitar added a new dimension to this instrument. He wrote "Swingin on C", "Harlem Shout", "Blues In The Groove" and made other arrangements for *Jimmie Lunceford* and his presence in that trombone section added much to the precision of that powerful Orchestra. Also, his work with the *Bennie Moten* and emerging *Count Basie* Orchestras put his definitive stamp on those swinging aggregations. He wrote "Wham! Rebop Boom Bam", "Swinging the Blues", "Topsy", "Time Out", "Out The Window", "Every Tub", "Magic Carpet", "John's Idea" and also had an involvement with the famous hits "Moten Swing", "One O'Clock Jump" and "Jumpin At The Woodside." His arrangements for *Glenn Miller* achieved great fame for this popular band leader, especially his arrangement on "In The Mood" and his participation on trombone on his composition "Slip Horn Jive." His composition "I Don't Want To Set The World On Fire" was popularized by *The Ink Spots.* In his senior years he performed my *Newport Jazz Festival* in Rhode Island with *The Harlem Blues & Jazz Band,* and at my *New Orleans Jazz & Heritage Festival.* In all, a monumental and innovative contributor to the world of Jazz."

George T. Wein,

Pianist, Producer, Impresario. NEA Jazz Master,
Lifetime Honorary Trustee of Carnegie Hall
Creator and Founder of the Newport Jazz, Newport Folk,
New Orleans Jazz & Heritage and Playboy Jazz Festivals
White House Honoree (1978 and 1993).

Table of Contents

My goal in the creation of this book about my dad Eddie Durham is to chronologically document articles, posters, quotes, etc., and intersperse them with conversations and my interviews of family, peers, colleagues, and scholars. This is to resolve the lack of any comprehensive writing on our musical Durham family. When all volumes are completed, a *Durhamipedia* will result. I hope you are enlightened by my labor of love.

Topsy M. Durham

Eddie's Statement

The following is a transcript of an interview by NBC news reporter Carole Jenkins:

Carole Jenkins: "Well the Greenwich Village Jazz Festival is in full swing and slated to play is Eddie Durham, one of the greatest and least known giants of the Swing Era. A composer, arranger and father of the electric guitar, Durham created many of the hits of the big band era and this past week he was honored on his 80th Birthday. For Count Basie he composed [& arranged] "One O'Clock Jump," "Swinging the Blues," "Jumping At The Woodside" and many other Jazz standards. For Glenn Miller he wrote the classic arrangement of "In The Mood" that has become the anthem of the Swing Era, and he created other hits for Benny Goodman, Artie Shaw and Jimmie Lunceford. He is Eddie Durham and the other night over 200 friends and fans gathered at St. Peters Church. The occasion …a musical tribute on Durham's 80th birthday."[1]

Watch the Interveiw   *www.youtube.com/watch?v=oBx373pLD60*
See Eddie at his Party   *www.youtube.com/watch?v=9A3UsDU0wLQ*

Eddie Durham: *"I feel very happy about it because I love to see the musicians play this kind of music. It's real sensible ya know, you can understand it."*

Carole Jenkins: "A Big-Band played Durham's music and musicians sang his praise…" (*NBC News* August 1986).

Titled, Written, Arranged, Composed, by ©**Topsy M. Durham** *Sketches & Book cover design* ©**Charles Frazier**

western union

Telegram

BJA095(1621)(1-0143701230)PD 08/18/86 1617
TWX ASCAP NYK DLY PD
0453 DLY NYK NYK 8/18/86
PMS EDDIE DURHAM
1911 DORCHESTER ROAD
APT. 5-H
BROOKLYN, NY 11226

ON BEHALF OF ALL YOUR ASCAP COLLEAGUES, I SEND BEST WISHES AND
HEARTY CONGRATULATIONS ON YOUR BIRTHDAY CELEBRATION. YOUR
CONTRIBUTIONS IN THE FIELD OF JAZZ ARE A CONTINUING SOURCE OF
PRIDE TO US ALL.

MORTON GOULD
PRESIDENT, ASCAP

SF-1201 (NY) (A-6/82)

ZCZC TRB3007 RM09862 QAL3005 DDY258000 G234097
ZXNY CO URSS 052
NEWYORKNY 52/50 02 1631

MR. EDDIE DURHAM
C/O MR. H. PARKS
519 WEST 158TH ST.
NEW YORK, N.Y.10032

DEAR EDDIE,

HAPPY BELATED 80TH BIRTHDAY AND ALSO FOR YOUR CONTRIBUTION OF
YOUR GREAT MUSICAL GIFTS AND TALENT TO THE WORLD OF MUSIC.

BEST REGARDS,
GEORGE AND JOYCE WEIN, MARIE ST.LOUIS AND EVERYONE AT
FESTIVAL PRODUCTIONS

CONFIRMATION
OF TELEPHONE MESSAGE VIA RCA
TO ED BY SB DATE 9-2 TIME 2105
☑ MAIL
☐ MESSENGER CHARGE $6.00
AUTHORIZED BY.............................
TO REPLY PLEASE CALL
NEW YORK 212 806-5000
OUTSIDE NEW YORK STATE
CALL TOLL FREE 800-VIA-RCAG

2

Panegyric

"We are here tonight to honor the legacy of my dad, Eddie Durham. Scholars can tell you why he was a genius. I'm here to talk about why he is a hero. You might learn about, or maybe you know him to be an arranger, choreographer, composer, mentor, musician, performer and yes, also an innovator. You see, I've listened to the interviews of him and eventually, he is always asked the question: 'so Eddie, where were you in the 60's and 70's? You dropped out of sight'. This might sound unconventional for what is normally portrayed about musician parents, but you see, my dad was mostly home and we knew him as a loving, kind father, a carpenter, a mechanic, who happened to occasionally play guitar, trombone and piano.

We lived on Jefferson Avenue in Brooklyn. As children, Deborah, Eric, Marsha and a few years later Lesa and Terry, played on the plastic-slip covered couches which sat in front of the textured, red velvet wallpapered walls, where a picture of Luella, dad's mother hung. We climbed on his shoulders and rubbed Vaseline in his hair. As all parents seem to their children, he was such a giant to us. We did all the normal things families should do together. Some Friday nights he drove the family to Atlantic Avenue in Brooklyn for the best take out fried fish in Brooklyn. A few times we attended his local shows. We watched him set up and play and then we all rode home in the brown paneled station wagon, a style of car very popular at that time. Sometimes we would go to a formal dance as a family. One time my little brother, who was about three years old at the time, danced in his fancy light blue suit and he came home with a pocket full of coins people gave him.

In the summertime we went on road trips to places like *Pinegrove Dude Ranch*, went on midnight hay rides and learned how to ride horses. I suppose dad was remembering Texas then. Each year we spent a week or two, at a rustic cottage in the woods - where the McHarris family with their five children would always join us. We rode in the back of that station wagon with the seats folded down, trying to scare each other with stories as we watched the trail of pitch-black night sky and the multiplying stars rolling by. Mom always had plenty of snacks on hand. When we arrived, the first order was to marvel at all of the stars in the sky, which we could barely see in Brooklyn.

Dad repeatedly relayed stories of his school days in Terrell, Texas, with Principal Professor Burnett, who, he said, could play "Poet and Peasant" on his horn, while doing math on the blackboard and how much fun the bands at school were, where he was always the youngest in the bands. He told us of his dad, Jose, and exactly how he made his own fiddle for the square dances, where he and his brothers would go along as a family. San Marcos can be proud that although my dad left Texas most likely as a pre-teen, he did take his San Marcos indoctrinated family and community values with him around the world. It seems that his brothers and cousins' addictions to alcohol prevented Eddie from indulging such, at least by the time he fathered us. Alcohol did claim the lives of his father, at least two of his brothers and two of his cousins.

Family was never secondary. Although his music buddies were his family, once he fathered children, he kept his work local and dedicated two decades to raising his five children.

My brother, Eric, led a few pre-teen bands. My mother, Lillian, was their manager and her uncle owned a club where he allowed them to perform. Dad would drive them to their gigs.

When asked by NBC's Carol Jenkins …, *"How would you like to be remembered?*," my dad replied *"as a person who gathered together music that needed to be arranged and organized."*

He would be proud to stand before this gathering tonight knowing his legacy will help rebuild his hometown (Dunbar) neighborhood and bring people from around the world to get to know San Marcos' culture and the place where the gentle giant, was born.

*I'm **TOPSY DURHAM**. Thank you for attending this weekend event."*
(My Speech: **2nd *Eddie Durham Music & Heritage Festival***, San Marcos, Texas, 78666).

GitWhatchaGotGood

Some of Eddie Durham's sayings were:

"New York is going to become a place for the rich and the homeless."

"To make a long story short..." then, ten minutes later... *"So, I say'd that to say this..."*

"To be a genius you have to leave the paper [sheet music]. *"*

"Too Many Chiefs - Not Enough Braves."

"A roach will walk a mile for a crumb."

"If he ends on that note, I've gotta come in on this note."

"I hope you live at least half the life I lived."

Eddie's showman sneeze to us his children *"WhoIshShee."*

"Everything runs from a bullet!"

"Next year I'll be 79, I'll be a baby before I die."

"I left you millions, but you're gonna have to dig for it".

"Git Whatcha Got Good."

Accolades

"I find him very interesting that he didn't speak English until he started traveling with bands, he only spoke Spanish. Musicians taught him to speak English. Those sorts of things are very fascinating in American history. Our children should be taught about 20th-century American heroes, how we all should appreciate them. It's ok to teach them Columbus discovered America. They already know that the Indians were here first, so how you gonna discover anything. So, in the next century, we have to start getting our own heroes and Eddie Durham is certainly one, because he accomplished so much, despite all of these obstacles you will surely talk about. When we really start checking out his accomplishments we see it was diversified. In fact, if you try to look at it on paper, you'd say *nah, nah, nah - one person couldn't have done all of that*. And he could tell you the principle behind all of that. He'd explain it to you so simply that you'd say, why didn't I think of that. But that was just his gift to make it sound simple." ***Benny Powell****,* American Jazz tenor/bass trombonist, Bandleader (1930-2010).

"It is so exciting to learn about the great Eddie Durham as a true jazz pioneer and innovator. I realized that I've been listening to his arrangements for years through top bands including Bennie Moten, Jimmie Lunceford, Count Basie, Benny Goodman – but it's so important to discover that Durham's arranging helped create the exciting sound and swing of these bands. His electric guitar playing style was ahead of its time. Creating his "All-Star Girl Orchestra" in the 1940s gave women a unique opportunity to be featured on instruments that were considered 'non-traditional', and to be taken seriously. This helped to lay the foundation for girls and women to pursue their musical dreams, and continue to break down barriers as jazz instrumentalists and bandleaders to this day. Thank you, Eddie Durham for your wonderful addition to our rich cultural history. *Catherine Russell*, Educator, vocalist, multi-instrumentalist (toured with Steely Dan, David Bowie and Wynton Marsalis). *Grammy* award winner. Appears in the film *Bolden*[2]. Daughter of pianist/composer Luis Russell and Carline Ray (guitarist, International Sweethearts of Rhythm).

"As a gentleman, there are few who share the dignity of Eddie. As an innovative force, there are very few who could even think of challenging him for importance on 20th-century music. The granddaddy of the electric guitar and the writing backbone of the southwestern swinging tradition we know best through the Count Basie Orchestra is involved with an individual who is perhaps the humblest genius we have ever encountered." *Phil Schaap*, Grammy Jazz Historian, Editor-*Jazz at Lincoln Center*, Professor-*Swing University*, Archivist, Curator, Engineer, Producer, co-Author with Paul Devlin and Albert Murray, et al.: *Rifftide-The Life and Opinions of Papa Jo Jones*.

"Eddie Durham did more to influence the big band era than anyone alive. He left room for unparalleled soloists in the Basie band to expand and heretofore, these things were not heard of in other big bands. Eddie freed up the drums through Papa Jo Jones and this was a precursor to contemporary drumming." *Max Roach*, Drummer (1924-2007).

The Beatles drummer **Ringo Starr** stated that he "*was never really into drummers,*" but identified Cozy Cole's 1958 cover of "Topsy Part II" as "*the one drum record*" he bought."[3].

"He was one of the most intelligent, musically talented, funniest, and most soulful men I ever met. Most folks, especially from that era, had to be. So brilliant and yet, he never did get his just reward from the music industry. This project will create an atmosphere that demands coming to terms with who Eddie Durham was and come to a reality check. He was a great storyteller." *Loren Schoenberg*, Conductor, Tenor Saxophonist, Pianist, Grammy Jazz Historian and co-Author with Wynton Marsalis: *The NPR Curious Listener's Guide to Jazz*, Producer, Sr. Scholar-*National Jazz Museum in Harlem*, Archivist.

"In addition to Eddie Durham's myriad accomplishments and contributions to jazz and American culture, he also played a major role in the history of American female jazz musicians. When I was writing my book in the late 1970s, Eddie was incredibly generous with his knowledge, insights, and experience. During the 1930s and '40s, he was associated as a manager, coach, or arranger with *Ina Ray Hutton and her Melodears* and, later, the legendary *International Sweethearts of Rhythm*. He also organized *Eddie Durham's All-Star-Girl Orchestra*. I had the honor and privilege of interviewing a number of women who were part of these outfits. They were taught or coached by Eddie and were also on the road with him. Not only did he play a key role in their great musical success, but it is also significant to note that Eddie had the trust, respect, and admiration of every woman I spoke to. At a time when women who wanted to express themselves through the art of jazz faced daily prejudice and indignities from many of their male counterparts, Eddie Durham stood out as a pillar of support. Eddie, himself, was modest, unassuming, soft-spoken, wise, and brilliant. This book, which finally tells his unique and fascinating story, is a great cause for celebration! Kudos to Topsy Durham, for making it possible! *Sally Placksin,* Author: *American Women in Jazz: Their Words, Lives, and Music,* Writer/Producer, *Jazz Pioneer Eddie Durham (National Public Radio)*, Writer/Producer, *NPR's Jazz Profiles, ASCAP-Deems Taylor Award, Wilbur Award*, Appears in the film *Sweet & Lowdown*.[4]

"Sometimes I would drive Eddie home to Bushwick, Brooklyn after the shows. The little black children on the block always came running up to him and I naively thought, Wow! that's great, these kids know who Eddie is. But then Eddie burst my bubble and told me, *"I give them pennies."* He seemed to always be able to tell me what was going to happen next week." *Albert "Doc" Vollmer,* Manager, *The Harlem*

Blues & Jazz Band. Historian, contributing articles to *Just Jazz Magazine.* "Hot Steamed Jazz Festival's" Lifetime Achievement Award, New York City Council *Citation,* The Peekskill Mayor's Cross Cultural Connection, Inc.'s *Jazz Visionary Award,* The New Jersey Jazz Society's Award "*To Dr. Albert Vollmer for your life's work in honoring Jazz's Senior Citizenry through the **founding** of the Harlem Blues and Jazz Band.*"

"Eddie was director, arranger, manager and mentor for many all-women orchestras. They were prima-donnas, but he never lost his cool. There was the *International Sweethearts of Rhythm.* I was in *The Darlings of Rhythm,* a darker-skinned group with excellent musicians, but we didn't get the same recognition and publicity. Eddie was the thread through all of that, he knew all the girls and he would write and arrange for them. In fact, *The Harlem Playgirls* members came into *The Eddie Durham All-Stars.* In 1950 I recorded "My Whole Life Through" which he co-wrote. He helped dozens of female musicians become members of Musician's Unions." ***Sarah McLawler,*** B3 organ pioneer, pipe organist, bandleader, vocalist (1926-2017).

"My dad was the type of person who would see your weaknesses and your strengths and he would know how to utilize that to teach you things. He would show me shortcuts on how to remember keys for songs. My Dad was one of the first guitarists to give a note on the guitar some vibrato and to slide into a guitar note. Now, we take that for granted but back then, guitar players weren't doing that. I was playing straight up and down but he told me to "*develop your downstroke because you'll have more dynamic control over the notes with the downstroke.*" That helped strengthen my fingers. I remember being at *The West End Cafe* with him. I was touring full time with a cult, funk band who I recorded with as a guitarist and wrote several seminal hit songs on their first three albums. We opened nationally at stadiums for *Parliament-Funkadelic.* But no matter where I went, I always kept my guitar with me, even in New York where I lived because I'd drop in clubs to sit in. I dropped in on him at *The West End* once and my dad asked me to "*sit in with us on a blues song.*" I remember Shelton Gary was playing drums. I thought - I'm not getting up here with these great guys! But I'm glad I did - because that's still one of my fondest memories. When I think about him, he really comes to life!" ***Eric R. Durham, Sr.,*** Guitarist, arranger, bandleader, composer, producer.

"Eddie would breathe opposite the way you normally breathe, he would say, put it in the diaphragm and then you control it up on the lips and you can keep that pressure off your lips. This technique was later developed into *circular breathing*, but it was Eddie's invention. Eddie's charts were written to swing. "Swinging the Blues" was one of the main tunes that we had in Basie's book." *Grey, Al* , Trombonist (Benny Carter, Lucky Millinder, Clark Terry, Dizzy Gillespie, Count Basie), Bandleader (1925-2000).

Eddie Durham's charts opened the gateway for the lindy hop, jitterbug, and swing dance craze which almost a century later is still danced in vintage regalia in competitions globally. This dance outlasted every other dance in the United States, perhaps in history. *Barbara A. Jones,* Educator, Producer, Swing-dance historian, President, *The Harlem Swing Dance Society, Inc.*

"The Circus and black musicians traveling with the Wild West show - that was an education for me. Then the things I learned from his family, for instance, his never getting angry, cooking, encouraging people the way he did, without putting down the kind of music they played which wasn't his kind of music. To me, Eddie Durham is one of the great musicians of this century. I don't mean that lightly, I mean up there with Duke, Armstrong and Lester Young. Consider that he played two instruments, which is unusual, trombone, and various guitars. He wrote the music and composed and arranged. You know he's a multi-threat person; that's remarkable. But what's most important is that he was an originator. He had a genius for writing, composing, and arranging - there's no question about that. He's had quite a career and you can't just learn about it in a weekend. People like Eddie Durham forget more than we ever learn." *Douglas H. Daniels*, Professor, Author: *Lester Leaps In, The Unforgettable History of the Oklahoma City Blue Devils* and *Pioneer Urbanites.*

The Durham Brothers

By the time little Eddie Durham was seven, his two eldest brothers Joe Jr. and Earl were in their mid-teens, and before Eddie was born, they attended square dances in San Marcos with their father Joseph "Jose" Durham, Sr., the town fiddler, who built his own fiddle. This exposure was the foundation of the Durham family musical training. They all learned to play the fiddle and somehow Joe Jr. learned many other stringed and winded instruments, and taught his siblings. The early death of their father, Jose, forged Joe and Earl to the head of their household. Joe Jr. tutored his siblings in music and both he and Earl formed *The Durham Brothers Orchestra,* which Earl led. Fundamentally, this was their own home-grown music school with *at least* six pupils in attendance every day.

According to Eddie, his brother Joe Jr. occasionally volunteered serving as a *Musical Director* in the *Homecoming Band* for *Teddy Roosevelt's Roughriders*, in the *Cavalry Band.*

The Durham Brothers Orchestra (DBO) consisted of four (of the five) Durham brothers along with three cousins: **Joe Jr.** (tuba, trumpet, fiddle/violin, piano), **Earl** (tenor/baritone sax & clarinet), **Eddie** (banjo, guitar, valve & slide trombone), **Roosevelt** (fiddle/violin, piano, vocals); Three cousins: **Allen** (trombone) & **Clyde** (bass horn/tuba), and **Herschel Evans** (tenor/alto sax). Family friend **Edgar Battle** (trumpet) soon joined as well. [5] They otherwise performed and traveled together as *The Durham Brothers (Jazzy) Orchestra* and later as Edgar Battle's *Dixie Ramblers* from 1916-1929, with some exceptions. They performed in school, but during school breaks they backed up the traveling territory and national shows such as *Mitchell's Joy, J.Doug Morgan's Traveling Dramatic Show, The 101 Wild Ranch Circus' Negro Brass Band & Minstrel Show, The Mamie Smith 7-11 Show, Elmer Payne's 10 Royal Americans and* [drummer] *Eugene Coy and his 12 Black Aces.* This formative period is referred to as "Durham Brothers Orch." throughout the Appendix, which chronicles their respective known discographies. *(Appendix "A").*

Eddie recalled: "We always used an outside drummer but our family band performed local gigs, and at school as 'The Durham Brothers Orchestra'. We all got on the circuit with the Alabama Minstrels and the Georgia Minstrels, I was playing trombone, not guitar. Edgar Battle was with us. Harry White out of Detroit, was there. We played with "Mitchell's Joys."

Roosevelt is the only one younger than me, he's named for Teddy. Four brothers traveled with the J. Doug Morgan Dramatic Show. That was the biggest show out west at that time. It was a great dramatic show. A white fella named Neil Hellam played the dramatic stuff. They played in nothing but their own tents. I was about 12 years old, and I duck back to school for a while and come back out. Sam Price remembers all of that, he was there at that time. I met him when I was in school in Terrell, Texas. At the school in Terrell, I had a music/math teacher named Professor Burnett [William H. Burnett] He could play "Poet and Peasant" on his trumpet and do math on the blackboard, simultaneously. There were music and bands in all of the schools".6

Family History

<u>Berry Durham</u>

In the process of compiling information for this long-overdue reference book about my prodigious dad Eddie Durham, I uncovered some astonishing facts about our five generations of Berry Durham's. Although Chapter One only includes Eddie's grandfather, Berry III ("Nunce"), the endnotes unveil more detailed historical ancestry. The consistent military and governmental connections by the Durham's over the decades are atypical. It also may be too numerous to simply be a coincidence. Colonel John L. Durham who arrived in San Marcos in 1849 might be the key master.[7]

Berry Durham, III, nicknamed ***"Nunce,"*** was born in the United States circa 1850 in deep south Mississippi. He was not a slave, but to put his birth period into context, by Law, slavery was supposed to officially end on Juneteenth 1865. Since "Nunce" was very fair-skinned and easily passed as Caucasian, it's undeniable that one of his forefathers most likely descended from a slave owner with the surname "Durham." Hattie Davis was his Native American spouse.[8] *Nunce was a wrangler and a haggler, and you didn't mess with his family; a true Texan who would really hurt you with his Colt 41 gun!*[9] Marrying a Native American was common as it ensured freedom from slavery for your children, much like marriages today between Immigrants and Americans ensure citizenship for their children. Apparently, Nunce and Hattie lived in Mexico, then moved to Texas' Lampasas County,[10] and finally settled in New Braunfels, Comal County. They bore four children in Texas:[11] **Joseph [Sr.]** (author's grandfather), Will, Tom, and Eliza. (Booker T. Washington taught Eliza's daughter Claudia !).

Berry Durham, threats to kill--not guilty. San Marcos Free Press (Texas) - Thu, Mar 17, 1881 p3

Joseph Durham, Sr. a/k/a "Jose"

Eddie Durham's father (author's grandfather) was Joseph Durham, Sr., (b. circa 1872) *"but his Spanish name was Jose."* The family spoke Spanish. In 1893, Jose married Lou Ella "Rabb" (aka Luella; formerly "Fannin"), and they bore five children, including Eddie.

Lou Ella Rabb-Durham

Eddie's mother, Luella (b.Nov.1876 or 77, d.June 19, 1945), was African American and Mohawk Indian. Her Indian territory was near Lampasas, Texas. For a short time, she was a school teacher and, therefore, literate. Luella's father, Daniel Rabb, was an escaped slave from Louisiana who changed his surname from "Fannin" to Rabb (d.April 16, 1916). Her mother, Louise McMillan (d.January 29 circa 1892), raised Luella and her siblings in Gonzales and Waelder, Texas, on land that Daniel purchased and developed into a booming thriving syrup, cattle, and turkey business.[12]

Eddie recalled: "Mohawks are very dark Indians with rough, long hair. She was home raising the kids and farming too. Her parents are Daniel Rabb and Louise of Texas. They eventually settled in Newark, New Jersey."

According to "Glady's" letter to Eddie, Jr., the name 'Rabb' was taken after slavery - and the real surname was 'Fannin'.

Eddie recalled: "In those days, the population was between 1,000 and 2,000, and mostly farming and cattle. Most people spoke Spanish, and so did my family. In San Marcos, the Rio Grande flooded just before 1910 [April 15, 1910], and that's the only time they took a census. I have a copy of it because my eldest son, Eddie, Jr. [b.1928], did a family tree, and so many children born to "Rabb." My eldest brother gave me a few extra years because he thought it would help me not have to go off to war. My mother wasn't well enough to testify,, so they asked my brother. I had three brothers, Joe Jr. Earl, and Roosevelt, and one sister, Myrtle, who played piano. My hair was long [to the waist], and my mom kept it plaited."

Joseph's intention to have his younger brother Eddie showcase his talent rather than serve war actually worked out advantageously but in a serendipitous path. Eddie's reputation and career history by 1940 earned him the honorable placement as Musical Director for the Mary McLeod Bethune sponsored and subsidized *United Service Organizations ("USO")* tours with all-women orchestras. USO Tours provided entertainment to members of the Armed Forces and their families. His brother Joseph had already served as Musical Director for Teddy Roosevelt's Roughriders *Homecoming Band* and much later family friend Edgar Battle for Eisenhower's sponsored international USO Tour.

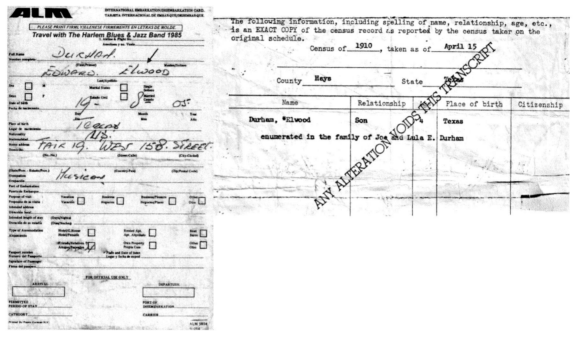

1. **Joseph Durham, Jr.** (circa 1894-d.1947)

2. **Earl Durham** (b.1898-d.circa 1968)

3. **Myrtle Durham** (b.1902-d.1952)

4. **Elwood "Eddie" Durham** (b.1906-d.3/6/1987)

5. **Roosevelt Durham** (b.circa 1907-d.1961).[13]

They are each born four years apart, except for Roosevelt. In between them, two children died in childbirth. But Eddie insists: he was *"born on August 19, 1909, Roosevelt was the youngest, and my dad Jose died quite young"*.[14]

Eddie recalled: "My father was a farmer, a bronco (broke wild horses), a jockey, a gambler, heavy drinker, and a terrific fiddler, and he wore a waxed mustache all the time. He was a sharecropper, planted what he wanted, handled all the money, and the owner would take his word.[15] Everybody in those days traveled on an honest basis, had pride in telling the truth, and tried to make as much profit. Weren't any rip-offs. How do you think we existed? We couldn't understand that you couldn't eat with 'em, couldn't sleep with 'em, but the only person they trusted to cook their food was a black person. They wouldn't have a white cook under no condition, and they wouldn't trust their kids with anybody but a black person. But I guess back in slavery time was different. It was pretty sick in this country. A lot of Jews changed their name to be a Manager in the South. So, we would move out of the territory, wouldn't be too close where they worked before. We moved to Terrell, Texas.

My father had a riding saddle, plus a special saddle he put on the horse to break it. He'd rope the horse, feet and all, so he can't move, throw the saddle on and let him loose and get on him. But if he needed money, he'd go to another ranch - he knew everybody. "So and so, you got a horse I can break this mornin?" It could take two days to catch the horse they wanted, but he'd lead him in and bring him in the corral and ride him. And I never saw him get throwed! He rode in some rodeos, not racing, but he was a jockey, with the trotters and the pacers, with a two-wheel carriage behind them. For a half hour, they'd ride horse after horse. Eighty guys standing in line. They'd get on a horse and ride, and they'd buck. Most of the times, they'd throw them ten feet over. But if you didn't get throwed off, you'd have to jump off. You weren't allowed to stay on long enough to break him 'cause that horse would be no good for the show the next day; he's not a bronco anymore.

Kids would ride the pony horses, already broke, small like the Indians ride. If they got on a cowhorse and didn't know how to ride him, he'd throw you right off. Cause if that horse sees a cow, he's going that way because they trained him to round up the cows. He turns every way the cow turns, right in front of him. But the rider knows how that pony horse was going to turn by watching the cows.

My father would get an old cigar box and cut it in the shape of a fiddle, cut out that F-Hole with a sharp knife, fill in the sides with wet stuff and bend it, dry it out, and seal it. He cut the neck out of the trees, Cedar, I think, one he could dry, drill holes to make the neck. Carve out the pegs and make the bow with the horse's hair from the tail. Put resin on it, which leaked from the trees. He used a Willow Tree branch as the bow. Everybody made fiddles all the time. Guys sitting around just talking would always whittle with knives and carve out many things. Cut a little bit from the side and put it under the chin.

6

He played fiddle for 100 people or more at town events to dance by rhythm for several hours, like 9:00pm-1:00am. He put hat straws between the bridge of the fiddle and the bow. His theme song was 'Turkey In The Straw', but he played some ragtime too, and 'Yankee Doodle Dandy'. He would give us $3 to play with him and be the drum with hat pins. His sister, my aunt [Eliza], was in California. We would go buy hat pins, about eight inches long. We hold them like drumsticks and beat them across the fiddle, not with the ball. You couldn't beat on it behind the bridge. As I remember, it would be on the strings in between. He bowed about an inch from the bridge, and we were just 2 or 3 inches above his hand. It would sound like a drum, and we'd be just as loud as him.

*I'd go and shoot a few rattlesnakes. The rattles come in sets, so if the snake was 10 years old, you'd have 20 rattles... dry them out for about four days and drop 10 of them in the fiddle. When he would hit that fiddle, boy, them rattles would sound loud with that wood, like an amplifier! I'd go turn over rocks, shoot the rattlesnakes, cut off the tail, dry them out, and sell them for 25¢ downtown, and they'd sell them to fiddle players. It's dangerous if you're not a good shot, quick, and not get too close. See, they curl up to strike you. But if you kill one, the others slither off - **everything runs from a bullet**! Gotta wear boots and jump back 'cause you know there's about ten of them under there. They was infested out there in the West.*

So, later on, I imagined it would be the same with an acoustic guitar. Then they took the cat's gut, stretched it, let it dry out, then cut it and made a string. Now they have a substitute for that, like nylon or something. There's horses' tail in the fiddle bow today."[16]

Joseph Durham, Jr.

Eddie recalled: "Joe Jr. my eldest brother, was born 1894 and died in 1947. He played bass, trumpet, violin, and piano, and subscribed to music lessons from the U.S. School of Music, which taught him enough to teach us the basics of music. Our dad was a natural musician, but Jr. would stay on me to learn music, not just play it. Jr. bought a trombone for me. He performed on trumpet in the minstrel shows and with Jap Allen's band. During the Spanish-American War he joined the legendary Rough Riders, volunteers

7

organized by Colonel Teddy Roosevelt, Jr. Pancho Villa was there when they were fighting across the border in that last War. Camp Travis was in San Antonio, but they went from camp to camp. Then the 10th Cavalry merged with the 24th Infantry, and they moved to Leavenworth, Kansas, as the Guards for Teddy Roosevelt."

The 24th became the first black regiment to serve in the eastern United States when stationed at Madison Barracks, New York, between 1908 and 1911. It went to the Mexican border in 1916, where they stayed until 1922. Joe Jr. did not serve as a soldier; he served by entertaining them as Musical Director of Teddy Roosevelt's *Homecoming Band.*

Eddie recalls: "Colonel Roosevelt returned a hero, and he became Governor of New York, and then he became Vice President under President McKinley (who was assassinated), and then Roosevelt became the 26th President of The United States of America, from 1901-1909. Teddy Roosevelt would ride with the cavalry. In those days, the President rode horses with everybody else. I've seen him ride.

*Joe Jr. learned to read and stayed deep into books and music. He bought me a guitar when I was 10 (he was 22). When I didn't have school, I would go out to stay near where he was stationed. **He would teach me there.** In those days, it was just light guard duty, like the National Guards. You might notice I have a brother named Roosevelt. My youngest daughter's middle name is Eleanor".*

As a pre-teen in the fourth grade (around 1916), Eddie began performing with the family band, *The Durham Brothers Orchestra.* Until 1922, the Homecoming Band to the Calvary was in Texas. Joe Jr. and the next eldest, Earl, eight years Eddie's senior, were most certainly, at the behest of their parents, traveling guardians for Eddie, Roosevelt, Allen, and Clyde. Each performed in *The Durham Brothers (Jazzy) Orchestra* until at least 1927. As their teacher, Joe Jr. naturally understood the general limitations of each one of them. He recognized that Eddie had the aspiration, and the ability to diversify his skills, and he certainly observed that Eddie seized every opportunity to do so. No doubt, brother Joe participated with Eddie when he experimented with arranging harmony for the brass section in the circuses. Joe would later recommend only Eddie to attend music school.

Eddie didn't need to learn to speak English when he traveled with his brothers and Edgar. They all spoke Spanish, and read the universal language of music very well. But not much later, while touring, he was taught to speak English by a fellow musician who was a teacher.

Joe Jr. left Jap Allen for Blanche Calloway's Orchestra. Regardless of his own personal music career, all of Joe Jr.'s familial students graduated into professional, lucrative careers. They were not struggling financially, even during the Great Depression. Joe Jr. convinced their cousin Herschel Evans to switch from alto to tenor saxophone. Ultimately, this solidified Herschel's career as the dueling tenor with Lester Young. Like Lester, Herschel also did not read much music, and in this sense, Eddie later mentored both of them in the Count Basie Orchestra (Basie also could not read or write music). Eddie worked through their strengths and weaknesses. When writinge etched both as soloists and created the perfect, perhaps first, duo and duel scenarios.

Eddie recalled: "After my oldest brother married, he organized Blanche Calloway's last band for her. She made him a trustee, and he went to Kansas City and brought Ben Webster back. Joe was a technician and as fast on cello as Oscar Pettiford was on bass. Jr. was with Nat Cole for a little while, and he was playing some bass! He was way ahead. When Nat got on top, he tried to get him to go in his trio, but he just hung around his wife and wouldn't leave. Then he was working in a shipyard, and playing gigs, and he never really made the most of what he had."[17] (Joe Jr recordings).

Their father, "Jose," a country and ragtime music fiddler, was their first exposure to rehearsing, organizing, preparing for, and performing a live musical show. He encouraged them to perform. Then, first-born virtuoso Joseph Jr. learned to read music, and he taught his siblings to study music and play an array of instruments.

Myrtle Durham

Myrtle was born in San Marcos, Hayes County, Texas (b.1902 d.1952). Like Roosevelt, she also learned to play piano but primarily performed in church. By the 1920s, all of her brothers were touring. By the late 1930s, she and her mother, Luella, moved to Kearny, New Jersey, where Joe Jr., Roosevelt and Earl later joined them.[18]

In 1931, Joe Jr. recorded with Blanche Calloway's band in Camden, New Jersey, two hours from Newark. In 1929, Eddie fathered his first child, Eddie Durham, Jr., with Hattie Nell Donaldson, who lived in Newark, but he toured constantly. While working as a staff arranger for Glenn Miller in 1938, Glenn put Eddie in an apartment four miles from Newark. From 1938 onward, Roosevelt led his own band based in Newark. Edgar Battle purchased a house in Newark before 1950 with a garage that became *Cosmopolitan Music Studio*. Over the decades, New Jersey became a central meeting point, and although half of them toured, they kept close family ties. Eddie visited cousins Allen and Clyde in California in 1948 and called for his brother, pianist Roosevelt (discharged from the Army in 1945), to join him on the *Cavalcade of Jazz* tour in the 1950s.

Earl Durham

(tenor/baritone sax, clarinet, bandleader)

Eddie recalled: "Earl, who played saxophone and clarinet, eventually went to Connecticut and stayed there. "Earl was the leader of our family band. He led a band in Hartford, Connecticut, where they called him the king of tenor and baritone saxophone, and clarinet. He pawned everything, from drinking. So I brought him to Newark, New Jersey, by my sister and mother. She put him in the hospital, and he got better... for a couple years. But he slipped back. He lived until about 70 years. He was living in a Hotel on the 7th floor, so I took him to my home in Brooklyn on Jefferson Avenue in Bushwick. I left him there one night and went to play; come back, the house is burning down. He fell asleep with a cigarette. My wife and kids weren't home when it started, they were at the Kingdom Hall. I didn't have insurance, but I built it back the way I wanted."

Earl was once Eddie's guardian, and later, Eddie became Earl's.

Eddie recalled: "I traveled around the country with Ina Ray [Hutton] for a year, and we were at the Rose Bowl ten weeks. They had a ten-week run on the radio called "The Choice Hour," coast to coast. Their competition was Bing Crosby on at 10:00. So I went out to write music strictly for that broadcast and **Earl was there**. But then, I scored regularly for The International Sweethearts of Rhythm. "

Eddie Durham

Eddie recalled: "I played banjo first, then four-string guitar. Later on, I added trombone and six-string guitar, and played both in the band... After our band split up, I went with the 101 Ranch Circus on trombone. Edgar Battle was there too, and that's where I really taught myself to write to express my own voicing because we had a lot of horns to play around with.

Before World War II, I did arrangements for Glenn Miller, Jan Savitt, Ina Ray Hutton, and Artie Shaw [with Billie Holiday]. I even had my own big band that featured Buster Smith on saxophone. It's hard for me to remember all of the bands and arrangements I wrote. I didn't play too much in the 1950s and 1960s, though I did get involved in the Harlem Blues and Jazz Band, and I played all sorts of combinations with Sammy Price, Kelly Owens, Hal Austin, Jerry Potter, Frank Foster, and more musicians than I can count. In 1941 I took over an all-woman band, The International Sweethearts of Rhythm out of Piney Woods, Mississippi."[19]

Roosevelt Durham

(fiddle/violin, piano, vocals)

Roosevelt, the youngest (b. San Antonio 1907; d.Feb.1961 New York)[20] was a vocalist and learned to play fiddle, violin and piano from his dad and eldest brother, Joe Jr.

"…His brother, Roosevelt, also attended school in Terrell for about two years. …William Henry Burnett (trumpeter) was born in Ellis County, south of Dallas, in 1872, attended *Lincoln University* in Pennsylvania where he obtained an M.A., and was principal of the Black high school in Terrell for forty-four years. The school provided musical and military training in addition to the usual curriculum. The student body included girls as well as boys. …Durham recalled that he *left Terrell, Texas for the 101 Ranch Show. …with his brother Joe Jr. on trumpet…*"[21]

Eddie recalled: "Roosevelt, my youngest brother and I were about ten months apart. I was born in San Marcos, Texas, in 1906. I had another brother who died in childbirth, and a sister four years older than me. My oldest brother went in the army during World War I, and it was when he got back that he was teaching us youngsters…."[22] "Roosevelt attended school in Terrell, where we moved after living in San Marcos."

Since Eddie was born in San Marcos, this is indicative that as Eddie states, Roosevelt is his younger sibling. Roosevelt's military records show him born in 1907. Therefore, I proceed in this book with 1906 as the year of Eddie's birth, not 1909 as some have speculated.

Roosevelt completed up to the third or fourth grade (until about ten years old; Eddie until he was twelve). Nevertheless, Roosevelt served in *the United States Army* in *World War II*. He was drafted January 1942, and received an Honorable Discharge from Fort Dix, on October 1945. He earned the *Asiatic-Pacific Service Medal, Good Conduct Medal, Philippines Liberation Ribbon* and *American Service Medal*. He returned an alcoholic and died on February

9, 1961 from pneumonia while being treated for nephritis. He is buried at *Long Island National Cemetery*, New York.

"Roosevelt often engaged in cutting contests and had his own band at Fisher's Tavern with vocalist Leatha McCraw. There were some very fine players around, but none, with the possible exception of Roosevelt Durham... approached a talent anything like [Donald] Lambert's. Lamb could play two songs at once, intertwining them while quickening the pace to a frenzy. Willie Smith was good, too, but he couldn't do nothin' with Lambert... "23

"Eddie's brother Roosevelt used to play blues piano and sing. No one's heard Blues like this. No one. He would make up the words right then and there, and the next time he sang that song, it was blues, and it was about that chick, but you would think it was about two other chicks. Make you happy and make you cry at the same time! He would sweat a lot, a lot. True blues, when he played." ***Rudi Sheriff Lawless***, Jazz drummer (1933-2017).

Eddie recalled: "Roosevelt stayed with the Minstrel shows as a pianist until I sent for him. He loved an old, bad piano sound, and he played so much piano that he could make an old piano sound like it wasn't there. But that wasn't justice to him. He was named after the Roosevelt first-family"24 We were together quite a while..."25.

"I met Eddie and his brother Roosevelt once or twice in Harlem. Roosevelt was a great stride pianist. He was very jolly, laid back and a happy man." ***Jean Davis***, trumpeter.

Roosevelt Durham (pianist/vocalist)

1916-1929 The Durham Brothers (Jazzy Jazz) Orchestra
Fisher's Tavern Roosevelt Durham's Band (Newark, N.J. 1938)
Villa Maurice Club featuring bands led by Roosevelt Durham ... and vocalist Leatha McCraw...(floor shows 1938)26
(U.S. Army 1942-1945)
Wynonie Harris (1951)

Clyde Durham (brass bass)

1916-1929 The Durham Brothers (Jazzy) Orchestra
Terrance Holder (1925-28)

Andy Kirk (Nov. 1929-Dec. 1930)
Gene Coy (1928, 1933, 1938)
Lionel Hampton (July 1936)
Teddy Buckner (Aug. 1936)
Floyd Turnham (until Sept. 1939)
Les Hite (Sept. 1939-Aptil 1942)
Fletcher Henderson (Los Angeles April-May 1944)
Armed Forces Radio Service transcription sessions, known as "Jubilee" programs
recorded specifically for black servicemen in World War II)

Allen Durham (trombone)

1916-1929 The Durham Brothers Orchestra
John Williams and His Memphis Stompers (1929)
Terrance Holder
Andy Kirk (1929-31)
Mary Lou Williams (1930)
Buck Clayton (1936)
T-Bone Walker (T-Bone Blues 1940)
Les Hite (1940-'42)
Allen Barry (1943)
Lionel Hampton (1933/1936/1944)
Buddy Banks Sextet (1945)
        (Allen Durham recordings/Appendix "A") *(Allen film soundies)* (Allen photo Buck Clayton Band)

Herschel Evans (alto & tenor saxophone)

Herschel Evans was in *The Durham Brothers Orchestra*. He joined his Durham cousins in *Mamie Smith's 7-11 touring show,* and then in *Edgar Battle's Dixie Ramblers.*

Eddie Durham recalls: "Herschel Evans was another cousin, and he joined us in Dallas. He was playing alto then, but he couldn't read and we tried to teach him. We put him on tenor, and he was better on that than on alto… We used four saxophones in four-part harmony, and just about the first time down he didn't hit on anybody else's note. So if he didn't play the note you played, he'd found his own!"[27]

"Herschel couldn't read much… He was from Lampasas area and recorded with Buddy Tate when he cut two side albums with Troy Floyd. It was in-between Jazz, but not too much Dixieland. Herschel played with the *St. Louis*

Merrymakers where he first met Buddy Tate. Early on Herschel played with territory bands in Texas, sometimes on tenor, sometimes on an alto that, according to Buddy Tate, had *"about a hundred rubber bands around it."* By the mid-1930's he was working with name bands such as Bennie Moten, Dave Peyton, Charlie Echols, Buck Clayton and Lionel Hampton. …In 1936 he joined Count Basie to form a team with Lester Young. …Their music, which echoed their personal contrasts to the note, instituted Basie's life-long tradition of battling tenor saxophones, and was to pass into general jazz lore. But says Jo Jones *"There was no real friction: Lester and Herschel were brothers in rivalry."* Evans's hit record *"Blue and Sentimental"* showed his heart-on-sleeve tenor to perfection, but he was not with Basie long. Late in 1938 he became ill with dropsy, and said Dicky Wells, *"swelled up so he couldn't get his hat on. It could have been cured if he had gone to the doctor earlier."* Buddy Tate dreamed that Evans had died and that a telegram came from Basie offering him the tenor chair; the telegram arrived in 1939. Buddy replaced him with *The Count Basie Orchestra."*[28]

"As much as Lester and Herschel are seen as stylistic polar opposites, the truth is that they borrowed each other's ideas, enjoying how they could adapt them to their own ends. Jo Jones maintained that after Evans' death in early 1939, Young memorialized him for the rest of his life by always throwing in at least a passing Evans reference on every gig he played." [29] ***Loren Schoenberg,*** Grammy Jazz Historian, Producer, Sr. Scholar-National Jazz Museum in Harlem, Archivist, Conductor, Tenor Sax, Piano*).*

Herschel Evans

1916-1927 Durham Brothers (Jazzy Jazz) Orchestra (w/Edgar Battle)
Blue Moon Chasers (TX 1927)
St. Louis Merrymakers (TX)
Terrance Holder / Sammy Holmes (TX)
Troy Floyd's Shadowland Orch. (Texas June 21, 1929*-32 (w/Buddy Tate)
Grant Moore
Bennie Moten's Kansas City Orch. (1933-35)
Richard M. Jones, Hot Lips Page (KC)
Dave Peyton (Chicago 1935)
Jones Chicago Cosmopolitans (Sept.1935)
Charlie Echols (LA)

Mildred Bailey (NYC June 1937 w/Buck Clayton)
Count Basie (1936-Dec.1939 w/Eddie Durham & Buck Clayton)
Harry James (NYC Dec.1937/Jan.1938 w/Eddie Durham & Buck Clayton)
Teddy Wilson (NYC Oct.-Nov.1938 w/Harry James & Billie Holiday)
Lionel Hampton (NYC Dec.1938) at The Paradise Cafe
Buck Clayton Band "Brownskin Revue" (w/Allen Durham)
   (Herschel Evans recordings "Appendix A") / *(Picture Allen & Herschel, Buck Clayton Band-1930s)*

Henry "Buster" Smith

Eddie recalled: "I met Buster in Dallas, TX when I was going to a musical school in Terrell, TX. There was Principal Professor Burnett and the whites backed him in anything he wanted to do. We had the best band in Texas and the best musicians came out of it. So I used to go 30 miles to Dallas to see a girl on Sunday's and I met Buster, a little older than me, and I started playing with his band at dances. He was a well-schooled musician, the greatest, could read and write. He's the guy that really did the "One O'Clock Jump," originally named "Blue Balls." Parts got added in 'cause his didn't have nothing to do with the trombones, because everybody was hitting the same way, and always could come up with something. A guy would say, "Now, let's see you put something in this, genius" And I'd just start it off. Then they started calling me circus boy... "there's old circus." But Buster didn't like to travel, wouldn't fly at all, didn't like boats... superstitious. He'd ride a bus or train."

Since Eddie Durham and his brothers were born in Texas in 1906, their mode of local transportation would have been on horseback, and touring would have been by train. They were born into a different world. Our generation cannot comprehend the world that they were born into, and grew up in with no radio, no telephone, no television, or computer. The first airplane is in 1903. Then add to it the racial factor, the complexity of their Indian heritage. That world is very hard to get in touch with today and people must remember, when you assess their careers and backgrounds, you must use imagination and visualize where they came from, what they emerged out of, and factor in these things. It's a world long before the modern technology we can now take for granted.

NINETEEN 20's

<u>Edgar *Puddinghead* Battle</u>

Eddie and his brothers met Edgar Battle very early in their careers, around 1921 with *Mamie Smith's 7-11* show. For the rest of Edgar's life he stuck around Herschel and the Durham brothers. He formed the *Dixie Serenaders* whilst at *Morris Brown College* and toured the southwest with them as Edgar Battle's *Dixie Ramblers*. In that respect, they traveled with a college-trained musician. Battle recorded with Blanche Calloway alongside Joseph Durham, Jr. (and Cozy Cole). He played trumpet, valve trombone and alto sax and wrote for Cab Calloway, Fats Waller, Earl Hines, etc.

"Of jazz musicians whose names sound like a description of a food fight, *Puddinghead Battle* just has to be the most versatile and accomplished. He would deserve such praise even if he didn't possess a silly nickname coupled with a violent surname. …Battle fought with trumpet, trombone, and saxophones as well as keyboard, both as a performing instrument and for composition and arrangement. …In 1921, Battle formed the Dixie Serenaders and used his college, Morris Brown University, as a base of operations.[30]
Eugene Chadbourne

Eddie recalled: "He [Edgar] was leading his band the Dixie Ramblers in 1927. I toured the Southwest with his band for a couple of years, then we joined drummer Gene Coy and his Happy Aces in Shawnee, Oklahoma. Edgar was later with George White's Scandals. He went overseas with Noble Sissle in the Eisenhower U.S.O. He made about $60,000 by the time he came back. So he went upstate to Otsego and bought 180 acres of land, but when he needed money, he sold it off, until it was down to 30 acres by the time he died. In his last year, he wrote a lot of tribute songs for 30-piece bands but didn't do anything with it, 'cause it's got bad spots where it's overloaded and you can't play it. Anybody could edit it. Benny Morton played it. He'd get right up to the door of a deal and close it, saying, "I got to have $400,000 or I can't do this." Everything had to be so big, and the backers would back off. He wanted to give up nothing, not even a percentage. See a lot of guys can write a great arrangement, but you got to perform a miracle …and have a hit, …a *guy who can promote it and a band that can perform it. Especially since the producers with the record companies, are looking to get their name on the record as a producer. He wasn't giving up nothing. So his stuff stayed.*

Battle could sure execute on trumpet and he wrote a lot more than I did, but I only wrote what a Band could use. I wrote one for Battle with his six saxes, top to bottom, all six-part harmony, commercial melody. But the bands weren't ready for this, they couldn't read it and they couldn't hear above a triad. I liked to create and experiment. My brother Joe played 1st trumpet and Battle played 2nd trumpet in whatever band we were in all together".

A large, shrewd businessman, Edgar later formed *Cosmopolitan Music Publishing*, promoting most notably, Durham's "Topsy I & II" (Love Records 1958) albeit claiming himself co-composer. Battle is also co-writer on "Slip Horn Jive," "Blues In The Groove," "Echoes of Reeds & Brass," "Tempermental," "Little Eva," "Fantasy," "Rhythm Rag," "Time Out" and "Topsy III- VI"; and with Eddie and Irving Miller on "Southern Nite Life," "Weird Lullaby," "(In A) Blue Mood," "Rabbit Foot Stomp" and "Streamline Express." Battle co-wrote "Strictly Instrumental" (Marcus, Seiler, B. Benjamin) recorded by Harry James and Jimmie Lunceford, among others.

Battle and Herschel co-wrote and performed on "Texas Shuffle" and "Doggin Around," recorded by Count Basie. Battle's trumpet solos are featured on two popular songs recorded by Andy Kirk in 1930 - "I Lost My Girl From Memphis" and "Loose Ankles," (with Allen Durham, Claude "Fiddler" Williams, and Mary Lou Williams), who Eddie Durham mentored.
"Edgar Battle (Memoriam) by Eddie Barefield Sextet on Amazon"

Durham and Battle scored an Operatic "Jazzphony" for an adaptation of Harriett B. Stowe's "Uncle Tom's Cabin", including "Topsy III-V." Also discovered are manuscripts in a hard-covered black spiral book, "The Black Book", representing portraiture playing styles of 33 famous musicians, including themselves. To his laudation, Battle left instructions that all of his music interests revert to Eddie and his heirs, upon his only daughter's death.
("Jazzphony Opera": see Appendix "A") ("Black Book-Portraitures": see Appendix "A")

Band's Names

Eddie recalled: "In them days, they always wanted to let you know that it was a black band, so they named them 'The Blue Devils', 'Gene Coy's Black Aces', 'Andy Kirk's Dark Clouds of Joy'. Ace is the top card, dark clouds bring joy because it brings the rain, but they are mostly referring to color complexion."

Circuses/Minstrels

Before film, phonographs, radio, TV, or even zoos, only newspapers advertised the annual mirific traveling Circus. Country-wide, everyone anticipated its arrival, and it was never under-attended. Arriving in trainloads with colors, sounds, and odors, it showcased freakish, bizarre, silly, extraordinary people, their costumes, the trainers with exotic animals, and the finale of two music bands. Sprawling in splendor, the circuses spent more money on colorful, eye-catching banners and advertisements than any other business, perhaps to date. The circus also utilized electricity before any city had street lighting, and in fact, their electric Generator was its own advertised attraction. One circus showcased the first theatrical musical, *"Jerusalem"* - the first "off-Broadway" show.

For African Americans, the circus provided unparalleled advantages and contrasts. Although handymen were replaceable from town to town, bands typically were not. Bands also did not perform death-defying acts but were afforded the benefit of exposure to show business in its enormity. An endogenous microcosm of varied talents. Perhaps in no other setting during segregation could 'negroes' insulate themselves within a national tour with performers of many races. As part of the Circus, African Americans constantly traveled by train through segregated territories. This experience was immeasurable as they performed in cities at the largest venues, where they otherwise would not have been invited to perform. They received guaranteed free room, board, meals, and a regular, albeit meager, salary. Best of all, it was consistent.

The animated advertisements prior to their arrival, along with the impressionable finale of a negro marching band, spread black music genres nationally. Ragtime and Blues music were popularized by the circus a generation before *The Harlem Renaissance*.[i] This exuberant diversity of talent left communities awestruck, and this impressed Eddie. The choreography, discipline, perfection, and professionalism Eddie embraced as a teenager were an impressionable experience. It is stamped in his legacy of arranging and showmanship. This is where his professional career began.

101 Circus

The Miller Brothers Ranch was a 110,000-acre cattle ranch in the Indian Territory of Oklahoma… The Ranch was the birthplace of the *101 Ranch Wild West Show*… It was the largest diversified farm and ranch in America at the time… In 1903, when Colonel George Miller died, his three sons, Joseph, George Jr., and Zack took over operation…[ii]

Eddie recalled: *"Edgar Battle, Joe Jr. and myself toured the United States by train, with the [Miller Brothers] 101 Wild Ranch Circus [Negro Brass Band & Minstrel Show]. My last show was at Yankee [baseball] Stadium in New York, I think, 1921, and then they tore down the Stadium within the next year or two, but the Circus continued to Europe. We were with them two Seasons, but the Show was off during cold weather. It was bigger than Ringling Brothers because they had elephants, wild animals like snakes and lions, four tribes of Indians, some from California, all in the stadium-like Arena, with Chief White Horse and Chief White Cloud performing with hay, settlers, canvassed wagons, horses, rifles with blanks for trick shooting and bow and arrows! It was a Wild West Show, just like in a film. There were always two bands. There was a 30-piece white band to parade all day, a black band for the minstrel show at night, and Archie Mays and Bennie Hudson were part of the comedians on the horse-drawn Wagons. If a Wagon broke down, Big Jimbo the elephant would come and push it out of the way! I played trombone. Trumpeters there were Amos White and John Mason, who brought me in, John was the leader. There were girls in the Bands, too.*

"We had four trombones, two or three french horns, and peck horns, but we didn't use all of them when we played for the minstrel show. They had very good men in those days, and they could read rings around me. They had trumpet players who could triple-tongue and double-tongue when they were

20

playing high-powered marches. They could play a little jazz but stayed very close to the melody. I was trying to solo a bit, and it wasn't hard for me to learn the value of notes, but a guy who could swing a break was something new to them. ...The minstrel show was like a sideshow, not in the big tent where the circus was. It didn't start till the big show was over."[iii]

So, when we played for dances at night, I asked them if I could swing in the jazz breaks. They were all trained musicians playing solid trombone-no faking-so jazz breaks on trombone were different".[iv]

"But the Circus is where I first began to arrange because I say, 'gotta be more than a triad of music'. So, at night, I'd give a dance - and then I'd also play guitar. I went around and told some guy, 'man, I can bring the band down here after the show tonight'. Charge 50c at the door. And that's how I learned quite a bit of harmony because it wasn't in the books. And I'd get 'em together and write for 'em. They wanted to be amused. They'd say, "What are you gonna do for a piano?" The band would play any music I wrote, just to be there, and some white musicians, too. Ragtime-type stuff. The Circus paid about $20/week plus room and board, but at night, we'd split up the extra money. We'd play 'till 11 PM, and I'd be experimenting with voicing four french horns, trumpets, and four trombones, obbligato, and tailgate the horns, with a bass drummer and a separate trap drummer, one playing after the beat, piano, French horns hitting the backbeat and that become a compliment, just like the piano. Then, later on, reed work by the Clarinets. So I always experimented, and I learned four and five-part harmony. When I went to New York, I met Bingie Madison, who was voicing, and Don Redman (with Fletcher Henderson), who was doing six-part harmony, and I studied with him, and I got away from that triad. He taught me chords that had no name yet but called them double-augmented, tonic fifth, third, and sixth parts. But when I went to the Bennie Moten Orchestra, they were still in 3-part harmony. I met Fletcher Henderson.[v]

31

The Big Stone Gap Post (Virginia) - Wed, May 4, 1921

Miller Bros.' Shows Coming.

Beginning May 16th and continuing for one week Miller Brothers' Circus and Exhibition will exhibit at this place. This is the same show that exhibited at the ball park here about a year ago and was considered one of the best of its kind that ever visited Big Stone Gap.

Eddie Durham was a teenager when *The Durham Brothers Orchestra* toured as a show-stopping unified finale entertainment band with the Southwest minstrels and circuses. Eddie is suddenly surrounded by exacting showmanship, brass choreography, the enormity of arenas, stadiums, crowds, and an array of acts accompanied by varied genres of music. These include a silent-clown storyteller, the suspense of a snake-charmer or sword-eater, and something he was familiar with from his father and eldest brother - the rodeo. Although Eddie is performing on trombone, there's a foreshadowing to guitar amplification being showcased at the circus - portable electricity! The circus pivoted Eddie Durham into a regimented discipline and allowed him to bond with an array of musicians, as the brass section welcomed his experimental composing and arranging with six-part harmony. Here are a couple of examples of the scope of the Miller Brothers 101 Ranch Circus…

"Not satisfied with all the varied attractions under roof at the International Wheat Show at Wichita, assembled at a cost of many thousands of dollars, and surpassing by far those of any other exposition in the Southwest, the directors have this year capped the climax by contracting for a standard Cowboy Circus and Wild West show, to be staged at the Wichita ball park, October 12th-16th. This circus features some of the champion cowboy riding and roping artists of America, having its own herds of cattle and horses, including buffaloes and even a huge ostrich. Everything in the "Wild West" category is there to be ridden; and ridden they are, according to all reports… The youngest brother of a quintet, whose name is Guy, is the guy who puts it over all the rest of his brothers, and most everybody's brothers, when it comes to bronco busting and roping cattle… One of the "stunts" that Guy will pull at the Wichita race track show will have to do with a real "wild" buffalo… He will jump from the back of a running horse to the head and horns of the fleeing buffalo, and, matching his strength with that of the beast, will attempt to throw the buffalo. He is the only man ever known to attempt this death-defying act… Another feat of Guy's is the riding of an ostrich, and he is some wild bird from all reports."[32] *The Downs News and The Downs Times - Oct. 7, 1920.*

Eddie recalled: "*I had a lot of experience with Bands. I was with the Alabama Minstrels when I was a kid; my brother was there, and I was with the Georgia Minstrels. I got a lot of experience listening to things and doing things. That was the best school in the world. The part that I enjoyed, we had a comedian named Billy Hudson, and he had soles on his tap shoes about two inches thick, and you could hear him coming out on the stage and another comedian, black faces and white lips. Show would open up with the band. Then one of these guys would start laughing so loud on the corner. And the straight man would say, "What's the matter with him?" to stop him - and he'd crack a joke out of this world! Great comedians! John Mason was a great trumpet player for shows. We backed up territory Minstrel and Tent Shows such as "Eugene Coy's Black Aces" with Clyde and Allen [Durham] in Shawnee, Oklahoma, at The Bluebird Ballroom. When the minstrel closed, we went to the "101 Wild West Circus," and that's how I got in there. My oldest brother Joe went with me. He played trumpet, bass, tuba, and everything, so I started playing everything. That's where I learned how to write a lot. Cause when I was with the Miller Brothers, these were very large shows - they always had two big bands.*"[33]

"The 101 Ranch at Marland, OK, which consists of approximately 50,000 acres of land, claims the distinction of producing more diversified products than any other ranch in the country. Even oil wells are now producing on it. Colonel Mill will carry out a novel plan in that practically everything in the show will come from the Miller ranch. Wild steers, buffaloes, and horses have already been selected. Seats and tent poles will be hewn from timber on this land. Harness for animals in the show will be manufactured from the hides of their own cattle. Food for employees and hay and grain for the animals will be raised on this ranch and shipped to the show constantly throughout the season. Indians living on the ranch will make their own tepees from cotton they raised, and woven into tent material in an Oklahoma mill This also applies to the canvas tents used in the show. The show plans to portray the primitive life or various tribes of Indians, their methods of fighting, war dances, and peace council. The show will also carry a museum of bows and arrows with a history, pottery, baskets, human scalps, garments, headwork, and peace pipes. Wild animals will be transported in the parades by motor trucks, specially built in Kansas City. It was said this would be the first time wild animal cages would be mounted on motor trucks for parades. Five hundred employees will be carried with the show. Most of the circus talent will be employed in Kansas City, which is known as the second largest recruiting center for shows and circuses in the country."[34] *The Kansas City Times* (Missouri) Dec. 16, 1924.

K.Oliver/Armstrong

In 1922 Edgar is 15 years old and Eddie is a few years younger.

Eddie recalled: *"When I went to Chicago with the **Ranch Circus** in 1922, Edgar Battle and I heard Louie Armstrong with King Oliver playing inside an old ballroom. We climbed up on the windows to listen. The police hit me in the head, I think I still have the scar! But we could see their heads bobbing, it was a creole band, about five or six pieces.*

Joe Jr. my brother, put me in a trade school called the U.S. School of Music in Chicago, where I stayed for two years. Then I said, they ain't got nothing to teach me now, I can teach this school. I was living with a friend of Joe's, a Dr. Dorsey, who owned a drugstore, and, I worked at Starkey's Bakery, it was German-owned; you'd work your way through it. At the school, I learned a little bit more about dynamics and the correct wording but in Latin terms, like tempo, accelerando... But they couldn't offer me much more than a foundation."

"He [Durham] studied at the *U.S. Music Conservatory* … probably the *American Music Conservatory* at 306 South Wabash… After playing at the 101 Theatre in Atlanta and rent parties… Georgia Tom toured with Ma Rainey and eventually became better known as Thomas A. Dorsey, the Father of Blues Gospel, one of the most renowned African-American composers of the twentieth century. It would appear rather unlikely that Durham worked for Dr. Dorsey and had no contact with his musician-nephew who boarded with his uncle… Dorsey was very likely an inspiration for Durham."[35]

In fact, Dorsey was a big influence on Eddie Durham, who several years later recorded four gospel songs with Laura Henton.

"Dorsey created a new style of gospel which incorporated blues melodies and rhythms with his spiritual beliefs. Many of his songs went on to become gospel standards and he was a key influence on the career of the 'The Queen of Gospel' Mahalia Jackson, whose signature song 'Take My Hand, Precious Lord' was written by Dorsey after he experienced the loss of his wife and first-born in childbirth." [36]

Morgan's Circus

The *J. Doug Morgan Show* that toured the Midwest and claimed to be the "World's Greatest Tented Amusement Enterprise", saw its role as presenting "A Grand Triple Alliance of Musical Comedy, Drama, and Vaudeville." In the late 1920s the tent shows faced severe competition from "canned drama," especially talking pictures, and most failed in the Depression.[37]

Eddie recalled: "Doug Morgan's Traveling Dramatic Show was next (1925-'26). It was a white Circus, but the Band was black. Morgan bought me my first real guitar, a 4-string, so I wouldn't have to borrow one in each town and then give it back. I played guitar and trombone in that show. I was inspired by this show, it was a process of learning what came before me, in order to develop my own style. Edgar Battle played 1st trumpet and my brother Joe played 2nd trumpet. My oldest brother bought me a guitar when I was ten years old and I've been in bands since I was in the fourth grade."[38]

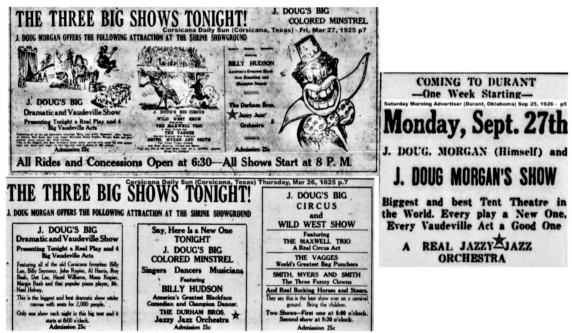

Eddie recalled: "When I was in Kansas City in 1927, I went to see the old soldiers that my brother used to be with. They were putting on exhibitions because anybody from the Tenth Calvary on a horse could hit his target falling, but they weren't allowed to use bullets. So they marched with wooden guns. If you were to shoot him off his horse, he'd kill you before he hit the ground. My brother taught me to shoot a rifle. I was young and having a good time, but very interested in music around 10 years old. When school was out I'd come to whereever my brother was at; his location was Camp Travis, in San Antonio. So I used to come there, and he'd get me a place to stay, and I could come over. And he'd help me with the music. They used to have exhibitions with the Tenth Calvary [which moved to Leavenworth, Kansas] and the Rough Riders, and they had hay downs, and they'd have to ride around and when they make a turn, they had targets for them, and they

couldn't draw until they fall off the horse. They fall off the horse and hit their targets. I was there and could see that. He was a great musician."[39]

Eugene Coy's 12 Black Aces

Next, some of the Durham Brothers joined drummer "Gene Coy and his 12 Black Aces" (1927)

Mamie Smith

"The phrase '*Race Records*' had been in use since 1920, when the success of an *Okeh* record "**Crazy Blues**" by Mamie Smith, motivated other record labels to record black female vocalists, many of whom would later be regarded as the classic blues singers. In time the term 'race' became a catchall for any type of black recording … The term '*rhythm and blues*' was introduced in 1949 by *Billboard Magazine* as a substitute for the word 'race' in a chart that had been headed until then, 'Top 15 Best Selling Race Records'".[40]

"With the Jazz Age in full throttle and the city's economy thriving, competition was stiff among Newark theater owners to attract top entertainers to their stages in the years following World War I. *Miners Theatre*, at Branford Place and Washington Street – Newark] was one of the city's major burlesque houses, offering huge productions… One of the most popular revues presented at Miner's that year was the 7-11 show that brought the musical *Durham Brothers* – Joe, Eddie, and Roosevelt – to town and starred Sam Cooke, Mae Brown, and Speedy Smith. Another was Lucky Sambo. Because of the business the show generated, Miner's manager, A. Johnny Mack, added a midnight show following the regular performance. Night after night, Lucky Sambo continued to pack the house, making it and the *7-11* the Columbia circuit's leaders in gross receipts."[41]

Eddie recalled: "All three brothers [myself and cousin Herschel Evans on tenor] and Edgar Battle were in the 'Mamie Smith 7-11 Show'. Edgar Battle (far left), Valentine Billington (center), and myself (far right) with my three brothers Joe, Earl, and Roosevelt (piano and clarinet) backed up 'Mamie Smith's 7-11 Show'. We had a nucleus. We played in the pit, twelve instruments among us, and you had to read. This show was by the Goldberg Brothers. We'd open with an overture, more smooth. There were about 70 people in that show too. We went all over the country as 'Edgar Battle's and The Dixie Ramblers' - the last show was at the Orpheum Theatre in New Jersey. We had three saxophones, my cousin Herschel Evans played alto and tenor, Battle on trumpet, maybe a nine-piece Band. I didn't record with her though; that was before that hit she had in 1920 was how she got the tour. Mamie Smith couldn't do the last two shows, so Miss Rhapsody did them. She was just a young girl, maybe still in her teens. Clyde went with 'Gene Coy's Black Aces', Allen went to Oklahoma City where Battle and I went after her 7-11 closed."[42]

"They played together for 4 years, and then joined a big musical show, disbanding when the show closed at the Orpheum Theatre in Newark, after touring for 8 months. This brought Eddie to New York for the first time, where he studied to be an electrician, but gave it up when he was offered a job with the 101 Wild West Circus to travel with the minstrel show and to write for the brass band, which he later formed into a swing band."[43] The New York Age, Newspaper (Dec. 18, 1943).

"Eddie used to tell me about growing up and about the Circus and Gene Coy's band. The one-story I do remember was how he learned to arrange. He said the circus had the weirdest, unusual combination of instruments, and that he had to learn to write for these instrumentations. Most people would look at that as a great disadvantage. Well, what Eddie told me he did, was when he had to write for two trumpets, a tambourine, a french horn, bass drum, and a maraca player, you really had to learn how to write. I think that's what at the root of his great genius and his orchestration." *Loren Schoenberg*

Jesse Stone

Eddie recalled: "Chauncey Downs was the next best Band in Kansas City, Chauncey was the front man. Keg Johnson and I were in the band with Eddie Tompkins-trumpet, Paul Webster-trumpet, and another trumpeter (1928). Every summer Tompkins and Webster went to Lunceford's Band and that's how I got in there, Lunceford heard we already had a brass section in town. We had a clique. But Webster and I, we could play it free.

The five of us also went into Jesse Stone's Blue Serenaders. Later down the line, we broke this down to a three clique, Tompkins, Webster, and myself in Lunceford's band. The other two left town. Jesse Stone was an Arranger, and he could slap music onto paper faster than anybody I know, and we liked that. He wrote "Huckle Buck." He was one of my mentors too. He's so underrated, ten years ahead of us."[44]

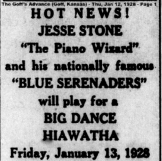

Blue Moon Chasers

Eddie recalled regarding Rattan's Blue Moon Chasers: "...with Budd Johnson, Herschel Evans, Booker Pitman and later Buster Smith [a.k.a. Prof] came in when somebody left. We left and went to The Blue Devils (1928), 'cause we got hungry![45]

"...in the summer of 1929 Durham, together with his brother Joe and Bill Basie, performed with *Elmer H. Payne and His 10 Royal Americans* in a Kansas City club, in fact, the largest in the city. That autumn they recorded in Chicago with Moten's orchestra and performed at the *Ritz* in Oklahoma City, and then at the *El Torreon* ballroom in Kansas City. They also broadcast over Columbia's *KMBC* station three times a week. Eddie continued to work with his [mentor] brother Joe, even when Eddie was with Moten."[46]

Mentors

Eddie is introduced to multiple instruments and music notation in his formative adolescence. He performed live in circuses with his brothers, three cousins, and an extremely organized friend, Edgar Battle. Joe, his eldest brother, is a virtuoso. He tours with the prolific writer Jesse Stone. Buster Smith is his best friend. Then, he happens to be working for and living with the Dorsey family. These random events were pivotal quantum leaps that were tantamount to a formal music education of the highest degree. It confers upon him the ability to recognize and assimilate from any other genius in his immediate orbit. For instance, Stone clearly influenced Eddie's early arranging and writing style, which Eddie later developed into the swing genre. Eddie's sit-down one-on-ones with titan pianist Art Tatum expanded his scope of string orchestration. He learned to speak English from a musician while on tour. Eddie learned voicing from Bingie Madison and six-part harmony from Don Redman.

Eddie recalled: "*Fletcher Henderson, Duke Ellington, Louis Armstrong - these were my influences. J. Doug Morgan bought me my first real guitar. Bingie Madison, who was voicing, and Don Redman (with Fletcher Henderson), who was doing six-part harmony, Art Tatum, Jesse Stone, my dad, and eldest brother - these were my mentors.*"

"I saw Jesse Stone and Eddie together. Ninety percent of the people I met were younger than Eddie. But I felt that Jesse Stone, a legend, was somebody that Eddie respected and had learned from very early on in Texas. Jesse wrote a big hit called "Idaho," and he was a very interesting arranger who wrote for Terrance Holder, and that's how he got famous. So Jesse was probably the first great arranger that Eddie knew and learned from on a one-to-one basis. Fletcher Henderson was conceived to be the best band then, and I'm sure Eddie heard and adapted some of his stuff, but with his own unique style. Duke Ellington was great too, but he was always in a category by himself. But when the *Bennie Moten Orchestra* came to the *Pearl Theatre* in Philadelphia in 1931 and 1932, when they made their east coast trips, Ellington, Henderson, all of them were knocked out by the Eddie Durham arrangements they heard that Orchestra play. And then, you can hear those bands kinda copy what they heard from then on." *Loren Schoenberg*

"Fletcher Henderson was considered the first Swing band. That's why John Hammond wanted Benny Goodman to organize a swing band like Fletcher's. Benny married John's sister, and then John took an interest and helped him put a band together. Benny loved swing music, and John was 23 years old when he used to come to Harlem when I was playing with Benny Carter in 1933. He played with Ben Pollack then, but he wanted his own band. We recorded "Big John's Special." Most of the songs you hear Goodman play, Fletcher Henderson played. Fletcher started writing for Goodman while I played with the Chicago band. The bands coming through the Savoy up to 1934 were Fletcher Henderson Bennie Moten - with Eddie Durham, McKinny Cotton Pickers, Chick Webb, Missourians, and Stanley "Fess" Williams. I went with the *Mills Blue Rhythm Band* in 1934. In 1940, the male bands broke up. Basie's band debut was around 1935 at the *Grand Terrace* in Chicago. They came in from Kansas City. I was there playing with Fletcher."[47] **Larry Lucie** (1907-2009), Guitarist, Bandleader

Art Tatum

Eddie recalled: "I learned a lot of way-out chords with Art Tatum. Every time I went out to Ohio with Lunceford, I'd stay with him a few nights. As long as you were buying him beer, he'd like to sit down and play. He showed me a

lot of things. So, I wrote down a few passages. I have one passage I've written four songs from already. I have to use the music with three lines 'cause the bass line and the trumpet player's line wouldn't take it. Put the melody up on the third line. So I picked up on them, and he learned 'em to me, and I wrote 'em down, and we sit there all night... So I say'd that to say this, I have some of those numbers I made, and I never did get them across to the band. I make 'em and stop. If I don't hurry up and get 'em I'll have to take them to the grave with me - I'd like to get some of 'em out! All kinds of augmented elevenths, and everything. So Teddy Wilson used to come to Connie's [Inn] with Willie Bryant's band, and he was always late! So he'd walk in, I'd be on the piano, and I'd hit chords with the band. He'd back up. I'd see him standing in the wings, and he wouldn't come out. All the piano players like to hear those inversions that I can do on the piano. I don't know why they don't even know 'em. But I got 'em from Art Tatum. And he'd stand right there, and he'd listen, and he'd catch him, say he's back there. And he always wanted to hear what I had to do. I make 'em and stop..[48] *Hear Asch Recording (NY452-2A; MA1255) of "Topsy" (Durham, Battle) with Personnel: Art Tatum (p), Tiny Grimes (g), Slam Stewart (b).*

"As children growing up, we saw our dad write music mostly while playing the piano." *Eric R. Durham, Sr..*

Oklahoma Blue Devils

The number one, most exciting, and innovative territory band was "Walter Page's Oklahoma Blue Devils"

Page's mission was to dethrone his former boss, Bennie Moten. But in the end, almost everyone joined Moten's Orchestra.

Eddie recalled: *"I joined Page when he came to Texas. They only recorded "Blue Devil Blues" but that was before me. They had soul and won the Battle of the Bands with Bennie Moten's band in Kansas City at Paseo Hall. George E. Lee was the #2 band. I joined sometime in 1928 and stayed under a year. Buster Smith, Bill Basie, Hot Lips Page, Dan Minor on trombone, who they never mention, Alvin Burroughs on drums, Jimmy Rushing and maybe Budd Johnson and Booker Pittman, myself. The leader was Walter Page when me and Buster came in… I was the first to leave [the Blue Devils] and as arranger and composer, I revitalized his sound, from a stomp to a swing, as evidenced by the Victor Recordings of 1929-1932. But we all came from The Blue Devils Orchestra. Anyway, in Summer 1929, I say, I'm going to Bennie Moten's. Big Page said, 'Let's all the rest of us go'. That's how they all drifted away.*

Their Winter home base is Oklahoma City's The Ritz Ballroom. Walter was playing bass on his baritone sax, and he played bass too, because a bass sax can play bass on there, just like a bass horn, too. He didn't have a string bass and we didn't have room for that bass. But he could pump it. So when he would come into Moten's Band, I wanted a little of that. He played staccato style just like the bass player, boom boom-boom-boom boom, not like a tuba but more like a string bass - it's in between. I didn't stay with this group long,

33

didn't record with them." For at least a decade, Bennie Moten had developed a working relationship with the political mob boss of Kansas City, Tom Pendergast, so despite the Blue Devils winning the Battle of the Bands, it's fate was sealed and most of the members left to join The Bennie Moten Orchestra."[49]

Laura Henton

Laura Henton recorded four gospel songs for *Brunswick* in Kansas City, November 1929. It is notable that while Eddie did not record with *The Oklahoma Blue Devils*, on these recordings Laura is accompanied not only by Eddie, but also pianist Bennie Moten and on tuba Joe Page [more likely either Vernon Page or Joe Durham]. A few months earlier Eddie recorded with *Bennie Moten's Orchestra*.

"...utilizing the well-known band leader Bennie Moten on piano, pioneering guitarist Eddie Durham, and a string bass player listed as Joe Page. The guitar voicings in particular are most unusual in a gospel context and even today sound fresh and up-to-date.[50] ***Ken Romanowski***

(Eddie / Laura Henton recordings: see "Appendix A")

NINETEEN 30s
Bennie Moten

1929-1932 *Bennie Moten's Kansas City Orchestra* (cover art on this book).

"Walter ["Big"] Page played the tuba and baritone saxophone with the same authority he displayed on the string bass, and when he finally threw in the towel and joined Moten in 1932, the stage was set for one of the truly defining moments in Jazz history. Page's propulsion of the band, along with Eddie Durham's discoveries in the realm of swinging Jazz orchestration, resulted in one of the first innovations to be made away from New York, where the pace had been set by Duke Ellington, Benny Carter, and Bill Challis. There is no precedent in Jazz for their fiery recordings of "Lafayette," "Prince of Wales," and "Toby.""[51]

"It was at Durham's suggestion that Moten hired trumpeter [Oran] Hot Lips Page, vocalist Jimmy Rushing, and pianist Bill Basie in spite of the fact the band already had two pianists, including the leader himself. Durham desperately wanted Walter Page's string bass, but the Blue Devil leader resisted until 1931 when he finally joined."[52]

"Durham's arrangements, in particular, and his compositions, along with the arrangements of Eddie Barefield - who became a Motenite in 1932 - and the addition of Blue Devils like Oran and Walter Page, produced the legendary 1932 New Brunswick recordings. These included the classics *"Toby,"* *"Prince of Wales," "Moten Swing,"* (foreshadowed in Durham's 1929 composition *"Oh! Eddie,"* as well as in *"Here Comes Marjorie"*), *"Lafayette,"* and other arrangements that presaged the big band music of the swing era. These are considered by music critics to be the first swing recordings. …These recordings "inaugurated a conception of orchestral jazz distinct from that of Henderson and the eastern axis, a conception moreover which was to bypass the inherent stylistic hazards of the Swing Era and provide at least one of the routes leading to modern jazz and bop.""[53]

"Even though I'm categorized as a bebop musician, my favorite area of the Jazz evolution is Kansas City. I grew up next to the hi-hat of Jo Jones, later on with Eddie Barefield, and Harry "Sweets" Edison. I saw that there was a particular style and character about Kansas City musicians that was just like no other. I was a Basie fanatic from the Bennie Moten days right up until the 1960s when the band started to change its character. But I was always intrigued from the standpoint of composition because that's what I studied formally in school. Realizing from these early recordings, particularly following The Moten Orchestra's transition from the 1920s to their final recordings in 1932, I suddenly came to realize that Eddie Durham was the primary factor in that whole style of composition."[54] ***Theodore Wilson, III***, acoustic bassist (son of pianist Teddy Wilson)

Eddie recalled: "When I went with Bennie Moten in 1929, he had only three saxophones and two trumpets. Although I didn't care for the instrument, I was playing valve trombone in order to help the trumpets. I worked very hard, playing awful high with the trumpets to give a three-trumpet effect, then switching back to make a two-trombone sound. There was a lot of pressure on the brass but those guys wouldn't play a sixth or a ninth chord They were playing the fifth, tonic, and third, and they couldn't hear the sixth. So then Moten brought Lips Page into the band. 'What's "he" gonna play?' ...Then I stepped the band up to ninth chords, and they could hear a ninth better than they could a sixth. Lips...could hear the sixth, so I gave him that and played the ninth myself. That's how we started getting five-part harmony in the brass, and they came to see why we had needed another horn. There was nobody playing their note, where before they'd been saying 'You playin' my note? Get off my note! ...They preferred a sousaphone in a dancehall because you could hear it better. Without amplification, a lot of guys weren't strong enough on bass fiddle. But Walter Page you could hear! He was like a house with a note ...The bass is one of the greatest things in the world for rhythm, but instead of writing a two-beat bass on the fifth and tonic, I kept it moving on chromatics to the chord. It sounded good, but when they saw it on paper, musicians said, 'This has gotta be out of tune!' Walter Page is the guy that created that walkin', walkin'... I wrote it long, but I couldn't control and master that swinging motion till I'd been in the band a long time."[55]

"Eddie Barefield added: "When I joined Moten, 80 percent of the book was written by Eddie Durham."[56]

"Eddie Durham's guitar solos on his early records are immediately identifiable. His trombone solos on the 1929-30 Moten recordings have never received the credit they deserve, probably because they were assumed to be by Thamon Hayes. Hayes' work, though very acceptable for the period, doesn't display the high range and technique that Durham's few solos feature ("Boot It" being the greatest example.)." ***Dan Weinstein***, *Violinist, Trombonist, Educator, Composer, Live sessions with Ray Charles*

"While on the road, Basie and Durham totally revamped the band's book, creating orchestral arrangements of *"Honeysuckle Rose," "I Can't Give You Anything but Love," "I Want a Little Girl,"* and other popular standards. The last vestiges of the stomps, blues, and breakdowns previously featured by the band fell by the wayside. Satisfied with the overhaul of the band, Moten lined up a late-spring tour … capped by two weeks at Coney Island and four weeks in New England. …The accented brass and reed sections gave the band a more aggressive and expansive sound, particularly on *"Moten Swing"* and the popular standard *"Blue Room,"* in which the sections totally absorb and elaborate on Richard Rodgers' original theme, building to a climax of riffs that totally transcend the melody in a joyous out-chorus. Taken at breakneck speed, *"Toby"* showcases the band's impressive soloists who were urged by shouting riffs from the brass and reed sections. Basie artfully paraphrases *"Rhapsody in Blue"* in the introduction followed by a round of masterful solos by Eddie Durham, doubling on guitar and trombone… More tightly structured and crisply executed than *"Toby," "Moten Swing"* heralds the golden age of the Kansas City jazz style. …In the bridge, Durham contributes for rollicking two-bar phrases on guitar… The collective improvisation from head arrangements, fueled by the driving rhythm section and the supporting soloists and riffing sections, established a new style of freer orchestral jazz that foreshadowed the Swing Era. …The lack of local work forced the Moten band to resume regional touring. Departing for Oklahoma in mid-January 1933, the band played dates in Muskogee, Tulsa, and Forest Park in Oklahoma City. Moten hoped to return to New York and replace Cab Calloway at the Cotton Club in February, but the opportunity fell through, so the band continued barnstorming through Louisiana, Georgia, Alabama, Tennessee, Mississippi, Arkansas, Oklahoma and Iowa. The constant traveling took a toll on the band's personnel. While on the road, four band members resigned, including the entire saxophone section. Moten gathered replacements on the fly, adding tenor saxophonist Herschel Evans in San Antonio."[57]

All of the songs mentioned above were arranged by Eddie Durham.

Eddie was briefly with saxophonist/tubist Andy Kirk in 1929, as guitarist. His cousin, trombonist Allen Durham toured and recorded with Kirk from 1929-1931, perhaps recommended by Eddie. Kirk was just as popular as *Bennie Moten's Orchestra,* who Eddie and his other cousin, Herschel Evans, began to tour and record with. Although Eddie Durham performed on both trombone and guitar, his solos with *The Bennie Moten Orchestra* are mostly on guitar.

Eddie recalled: "I arranged "Blue Room," "Toby" and "Milenberg Joys," maybe a little touch on "Prince of Wales." When I was with Moten, I played a straight guitar with a resonator. It was about the size of a ten-inch record, made of tin, and it went right under the bridge. When you hit it, especially near a mic, you got an electric effect, and it carried like a banjo. Later I made a record of "Honey, Keep Your Mind On Me" with Jimmie Lunceford, and it sounds like electric, but it wasn't...

Moten Swing

Of all the arrangements I did for Bennie Moten, "Moten Swing" was the biggest. We were at the Pearl Theatre in Philadelphia when the owner, Sam Steiffel, complained about us doing the same things over and over again... When Bennie said: we've got to have a new number, I asked him to let me lay off one show to get it together for him. I went downstairs and Basie came with me. He was often my co-writer. He'd put a little melody in there, so he'd have an answer when Bennie asked me 'What did he write?' This time he gave me the channel. Horace Henderson was there and saw me write it, in pencil. We took it upstairs and the band went over it once, and then played it on the next show. It stopped the show every time. When we went to the Lafayette in New York the following week, we played it as the last number, and it took seven encores. The manager said, 'If you play it one more time, I'm going to throw the doors open'. And that's what he did, threw the doors open to the street, and people crowded around the doors to hear us… After I left Bennie Moten…, I went to New York to join Willie Bryant's band."[58]

"Junior Warren, a young banjoist/guitarist, had just joined the *Howard Bunts band* when *Bennie Moten's* influential band came to town from Kansas City in the summer of 1932. [Warren recalls:] 'I learned a lot of guitar from Eddie Durham in the *Bennie Moten band*. They had played the *Forest Club* and Charlie Stanton [from the *Goldkette* office] heard them and got them a job at the *Graystone [Ballroom]* for a week….I had never heard anything like the Moten band in my life. Every chorus they set a different style of rhythm. You know, pushing rhythms where they pushed the soloists. They played riffs as background rhythm on every chorus. We didn't dance even though we had brought our girls to the *Graystone*; we forgot all about the girls! No band in Detroit played that well. The Moten band stayed at the *Biltmore Hotel* and we had jam sessions in the basement of the hotel on St. Antoine. I hung out every day with Eddie Durham, Ben Webster, and Eddie Barefield and we became great friends…"[59]

"Though the composer credits on the label are Bennie and Buster Moten, Eddie probably deserves the lion's share of acknowledgment for his reworking of Walter Donaldson's "You're Driving Me Crazy" into an immortal Kansas City jazz anthem "Moten Swing." Later versions by Andy Kirk, Basie himself (who used it as his theme song before "One O'Clock Jump" became popular) and Jay McShann (featuring the fresh genius of 20-year-old Charlie Parker) still don't supplant this first, and best, recording. Lips Page's solos here, alternating sensitivity and forcefulness, presage Buck Clayton's work in the late 30s. Barefield shows both his admiration for Benny Carter's alto, and his exposure to Lester Young when they worked together in 1931 in Minneapolis. Ben Webster also gets a nice bridge statement. The driving medium tempo allows the entire group to swing to the hilt." ***Dan Weinstein***

"People know that the national anthem of Kansas City Jazz is "Moten Swing," one of the most famous tunes ever written. And we were talking about it with folks, and I said, 'you know, Eddie Durham wrote that tune'. They'd say, "No he didn't." I'd say, 'Yes, he did', and they'd show me the credits "Buster and Bennie Moten." So I told them the story, to which there were many witnesses, this was not just a story Eddie Durham made up, all the other folks in the band talked about it too. One day they needed a new arrangement, and Eddie was backstage with Count Basie who was on the piano, and they put this song together, but it was mostly Eddie's idea, and Basie had some riffs. But Eddie's name is not on it [the copyright]." *Loren Schoenberg*

Eddie recalled: "From Chicago, I went to Kansas City and joined the Bennie Moten Orchestra. They played an old style. Bennie & Buster brought me into the band to write and to play. They only had two trumpets, and two trombones. Ed Lewis tpt played first chair, Booker Washington tpt and, Thaymon Hayes-first chair tb, Woody Walder-clarinet/tenor, Harlan Leonard-1st alto, Vernon on tuba, Jack Washington-tenor, Buster Berry, Mac Washington-drums, Bennie Moten-piano, we got Buster [Moten] an accordion. I came in first from the Blue Devils. Lips Page made five, he replaced Vernon Page, then they added a sixth. Big Page, he come in with his sousaphone, we switched him right away to the string bass. Wasn't any string basses around in the bands at that time. That was a problem too, 'cause the band didn't understand it. Vernon and Walter wasn't related.

Basie come in very shortly after me, asked to be my assistant arranger. That's how he got his name, Count. Bennie was well studied - a real musician on piano, could read and everything, in that bracket like Fats Waller. The guys would say "that guy is terrific with Eddie." Because Moten was a terrific reader, like Fats Waller, birds' eyes. So Moten would tell Basie to play something from a chart, but Basie would say, "I can't read that!" and Moten would say, "You supposed to be an Arranger?" Then I'd tell Basie to sit down and make up something and I'd write it down, 'cause Basie couldn't read or write music. Basie would start off an idea, but I would have to finish it and write it out. Basie would get up and say, "Finish it out." Basie would play a bit and a bit more and then leave. Bennie would always say, "Where is that guy? That guy ain't "no account, we don't need him." So I wrote a song called "The Count" and put it in the book as a joke and every time Bennie would call that song, everybody would laugh. Basie didn't know what it was all about. But it was dedicated to his name as the "no account." The joke went on for a long time. That's how he got his title.

*I started right off arranging for this Band, nobody else arranged after I came in. They had a funny, peculiar sound due to the tone and didn't like for it to be changed, but it had to be changed. I changed the dimension, with charts like "Everyday Blues" and my playing guitar. At the end of it all, "**Moten Swing**" took four encores at the Lafayette Theatre in Philadelphia, PA, then seven encores and on the eight, they opened all doors to the public. They couldn't do any head arrangements, that came in when I was with Basie. Bennie Moten couldn't 'head'. I could write out a background riff, for the sax to play and my cousin Herschel, who wasn't a good reader, but a good ear man, and those guys would play their harmony right with it, I didn't have to write it.*

For Herschel, I could write 4-part harmony, sax, and pass it out, invent it the first time and he'd play down what you're supposed to have for him. Lester Young was good at that too, but Herschel was the king.

For Lester, you'd have to interpret it to him and give him time to get it. They'd say, 'write it later when you get ready to publish'. So that's how Charlie Hathaway came in and got credit and Buck Clayton because they had to score the harmony. But I can make a lot out of skeletons. Nobody could read what I could write, all the way down the line.

Eddie Barefield was with me on "Toby," he was a writer too. Page could master tone on the fiddle and be heard without an amplifier, he was strong, had big arms and hands. He would hug the bass, he said, "for tone"- and when he hit (not pick) those notes the vibration would vibrate in any room and the stage would sway. He held the notes a little longer than most of them. The reeds went from three to four.

Banjo went out. I played guitar and they got Freddie Green right away. Lips playing the chord or tonic third and the fifth, I added the sixth. But the Band thought it was out of tune and that I was crazy, or, that Lips was there to replace somebody else because they only knew limited notes. Now I still had to put my note in, mostly on valve trombone, and this made five brass. I used valve trombone for trumpet notes, which came from the Circus.

On guitar with Moten, I played mostly my solo work because we had a trombone player and I didn't see much to playing a lot of trombone. So they'd run to Bennie without me and tell him, "He's crazy, it's out of tune"... but when I added in the fifth, which was the ninth chord, that sounded pretty to them. Moten told them to play whatever I write and that's how we got "Moten Swing." So the sixth note they didn't like that. That was an edge I had with the Count Basie Orchestra with Earle Warren, I'd tell him to make it a flat fifth. Guys would come up during intermission asking about notes they heard when he was holding a chord. I could dissolve odd background sounds, like organ harmony, to get a peculiar sound on the reeds. But what it was, if it was an F flat, F sharp, and it would be an F flat the way he'd make it, but I wouldn't let him put the signature there. They'd say, 'Oh Earle Warren sure can bend those notes'. But it was a trick. And if you didn't hold him down with his own thing, he'd go out in space with something else, no limit to what he could do.

This Band would promote their own dances, rent a big Hall or auditorium, write and promote, put some men on the door, and split the money after expenses. Moten got no more than the next guy because he thought that a sideman was worth just the same thing as the Leader, even though he played the piano and handled the business.

42

One O'Clock Jump

But in the rhythm section, they didn't like the bass fiddle walking too much, like "One O'Clock Jump," said it was out of tune, out of chord if it's a B flat chord. I was using everything else, chromatic and that bass, but it's dissolving all the time, just like a train moving. I changed Moten to walking on "One O'Clock Jump." I took a B flat chord consisting of a B flat, G, F, and D, I'm using an E flat and E natural, F sharps, A's, and chromatic for the dissolving tones. They complained that I was changing the style of the band. But after it got on record, then they accepted it because the public accepted it. But the band was always more critical.

I always had an idea and I liked to create. I voice the organ with the clarinet and the trombone and it sounds beautiful. I played both trombone and guitar with most all the bands and most of my solo work on guitar in all the arrangements. I don't know that much about Duke, but I know he liked to create; Don Redman, Fletcher Henderson, Art Tatum, and Jesse Stone too.

Nobody pulled out no book for me in those days - I always had or made the book for the band.

Now Ellington had a weird tone, semi-symphony, much greater than any of the others in that Band; far gone, his style - fifty years ahead of his time. Strayhorn's expression is great too, especially for Johnny Hodges, ballads, he wrote wonderful things, but pretty close to a white writer, white music, legitimate training - but Ellington's music come out of his head instead of the book - just compare "Warm Valley," "Untouchable" and the stuff Duke wrote after Strayhorn died. But a guy like Strayhorn will make a guy like Duke ease up a little.''[60] *(Eddie / B. Moten recordings: see "Appendix A")*

"The band to beat back in the old days was always the one led by Bennie Moten, who because of his emphasis on high-level musicianship and all-around classiness was sometimes called 'the Duke Ellington of the West'. Members of the old *Blue Devils Orchestra* brag about winning so many battles against so many other bands that Bennie Moten not only would not do battle with them but as a matter of historical fact, hired away most of their best members... About the evolution of the Kansas City Four/Four, Jo Jones, who as the drummer in the *Count Basie Orchestra* from the mid-thirties through the early forties was largely responsible for extending it into the national domain, has said: 'When Bennie Moten's two-beat one and three rhythm and, the two and four of *Walter Page's Blue Devils* came together in the Basie band, there was an even flow one-two-three-four,' (Walter Page himself playing what came to be known as walking string bass, with Eddie Durham and later Freddie Green chording on rhythm guitar, provided the anchor for the Basie rhythm section. ... Classic Basie: "Time Out," which contains a four-bar Herschel Evans introduction to a Lester Young solo, also features Buck Clayton, Eddie Durham (electric guitar), Basie, and Earle Warren "Topsy" features Buck Clayton, Jack Washington, Basie, and Herschel Evans, *Sent For You Yesterday and Here You Come Today*, one of the band's most popular Jimmy Rushing shout vocals, is a typical example of blues music counter-stating negative lyrics. "Moten Swing" the Kansas City Anthem, is credited to Bennie and Buster Moten, but was actually composed by Eddie Durham from the chords of "You're Driving Me Crazy." Durham laid out to do so during a set backstage at the *Pearl Theatre* in Philadelphia in 1931 because a ride-out number was needed for the finale. Eddie Durham, the guitarist-trombonist-arranger/composer, ...whose "Out The Window," "Time Out," and "Topsy" (Decca DXSB 7170) are almost always included in listings of the Best of Count Basie... Eddie Durham, whose arrangements for *The Blue Devils*, the Bennie Moten Orchestra, and Count Basie played a crucial part in making the Kansas City emphasis a fundamental element of blues-idiom musicianship."61

"The band then started a trip east that was "the damndest barnstorming trip you've ever seen in your life. We never did get paid. We used to work and get enough money to eat on, but we never made any money. We traveled all the way from Kansas City, and we were stranded in Zanesville, Ohio.. Columbus... Cincinnati... finally we get to Philadelphia and started this job at the Pearl Theatre... now we know we're going to get a week's salary, so we started tabbing our whisky... taking the girls out and we were having a ball... When the musicians lined up in the back of the theatre at the end of the week to get paid... a creditor who had sold uniforms to the band on their previous visit went to the head of the line and took all the cash. He also took the bus… So finally Bennie Moten went off and came back with a fellow named Archie. Archie went somewhere and got an old raggedy bus and loaded us up… and drove us over to Camden, Ohio. So we went to this pool hall and this guy Archie made a big rabbit stew. Where did this guy find a rabbit so quick in Camden? Then they took us over to a church and we recorded 8 sides, including "new Orleans," "Lafayette," "Moten Stomp, "Moten Swing," "Toby," and a couple others. I never did get paid for it, but nevertheless it went down in history… It was quite a band we had, with Lips, Dee, and Joe Keyes on trumpet; Eddie Durham and Dan Minor on trombone; Jack Washington, Ben Webster, and myself on saxophones; Basie and Walter Page in the rhythm section, with Leroy Berry on guitar and Pete Washington on drums; and Jimmy Rushing as vocalist. Bennie Moten played piano, too, but Basie played most of the time and Buster Moten conducted.

We were stranded in nearly every city on our way to New York. We just hung around the town until they got another raggedy bus. And those buses were always breaking down! One time in Virginia we were coming down one of those steep hills and the brakes refused to work. The hand brake came out in the driver's hand, and the bus went careening down through a town at about sixty miles an hour. Being stranded meant that you were in a town without work or money…Mostly it was hot dogs and chili, with booze. We weren't alarmed, because it was a common thing, and finally, somehow, we got to the Pearl Theater in Philadelphia …" *Eddie Barefield,* Jazz Saxophonist, clarinetist, arranger (L.Armstrong, E.Fitzgerald, Ellington, Dorsey, Goodman, G.Miller, P.Whiteman) (1909-1991) [62]

The *Bennie Moten Orchestra* performs a two-year residency at the *Harlem Club Paseo* in Kansas City, Missouri. Sometime in late 1934 before this residency ended, Eddie leaves for the *Willie Bryant Orchestra*. He joined the *Jimmie Lunceford Orchestra* in February 5, 1935 accompanying them on a one-month tour to Europe, returning mid-March 1937.

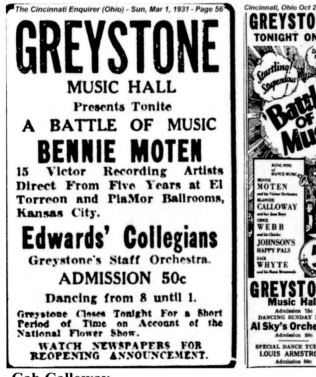

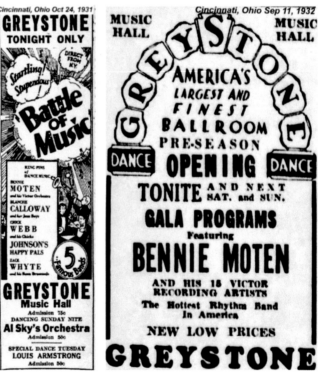

Cab Calloway

"The deepening of the depression brought on a serious decline in work. So between Moten engagements, Durham sometimes worked with Basie in a small 12th St. club in Kansas City. He was hired by Cab Calloway, who brought him a new trombone. The band went into the Main Street Theatre for a week beginning on June 24, 1933. The result was negative. As Durham puts it, "Cabell couldn't see me. I just left the new trombone on the stage and cut

46

out after the week was over."[63] Recall from the previous *Family History* section, that Blanche Calloway, Cab's older sister, made Eddie's eldest brother Joe Jr. her "trustee." Edgar Battle was also in Blanche's band.

Willie Bryant

Eddie recalled 1934: "In this band with me were Benny Carter, Stan Payne, Lorenzo [Glyn] Paque, Johnny Russell, Teddy Wilson, Cozy Cole, Richard Clark, and Edgar Battle. But Bobby Cheek, Jack Butler, and Taft Jordan were there before or must have been after me. ...I was in Kansas City... but he [Willie] wanted me to write arrangements and play in the band. He sent me seventy-five dollars to make the trip and told me he was playing at Connie's Inn. I think he'd heard about me because Battle was already in the band. I didn't get to play much with the band because an 802 [union] delegate stopped me and said I couldn't play because I didn't have a card. So I wrote arrangements and hung out with the band. Sometimes I played a little guitar or, if Teddy Wilson was late, I sat in on piano. ...I was on a couple of records... most of my playing was just sitting in with the band or gigging at joints and rent parties... I stayed with Bryant about six months then moved on.[64] I left Moten four weeks before he died [April 2, 1935]. I felt they had all they needed with my arrangements. Willie Bryant sent for me so I went to New York. We were at Small's Paradise and The Savoy Ballroom in Harlem. I was there for about six months. But I had trouble with the Union, with the transfer.

So I just wrote "Chimes in the Chapel" or they changed it to "Chimes at the Meeting" 'cause they didn't want to use "Chapel," but it had chimes, bells in it, got paid as an Arranger - and he recorded. But lots of nights I'd play peek-a-boo trombone but sometimes I'd play piano with the band, with Teddy Wilson – he was always late. He'd come in and find me stretching those big chords and tell me not to move – he'd let me play a while. Willie had a gold pistol, he was the Mayor of the town of Harlem, a ladies man."

"Chimes" was recorded on January 4, 1935. On January 26, 1935 Percival Outram of The New York Age Newspaper reported: "Willie Bryant, leader of a promising band featured by the Savoy Ballroom on the radio, is reported on the outside looking in. Willie kicked the traces over too often and the Savoy management severed the connection with the volatile leader."

(Eddie / Willie Bryant recordings: see "Appendix A")

Unions

Eddie recalled: "See with the Union, you had to put in an application, sweat it out while you wait six months, then go on the application as a 'traveling member'. And if you were in the city, you had to go out and play dates until you become a member, but you had to let them know when you went out and came back. You'd live in the city and go get your gig somewhere else. You could stay with both locals, like Chicago and 802 in New York, but you had two dues to pay. I belonged to four Unions once, for a long time, I believe Local 627 in Kansas City, 710 in Washington, D.C., I was on the Board of Directors there, and New York and Connecticut. Every time a delegate came I'd have to sit out. But I didn't like to be antagonized by the Union, sitting around waiting, so I left Bryant and went to Jimmie Lunceford next, to a band where I could play..."[65]

KC Nightlife

Eddie recalled: "Musicians were everywhere in Kansas City, Mary Lou, Lester, Prez, Herschel, Basie, Buddy Tate, Buck and others. Kansas City bands come off the stage at daylight. People would go straight to work from dancing all night long. We'd leave one job 3AM and go to another job. I'd finish at the Cherry Blossom, go down to Piney Brown's where Joe Turner was bartending, with my guitar, jump up on stage and Joe would come and sing, Jo Jones would have his snare drum, no sock cymbal - and that was another job until 7AM, we would get tips.

Ben Webster was like a kid when he got some wine, turn his back on the tracks and not move! He'd fight you! So, they'd call the cops and before they come, Ben would run and hide. They'd say, "What's that?" "Oh, Ben Webster in the middle of the street car track."

The liquor stores stayed open 24 hours in Kansas City, until they passed a law, and one store would open one minute after midnight. So, they'd stand in line on 18th & Vine Streets to get wine. All the musicians met there in the middle of the street after all the jobs was over." [66]

Teddy Wilson

Eddie recalled: "Teddy Wilson [Sr.] played a different kind of piano from anybody else, very smooth with that stuff, kinda like Ear Hines, but Earl was kinda rough. Teddy used more chords and stayed closer, nice style. I remember his piano playing anytime I hear it, that's all I go by. He was a nice guy. ...The rhythm guitar was supposed to strum and that's rhythm just like a pianist used to play. They don't play too much of that strumming. The only guy stuck to it close was Teddy Wilson, he could leave his piano rolls and style and play that strum. And that holds a beat.

Now, the kids dance by a drum only, because the guitars are gone off somewheres in space, as Basie says. They become united with the bass drum and the piano. If it ever comes united together, you'd say, boy, that's some rhythm."[67]

"I first met Eddie's daughter [the Author] while we were both serving on Jury Duty in Queens and both assigned to the same jury pool. Talk about irony! As we began talking, imagine the amazement when we realized our dads not only knew each other but how well! I hadn't met Eddie until the last year of his life, but I knew about him very well. You see, the need for dance was the big principal factor for the so-called Swing Era. Blues, as such, is really theoretically a multitude of styles. We're most familiar with what's called the "urban blues" the 12-bar Blues. But the really down to earth Blues, what we call the "rural blues" varied from many people. Not only in the Southwest and Kansas City but throughout the Delta region, and that is as varied as virtually as the many people who sang it, the famous ones, particularly from Kansas City and Southwest territory bands, notably Leadbelly and Blind Lemon Jefferson. Bessie Smith is urban blues, very structured 12-bar blues. But if you listen to any of these "field recordings," literally recorded in the fields, each has a very individual style. And I think that aspect got into the Jazz, from the standpoint of the soloists.

When you have a really true Jazz soloist, you can have five saxes and everyone is playing the same tune and each one is very different. That's a throwback to a true blues singer. But with that, coupled with this style of ragtime piano which is a very structured form, it provided at least a basis for a beat, something people could dance to. I would say that's what really moved from the freedom of the real rural Blues to the structure of Swing music Jazz, was this thing of being able to dance. The earliest swing bands were Elmer Snowden, Sonny Greer, Duke Ellington, and Fletcher Henderson. Jelly Roll Morton was kind of a musician all of his own, and he said he "invented Jazz and everything everybody else is doing, they were playing his music." But these are the beginning of organized bands who were really reading arrangements and who were getting into the structure and style of at least having a lead sheet. It's not like a note for note arrangement with guys just playing from their heads. This is an organized structure where everybody's playing in such a uniform way that it's easy to tap your foot and you can dance."[68] ***Theodore Wilson, III,*** Acoustic bassist (late son of pianist Teddy Wilson)

Guitar Innovation

"When we teach a person they are mostly playing mechanically. My father was a violin player and we had a family band. So naturally, I didn't have any problems with playing because I was with it all the time. And that's the way Eddie was, relaxed. When I teach, I teach like Charles Roth taught me, first master the chords, so you can actually *play* the guitar. I teach basic but the system I teach is the 120-chord system, 12 tone system, all the C scales and it's very easy. It's root position, position of the third, fifth, inversions E flat, and so on, back to F again. Then I teach diminished and augmented. People like BB King learned by ear and they played the same thing all the time."[69] ***Larry Lucie*** (1907-2009), Guitarist, Bandleader, Professor, Recording Artist

"Eddie Durham's innovation of the electric guitar is more forthright, his playing is more developed, his security with the set-up is more clear and the record documents a very early prominence of this new concept in sound. Earle Warren remarked that he and his twin brother, Robert, went to hear *Bennie Moten's Kansas City Orchestra* in 1931 play at the *Masonic Hall…* in Ohio. Being musicians, when the great bands came to town, they'd get there when the band got there and hear them rehearse or set up their gear or hang out and talk with them. As they started ambling up the stairs, they heard something that really sounded odd and they didn't really know what to make of it, they

50

didn't have too much experience with a microphone, but they understood that such things existed and that speakers and singers were starting to use them. They weren't common at all in Springfield and in fact, they knew that the place they were going into, didn't have one. But they knew the sound was different and they walked in and they heard Eddie Durham, setting up his contraption for that evening's performance. It was a lot of gear to get that electric guitar sound and he got it - and there's the first intersection in 1931, for these future colleagues in the Basie Band, he would lead the reeds, Earle Warren and the great Eddie Durham. So it's very prominent on these records. But what's even more prominent, is the sound of the original Count Basie Band - up and operational in *Bennie Moten's Kansas City Orchestra*, and Eddie Durham's riding a full five years earlier.

These records are a quantum leap forward from everything [recorded so far]. We hear Eddie Durham's composition and arrangement "Moten Swing." As great as that writing is, Richard Rodgers' Broadway show tune "The Blue Room" is to my estimation the definitive Eddie Durham arranging masterpiece of this period and his first such masterwork. It's of that higher order. They'd been appearing in Pennsylvania with a vocal group called *The Russell Sterling Trio* and they came out to Camden, NJ to make the records with them and did "Imagination" and Eddie Durham cooked up an arrangement for them. Jimmy Rushing sings Hoagy Carmichael's new tune "New Orleans" and Eddie Durham arranges that. *The Sterling Russell Trio*, for their flip side, did "The Only Girl I Ever Loved." Then in a 1, 2, 3 knockout punch sequence we get "Milenberg Joys" Eddie Durham arranges Jelly Roll Morton; "Lafayette" Eddie Durham arranges Eddie Durham; and "Prince of Wales" Eddie Durham arranges Elmer Schoebel and early Jazz.

These are the classics and if you don't know these records, you're going to be thrilled. If you know the early Count Basie swing era records, and you don't know these records, you're going to be thrilled and surprised. The genius behind the *Bennie Moten Band* is the same guy to write the *Count Basie* book five years later. The great Eddie Durham." Phil Schaap with you, this is *WKCR-FM* New York."70 **Phil Schaap**, Grammy Jazz Historian, Editor-

Jazz at Lincoln Center, Professor-Swing University, Archivist, Curator, Engineer, Producer

"T-Bone's first instrument was the banjo, which he preferred to the guitar because it was louder. ...He also played banjo and guitar with the Cab Calloway orchestra for a week — the gig won first prize in a talent contest — which led to a record deal with Columbia in 1929. ...In the early '30s, Walker had a street act with Charlie Christian, an ex-Dallasite living in Oklahoma City, who would be immortalized as jazz's first great electric guitarist. Let that settle in: The two greatest guitar pioneers of the twentieth century were a pair of Texans who played together for tips on street corners in Oklahoma City. The pair were probably introduced to the electric guitar by Eddie Durham, the San Marcos native who made the first known amplified guitar recording on 1935's "Hittin' The Bottle" with the Jimmy Lunceford orchestra."[71]

"Back to Eddie's pioneering work on electric guitar, he can be heard to great advantage with Lunceford soloing on the band's recordings of "Avalon," "Hittin' The Bottle," and "Honey, Keep Your Mind On Me," among others. Charlie Christian, the great electric guitarist in Benny Goodman's orchestra, can be heard on recordings quoting Eddie Durham's solo from the Lunceford recording of "Avalon," in fact there could be no greater compliment. In my own career, I've also played for a number of years with guitarist Les Paul's trio, and Les is often credited as the father of the electric guitar, but he freely acknowledged Eddie's historical role in developing and making early recordings on the instrument"[72] **John Colianni**, Jazz Pianist (*Les Paul Trio*, Bandleader, American Jazz pianist (Les Paul trio)

Eddie was in fact, a decade or more, older than Les Paul.

Eddie recalled: "For amplification, I used an acoustic but I rigged up my own homemade guitar, and in the dance hall we would use a mic, lean it over. Finally, I figured out a way to get an old amplifier with a mic. This is what I played on "Honey Keep Your Mind On Me." I played only downstrokes. I made a resonator with a tin pan. It was back in the early 1930s. I'd carve out the inside of an acoustic guitar and put the resonator down inside there. It was the size of a breakfast plate. I'd put something around the guitar to hold it. And when I hit the strings, the pie pan would ring and shoot out the sound. I didn't have to do that for long because I ran up on a National. It had a resonator in it. It was used as a steel guitar with a bar. I removed the bridge and put an acoustic type bridge on it because the other bridge held the strings up too high. When I was with the Jimmie Lunceford Orchestra there was one microphone that was used by the singer, but when I played my solo, Lunceford would bring that microphone right up to my guitar [to the F-Hole]. He was crazy about the resonator.

Then I tried converting radio and phonograph amplifiers and even drilled into the body of the guitar. With that rig, I used to blow out the lights in a lot of places. They weren't really up on electricity like they are now, no fuses. Later after D'Armand came out with a pickup, I was one of the first people to use it. I made an attachment where I could play into the sound system. If I wanted to I could be all over the joint. I couldn't play rhythm because it was too loud. I just played solos. I played with just about every guitar I could get my hands on, Nationals, Epiphones, Gibsons, Danelectros, and others.

Vibrato

I even rigged up my own vibrato arm before they made them on guitars, I took a clothes hanger and bent it and hooked it on my finger. The bridges were swinging bridges. They weren't stationary in those days and they had an apron-like tailpiece. The strings keep the apron in place and I hooked the other end of the wire to the apron. When you shook the wire, the bridge would move and you had a vibrato. Most of the time I used it with chords.

I came from Seattle out of Vancouver, B.C. with a girl's band. My band was going on at midnight, but in the Seattle clubs, they announced that all the guitar players have off, for one hour, midnight to 1:00 AM. But the boss allowed people to come hear me because I had out that "Honey, Keep Your Mind On Me," and now, I had an electric guitar and an amplifier. I set up on the stage and they used to blow the lights out. So they'd want me to set up the amplifier with two tubes in it. I said, 'if we cover this box, the guys won't bother me', 'cause they'd never want that amplifier. They called it my "starvation box."

I also used 12" megaphones for trumpet and 16" for trombones. The band would come out first with a big introduction. All the guitar players in town come over to that club, for free to hear me play that get up. I played two numbers. Christian went out with Goodman that year. (Hear Charlie Christian's recording of "Swing to Bop" and Durham's "Topsy"). I've always been fooling around with electric string on top of the reeds. I got that 12-string guitar, special made and I had Les Paul come down look at it, check the neck and he said the neck is true.

"I remember Ina asking me one day, 'Eddie, why do the two tenor saxophones have to be separated like that?' It was a good question because all the bands used to put the two tenors and the two altos together, but all of a sudden they began putting one tenor on each end of the saxes.73 Ina had tenors split up only because she saw Basie do that. I explained to her why he did that which was because Lester and Herschel didn't like each other's vibrato."74

Flat 11th's & 5th's

Arthritis kinda hit me in that hand and crippled one of my fingers, the little finger ...the lead finger. I don't know if guitar players know what it's all about but that's the finger that you make them flat 11ths and 5ths. So when I play guitar now I don't use those chords, I skip around 'em.

Palm Damper

To play my way, for inside chords you gotta use one finger to kill strings below the other one, I use both hands and the palm of my hands as a damper, just like the pedals on a piano. And when you hit the note, gotta use the palm of your hand to dampen it and if your guitar will take it, then when you come back with the next hand, your hand you do the same thing up here, you use both hands as a damper, it's like two feet working. That was my style.

If I had'a just stuck to the guitar and really studied it, I could've perfected it. When I play it you say, well that's Art Tatum with the piano. But I know

54

what needs to be done, it needed more positions. The guitar only had about 7 positions.

12-String Guitar

This 12-string guitar I got has 34 frets and you could get your chords down here because the guitar has got the same range of a trombone. Ain't got enough positions, it should be an octave, it's not an octave. So when you play it up in the first position, when you get down far enough to go into something else, you gotta go back to get it somewhere else. So that's what I really worked on. 'Bout the time I got it perfected I quit playing the guitar, on the count of arthritis.[75]

Dobro Resonator

On the resonator guitar, I took a stiff clothes hanger and hook on back and over to the swinging bridge, or the top, hook it in my finger so I could shake it when I play. I wore out my resonator so by the time I was ready to get another, they were all out of business and the neck was too thick for later stuff. That guitar has a piece of tin built in it, with little holes, but once I mic it, it sounded electric and loud. That's what you hear on "Hittin' The Bottle" (Lunceford Orchestra 1935 metal-bodied Dobro resophonic, non-electric guitar).

A couple years later they came out with something already made like that in the electrically amplified guitar. I got one and took it on the road. The Ballroom owners were always scared that I'd blow out all the lights, but the problem was that it worked on AC current and there was still mostly DC all over the country. I thought about that later, I should have patented my idea before they did. I think Epiphone was the first to make an amplified guitar. The Stella guitar, I used with Lunceford on "Honey." National made the metal resonator.."

"I first heard Eddie playing the Dobro guitar. When they first made it there was no electric guitar and it was made to give the guitar more volume. Cause otherwise, you'll drown if you play a solo. So Eddie seemed to be one of the first ones to play it, he was the first one I heard really play it. And then I went and got me one right away." **Larry Lucie**

Dan Electro Bass Guitar

Eddie recalled: "I used a Dan Electric which had a peculiar sound but I could very near take anybody else's guitar and get that sound. It's the way you grip and hit, and I only played downstrokes. Nobody else did that.

Frets

See, the only thing changes the tone of a guitar is the frets at the end. I think if you take a note and push down and hold it, you'd change it, but once you strike it, that's it. Electric guitar sure took off, changed history, brought in Rock 'n Roll. Now they build it in the foot pedal, just touch it and go. I used a real electric guitar on The Kansas City Six in "I Want A Little Girl".[76]

"I wanted to do a tribute to my father. It finally happened in his hometown in 2004. I took the song "Topsy" which I thought was relatively easy. But from playing the pop and Rhythm & Blues from my generation, the approach to the melody is very different. Straight ahead Jazz is very different. The fingering is unfamiliar and foreign. So I'm relearning how to play things. He used to talk about staccato & legato and when you attack with only downstrokes you get a different sound. He did a lot of arpeggio things and they don't play like that in Pop and R&B.

Tone

My father told me *"you have a nice warm tone in your fingers and everything is very definite."* I didn't understand that at the time, you know because I thought the tone is in the guitar. But later I noticed that you can give a guitar to five different people and have them play the same line, tempo, notes, etc., but each one will sound different, it's like a personality. It's like a sax player, some have a real sweet or creamy sound, a rough tone, a dead tone and some you don't wanna listen to. But he explained that some guitar players play, but the sound is not a rich sound - the feeling in the sound is not there. But after I had been playing with different people, they would say, "Oh, we wanna use Eric, we don't wanna use the other guy." It goes to the tone in the fingers, the way you attack the string and the attitude that you put in each note. And I got that from watching him. A lot of things happened because you're there and I was watching and hearing him as I was in the process of learning,

56

so I learned from him without even realizing it. But when I look back, I realize it now. I think that if he wasn't my father, I would probably be doing something creative but I don't think I would be playing the guitar." *Eric R. Durham, Sr.*

Eddie recalled: "*Buster [Smith] was trying to teach Charlie Parker how to hold the alto. Charlie wasn't reading and his tone was so bad and Charlie told Buster, "I don't want to play sax no more." Charlie didn't get into it fast enough so that sort of worried Buster, because the guys were cranky about tones. Charlie was trying to play like Buster all his life and he couldn't get Buster, so he materialized something that was of his own - which created history. See, Charlie's tone wasn't good to blend with the saxes, but it was a tone the public went for. Because you've got to play the same weight of vibrato. Sometimes it's too much vibrato or not enough, it works for solo work, but sometimes it won't, the other guys can't get it.*

White Bands have the Lombardo tone and the straight tone and that's why any white musician can sit down and play with Glenn Miller or someplace else. But black musicians get eight to ten different tones on his horn so when he gets in a band it's harder for him to fit. When you got other horses to team with you, you got to stay in line. Coleman Hawkins had a big-headed fat tone. Lester more whispery... His style of playing fit what he was doing, so it was just his solo individual deal. But I found a way to use it with the section, up as a C melody part, which we call the alto part, way up in the sixes and hard notes, laying right next to that second alto. I never let him play the root of the chord. If you ever move away from that, the weight will go away from the section, because he didn't have a big heavy tone, and that why the section sounded different. When he came out, they put in two regular tenors. Tone-wise, Basie's section started sounding like Fletcher Henderson. I was teaching Charlie Christian guitar at the same time, in Oklahoma City".[77]

"I was a very well trained musician and I had a good classical background so I could read anything, and I thought it was great. Then when I joined this band many of the girls had problems reading because they had learned their instruments the hard way, it was just put in their hands, it was like now or never, learn it fast and play, but what they had was a relaxed way of approaching the music. Their beat was different from out more up-tight white rhythm".[78] Rosalind "Roz" Cron, *International Sweethearts of Rhythm*.

"Lester didn't play down in there [with Evans]. Lester was another way." Young "had that C-melody sound," he said, "so when I made arrangements for him, like all the numbers I made for Basie, I had to use Lester way on top." If he put Evans on top, "it didn't blend good and you didn't get that…that jazz sound." This need to place Young according to his tone "made Basie's reed section different from any reed section." [79]

Transposition

"But after learning the guitar, I had all these ideas in my head and I got to the point where I wanted to learn how to put it on paper. Because I saw my father do it, it didn't scare me. But I don't think I would have pursued trying to learn how to put things to paper if he wasn't my father. Sometimes I would get up at 2AM and he would be in the kitchen and have all the charts spread out, he still did some arranging and I would see the different instruments at the top of the page. But I saw on his charts it said 'A', and the notes on the trumpet, the key signature was one thing, but on the sax and the trombone was different, but the title of the song was the same. So I asked him. He said, *"The keys for each instrument was different so I have to transpose for them to be playing the same thing in the same key."* So he took a half hour and he explained transposition to me. I was about 15 years old. I could always interrupt him, he never got upset. He didn't teach me to read music. He showed me techniques to pen things and when I got good at it, I would bring it to him and he would say that my *"Penmanship to paper is excellent"* - and I got a real kick out of that. Sometimes musicians will hire me just to write out charts. But I'm not a great site reader. I never felt I could fill his shoes. The more I do in this music business, the more I realize just how much of a genius he was." ***Eric R. Durham, Sr.*** guitarist. (Eric's discography: see "Appendix A")

Lawrence Lucie

"When I first heard Eddie Durham play guitar, I think it was a Kay or either the Dobro guitar, it was a straight guitar. This was around the early 1930s at the Savoy, with the Bennie Moten Band. I started playing it right after that.

There was no electric guitar at that time. We started playing electric guitar only for solo work because it was a little louder. I played rhythm guitar for 15 years, no electric. I only started playing electric mostly when I quit the big bands, that's 1945 when I went into Rock 'n Roll.

Every time I heard Eddie he was playing a straight guitar. With Jimmie Lunceford, he played straight guitar. Lunceford was a great Swing band, one of the greatest entertaining bands of all time. Eddie used to always solo with the guitar. His style of playing was more or less like he played the trombone. I guess he must of had inspiration playing solo like he played the trombone, made it original, and made it different because he was playing it like a horn. The guitar players were following another approach. But when we heard him playing it, making it sound like a horn, that was one of the things made it so appealing to Charlie Christian. So when he would play these solo breaks, he was playing melodic lines, making it sound like a horn.

I listened to Eddie Durham and Charlie Christian. When I heard these two guys, I thought about maybe playing solo guitar sometimes; up to then, I was strictly a rhythm player. I first heard Charlie Christian in Oklahoma City when I was on tour with Lucky Millinder, in 1935 or 1936. ...What I noticed was that Charlie did a lot of down picking, like Eddie Durham, and he wasn't playing any modern chords. Playing down is more powerful, more exciting and you can develop a fast technique.

Eddie Durham's style went to Charlie Christian and to Wes Montgomery. It's all built from, first beginning with Eddie picking up the guitar with Jimmie Lunceford, picking up the guitar playing those solos. I was listening to it and he becomes my favorite, my inspiration. So I was feeling what he was doing because it's like a beginning of something which nobody else is doing.

Down Picking

Eddie played all down-picking, but the average person would play up and down. Down-picking gives you that other sound. Playing up-picking is not as effective. Eddie Durham started something that nobody else has been able to do it, but those that did it sold the most records. Charlie Christian, he died at 22 years old and he was the world's greatest record seller. Then Wes Montgomery copied him exactly. The only thing is Wes Montgomery used his thumb. But it still comes from the Eddie Durham approach.

Eddie was a very good arranger. When he played trombone it was so soulful. But he was my idol when it comes to playing guitar, the feeling, style, and sound of a guitar. He added more to the guitar feeling than anybody. 'Cause I built my whole style of playing with Eddie Durham. Matter of fact, I took notice of his playing, even though I knew the guitar very well, I changed to that particular style. Now I'm playing everything down because it's more effective, more powerful, and exciting. You can develop fast down-playing."[80] *Lawrence Lucie*

"...I was contrasting two short episodes from two strikingly different records, that nevertheless contain a musical match. [Avalon and Gillie.] When Jimmie Lunceford's Orchestra, Lunceford a Missouri born, Denver raised man who emerged in Memphis, Tennessee who led a great, big band, it was characterized by its Arrangers and the fourth piece to fall into place in Lunceford's career was when he added the arranging touch of Eddie Durham, which he added in 1935 or late '34. In doing so he also intersected with the advent of the electric guitar, which was Durham's specialty instrument, he also played trombone, and he solos on both instruments in Lunceford recordings, Electric guitar, yes… that date back nearly 70 years. One of them is particularly precious in terms of understanding the pioneering cornerstone to the electric guitar that Durham represents, it's this one, "Avalon."

60

Durham's arrangement was excerpted, where orchestral strings and a little bit of a riff alternate with, I believe, improvised guitar breaks. But those guitar breaks no longer are improvisations, when five years, two months and twenty days later, Durham's pupil, perhaps the best known early electric guitarist Charlie Christian, recycles the improvisation as arranging, putting in an interlude in the midst of the Benny Goodman sextet recording of "Gilly" using it in almost the same exact context, although it's in the middle, as a fetching arranging device to help things head towards its home stretch, the same thing that Durham had used to introduce a completely different piece by a completely different Band over five years before.

So the point here is if you're really interested in the dawn of guitar, you must know about Christian. I'm not trying to trump Christian's ace, 'cause he's a genius and by Durham's own admittance is a person of greater technique on the electric guitar and regardless of his primacy as a pioneer, is a genius and the music's great. But the direct connection to Christian between Durham and Christian is under-documented, although it is very much a provable point. I've just added a little bit of this musical smoking gun to the many doubting Thomas's.

Durham was the rarest of geniuses, a humble one, and he rarely if ever, blew his own horn. He was not very careful about keeping track of what he had accomplished or even getting the financial reward that he deserved for such contributions. His career is in that regard, highly checkered and therefore, by the way people keep track of things, hard to illustrate quickly, in today's modern day and age.

Christian played with probably the best-known instrumentalist, Benny Goodman, who was showcased on *Carnegie Hall's* stage, on radio on a near-weekly basis as part of Goodman's *Camel Caravan Show* and on numerous records. While Durham also played *Carnegie Hall*, he didn't get there as quickly as Christian who actually was there for a short time. And although he's showcased on Basie records, he's not as well-known as Christian. And given Christian's magnitude and their contemporary status, most of the time the short-cut answer is - Christian is the first electric guitarist. But the first is, of course his teacher... Eddie Durham. The records that I played was an illustration of that. In 1935 Eddie Durham played a passage… and Christian incorporates it in a record over five years later playing with Goodman. …You'll hear Eddie Durham on electric guitar in 1935 in the introduction to his own arrangement of the well-known standard "Avalon." …The same passage of music used in a completely different context on "Gilly" with the *Benny Goodman Sextet*, five years later, Christian."[81] ***Phil Schaap***

"Originally, he had a friend remodel a standard microphone, wired to a PA system, to be inserted in the *F*-Hole of the instrument. This apparently did not entirely satisfy the guitarist, so he designed a movable bridge, connected to a metal wire coat hanger. By manipulating the coat hanger with his finger, he could produce a resonating effect. His electric model confronted Eddie Durham with a couple of problems. It was not unusual for his guitar to overload the mains of the hall, causing the lights to blow fuses. He almost electrocuted himself a couple of times. An even bigger problem was that his custom-built amplifier used alternate current, whereas most of the country still ran on direct current. Early in 1937 Durham, on the road with the [Lunceford] *Harlem Express*, met a talented seventeen-year-old guitarist in Oklahoma City, named Charlie Christian. Charlie of course was still playing acoustic guitar, and Durham showed him how he could get a crisper sound by hitting the strings in downward strokes only. He also showed him that by getting his instrument electrified, he could play at the same level as the horns. (Later, Christian was to devote a tune to their current problems: "AC/DC Current"). During the same tour, Durham came across Floyd Smith, guitarist in the *Jeter-Pillars Plantation Club Orchestra*, a meeting that resulted in Smith's adapting the electric guitar."[82]

Eddie recalled: "In the Spring of [1936 or] 1937 in Oklahoma City when I was playing on location with James Richmond and Buster Smith three or four weeks. This is when Charlie Christian started playing guitar. We used to go down to the pool hall (owned by Jimmy Rushing's father) every day. James Richmond would follow. Christian came in with an old acoustic guitar and asked me "how do you sound like that alto saxophone?" So I say, 'If you play the downstroke and fast, you're always going to get staccato instead of legato and you'll sound like Willie Smith, that's the secret to sound like a horn, the

62

downstroke, you get a sharper tone while the strings were bouncing back as the hand was on its way back up." So he said , "I'll play the piano," he was playing a little piano then. I say, Charlie that come from the downstroke, 'cause you can't make no upstroke on a saxophone. I say that's called staccato, and legato you gotta come up. But now when you come up, you can play fast as you wanna play, but you can't do so much down. So I listen to him some time and he did a lot of downstroke stuff. But after the style gets modern, you gotta come up some, to play fast, see. You get a lot of notes, you can make 30 seconds of anything you wanna make, but when you going down you can't do no more than a sax can do but it takes an awful fast wrist to play the downstroke. But he learned what I showed him on the guitar in a few minutes! I didn't have to teach him much. So I encouraged him. He moved on to the eastern style. The next thing I know, he's with Benny Goodman. He wouldn't have to read to do that part, can make that up."[83]

"There's a Charlie Christian solo on *Stardust* that I hear totally as a tribute to Eddie Durham. If you know Durham's guitar playing, then you know that what Christian played is a Durham solo. Many artists do that to pay tribute to someone who influenced them. Eddie used to tell me how he met Christian, who wasn't really playing the guitar that much, but he used to come to hear Eddie. So Eddie was the first guitar player to make great records with Lester Young on *The Kansas City Six*. Anybody who knew Christian will tell you that Charlie Christian was a total Lester Young fanatic. So it only stands to reason that Christian would know all about Eddie Durham, if only for Lester Young, but also because Eddie was the most famous, unique amplified-electric guitar player in Jazz around at that time.

Most Jazz musicians weren't really written about and especially Black musicians were not documented or credited. So if you think you're going to justify Eddie Durham's story by whether you can verify it from an old newspaper clipping, well then you're not a very good historian. Even though everybody exaggerates stories, Eddie was talking about stuff that happened 30-50 years ago, but Eddie Durham was not a liar. If Eddie told you something happened, you know it happened. I don't really even care about the stories or the documentation, all you have to do is listen to Charlie Christian, how he articulates notes on the guitar, the down picking. I remember I talked with George Benson about this once, in relation to Charlie Christian, that if you play up and down, you don't get the attack. Eddie used to talk about this all the time and he only played downstrokes, a staccato attack." *Loren Schoenberg*

Eddie recalled: "The year I was teaching Charlie Christian, two months later we went to Nebraska and Floyd didn't own a guitar, but he could play a little. I told him 'I'm leaving town tomorrow and he said, "If you come and go to my home and tell my mother what you're telling me, she'll buy me one." It cost $70. So I went to his home, I told her, 'This boy here, you'll never be ashamed of him, you'll be proud if you go buy this guitar.' So she gave him $70 and he went right down with me, he bought a steel Hawaiian guitar. About a year or two later, he went with Andy Kirk and he come up fast. So I say to myself, 'well I can't show any other guys anything else!' - here's Christian ready to teach me! But I was proud of them guys moving so fast... both of them making good music, "Floyd's Blues." That made me proud. Now T-Bone Walker could play much more Blues than any of the guys, extraordinary, soloing, jazzy-blues and swing-blues with a lot of effective gimmicks, a creator of that style - he could handle the whole guitar, but he wasn't with them big bands. Floyd reached the public quicker."[84]

Eddie recalled: "Freddie Green I think he's first place. He holds the rhythm good, plays the guitar like I think I showed him once or twice, how to dampen that guitar like a pedal on a piano with the palm of his hand, how to choke it with his left hand and that gives that ump cha swing. When they all get into that, then the rhythm guitar is more effective, like Chris Flory and Bill Wurtzel. That's kinda a weakness towards big bands today. They must concentrate on that guitar. That guitar is a powerful rhythm instrument in the Jazz Bands. The pianos don't chord anymore, they variate, otherwise and your rhythms tore up. But if the piano chords and the guitar chords, that's two different instruments with strings that play together. That's how Basie's band got that rhythm. Basie cause he laid down a lot cause he had Big Page there, he played rhythm just like a guitar. That's what's kinda missing in some of the bands today."[85]

Shelton Gary

Bill Wurtzel

Eddie Durham

"Eddie and I was in Oklahoma City at the same time and Charlie Christian was there too. I was with the *Mills Rhythm Blues Band* and Red Allen was playing trumpet. Eddie came and knocked on my door and said *"come down here and hear Charlie."* So I went down and Charlie was playing a *Kay* guitar, up to the microphone, picking downstroke only, like Eddie. We became very friendly the two weeks I was there. We used to go every night and jam. So we'd say, "Lets exchange ideas." Naturally, Eddie had to give Charlie some lessons and that's how he got that melodic sound. Eddie played pick, and so Charlie played pick. Charlie's playing the same style with a pick and Wes Montgomery is playing the same style, but with his thumb; a softer sound. [86]"
Lawrence Lucie

"Charlie Christian must be supreme because it's very hard to do a very hard thing for someone whose the creator, as an imitator. "Topsy" would be an appropriate piece to play regardless that Eddie Durham wrote it or regardless that Charlie Christian has a personal connection to Eddie. The "Gilly" "Avalon" thing is much more substantial because there's a real device there. Also listen to the rhythm guitar that Charlie plays on his very first record date, with Lionel Hampton, Sept. 11, 1939. If you're looking for Dizzy, who is not the trumpeter on this "Swing to Bop" that's Joe Guy. Dizzy actually is the trumpeter on the records that I'm mentioning. Charlie Christian through both his all downstroke rhythm accompaniment, he's in the rhythm section with Cozy Cole, Clyde Hart, and Milt Hinton, but also his obbligato behind

"One Sweet Letter From You," which is sung by Lionel - that sounds like Eddie Durham. So the earliest you hear Charlie Christian, he is employing things that he learned directly as a student of Eddie Durham.

If there were no documents and you came in to interview me (Jan. 6, 2010), and I was a little more playful than I should be, I could tell you 'hey man, dig this, that's Eddie Durham on this record' - and you wouldn't know, it's that close. But it is significant that Charlie liked new "Topsy," he undoubtedly knew it because the Basie band had recorded it, but if there was an Eddie Durham guitar solo on the original "Topsy" it would make it more substantial. The earlier you hear Charlie (before 1937) to his Eddie connection, it's more important because it's Christian's formative period. As early as you can hear Eddie play amplified guitar, with "Avalon," "Oh Boy!" and "Hittin' The Bottle," Charlie knows that record to the point that he's lingered on it to the ability to play cleanly, a very difficult guitar passage - and he pops it in as an orchestral device on a Benny Goodman record, over five years later, in the Fall of 1940! What Christian's doing in terms of his own inventions in 1941, he died in 1942, has less to do with what he got from Eddie Durham than these earlier illustrations and more clear-cut mimicking. Eddie isn't a be-bopper. All music is present tense when you're playing it or listening to it, Eddie Durham is who he is.

It's even funnier, nobody's paying attention to the fact that Charlie Parker's most overt early record display "The Bird" on the jazz scene, which in 1950 was labeled the "greatest jazz album EVER" and it might still be true - that's "Topsy" - that's "Topsy! I'm stomping all over everybody and it's really unforgivable, but I used Eddie Durham to cut through the gibberish and that's my guide. So Charlie Parker, not Charlie Christian, is displaying his trump as *'this is the piece I want to represent me'*, he calls it "The Bird," it's on the most important album made up to that point and time, is "Topsy." It is "Topsy." Just like they're saying it's not "Topsy" because Jerry Newman wanted to call it "Swing To Bop" in 1946 because he thought it would sell more records [for the label]. So you gotta make your choice of whether silliness or accuracy is your friend."[87] ***Phil Schaap***

66

"Because of Lunceford's fascination with the device [resonator], Durham, the arranger, was writing amplified guitar solos into the arrangements as well as trombone trio parts."[88]

Jimmie Lunceford

"Jimmie Lunceford and his famous C.B.S. orchestra will begin a tour of the deluxe theaters, beginning February 1… There are four new men in the musical aggregation for the present setup. Paul Webster, ace trumpeter; Elmer Crumbley, vocalist and trombonist, Laforest Dent, exceptionally fine vocalist [*sic*, sax], and Eddie Durham, arranger, guitarist and trombonist, are the three musicians forming the augmentation of the Lunceford orchestra."[89] The Pittsburgh Courier Jan 19, 1935.

Eddie began touring with Jimmie Lunceford on Feb. 1, 1935.

Eddie recalled: "Jimmie played big flute, I used to carry my guitar to his house - he wouldn't play with the band. I wrote out Avalon which were supposed to be quartets and Jimmie would look at the arrangements - and he quit playing trombone when I went over there. Sy was technical - cut in on my rehearsal and wanted everything played to perfection. But you gotta give musicians liberty like Basie, let them add some of their stuff in. Sy was tight on that. A concert we played, walked on the stand, some of the guys hadn't even rehearsed, so I fold up the repertoire and say, let's go to the head. The people thought it was the greatest thing they had ever heard. Say'd that to say this, black musician got a lot in his head and when he reads music it takes a lot away from it - when he leaves that paper, he becomes the Roy Eldridge, Coleman Hawkins. Jimmie was afraid of my arrangements."[90] "I could write flag-wavers like 'Harlem Shout, and they always opened and closed the show with a number of mines. When we were at the Larchmont Casino, there was a moving stand that used to excite people. The opener was always crescendo and loud. The band would be sitting on this stand, about a foot higher than the regular stage, and as they hit, the stand started moving forward, right up to the edge of the stage. It used to scare some people. They'd jump up and want to get out.[91] The only time I'd been to Europe [back then] was with Lunceford.[92]"

Europe

Lunceford's Orchestra played at the Apollo Theatre and then left for England on February 14, 1937.

"Attracting crowds of "10,000 and up" in the Scandinavian countries… They were requested to play for King Gustave of Sweden on March 8. His Majesty was given a sample of typical Lunceford "swing"… the same that has caused his critics to claim Lunceford's as the "finest colored or white orchestra ever presented" and to predict that "Lunceford can never be duplicated." European critics further declare that "Lunceford and his orchestra are making history." At every concert featuring the band, a background of the American flag was predominant. In Toghenburg, Sweden, the American Consul presented the smiling, genial Jimmie with a bouquet of flowers covered with "Old Glory." At Stockholm, the American Ambassador spoke in glowing terms of the kind of music Jimmie and the boys are producing for European consumption and enjoyment. … February 23, Copenhagen, Denmark. Feb. 24, 25- Oslo, Norway. Feb. 26-Gothenburg, Sweden. Feb. 27, 28-Stockholm, Sweden. Feb. 29-Ionkopink, Sweden. March 1-Orebro, Sweden. March 3-Return to Gothenburg. March 3, 4-Norrkopinga. March 5-Halsingborg. March 6, 7-Malmo. March 8, 9-Stockholm. March 10-Norway, Sweden. March 11, 12-Oslo."[93]

"Jimmie Lunceford, due Wednesday at Crystal Park, is described as follows in a Stockholm, Sweden, paper: This week I can not review any records of jazz orchestras; - after four hours of Lunceford-fever, all orchestras sound meaningless to me on discs. Lunceford was a great experience to me, a sensation that fully lived up to the advance notices. …The wanton but superior interpretation of "Black n'tan [sic, Tan Fantasy] ," the refined "Organ Grinders Swing," the heetoe "Harlem Shout" and the parodies on Ellington, Lombardo, Armstrong and Whiteman will stay long in my memory. The brass section with the thick coloring of the violently screwed muted trumpets and trombones sounded almost unreal. One was forever losing one's breath and it tickled over the temples from the substantial, expressive sounds. Sometimes it was exaggerated, got to be mostly technique and well trained rhythm-then, the audience clapped and shouted in ecstasy."94

68

Note: Eddie Durham is the only composer of "Harlem Shout." He arranged "Avalon" and "Bird of Paradise" for Lunceford's Orchestra.

The first show back in the USA was booked for one week beginning April 9, 1937, at the Howard Theatre, Washington, D.C. Eddie quit the Lunceford band on April 30th after a Battle of Music with Count Basie at Foot Guard Hall in Hartford, Connecticut.

"None of these popular black acts displayed Lunceford's versatility and finesse. None of them was able to swing as violently as the *Harlem Express*. The ability to play romantic ballads next to novelty numbers and hard-swinging killer-dillers or flag-wavers put the Lunceford band in the van-guard with both the dancers and the listeners. This versatility, combined with its unique stage show, sold the band."[95]

"Jimmie Lunceford Orchestra's display of the music was unique. ...They were individuals of incredible craftsmanship and artistic identity. He is the guide and coordinator and initially, he was the teacher. Literally a music teacher, who, when his better students grew up they all graduated together and became this great big band. But Lunceford had some friends from his graduate school work when he was getting his Masters in Music education, who were slightly younger than he, this would include Willie Smith (alto sax, vocalist, clarinetist, arranger) and Edwin Wilcox (pianist) and they're the initial cogs in the wheel that turns by arranging what vitalizes the music of the Jimmie Lunceford Orchestra. ...But a third personality of arranging came forward. He had a huge reputation within the band and to the leader. ...With Sy Oliver's arrival there comes to be for the first time a dominant arranger among a band that thrives on its arranging and its range of arrangers, as well as a unification of their individuality into something that could be one thing. But there was something missing musically and there was something missing in terms of balance with this Oliver dominance ... the flavor of the Kansas City, Oklahoma, Texas thing. Jimmie Lunceford understood that he didn't have it and understood how to get it in his own context, through an arranger. ...In hiring [adding] Eddie Durham, a ratio in proportion to the flavors of the Lunceford sound - as well as the addition to the Lunceford sound, was completed. And the start of a pinnacle episode in orchestral Jazz is launched, it is the zenith of the Jimmie Lunceford Orchestra, a band of arrangers who are all different and provide nevertheless, a unified wholesome quality that is so distinct as to be unique. A band whose identity is defined not by its soloists or repertoire or that it's run by a unique composer, but by its arrangers - - Edwin Wilcox, Willie Smith, Sy Oliver, and the last piece coming into place, Eddie Durham. …By bringing forward this emphasis of the last arranger to arrive for the glory time, the great Eddie Durham. …it is his arrival that concludes the development and peeks the quality."96

Eddie recalled: "They were tryna get me to come to Lunceford all the time. So eventually Lunceford came to New York, and they say, 'We'll git 'em'. I was with Willie Bryant. Cause when school would stop Paul Webster and Eddie would come back, cause Paul was taking up to be a mortician and Eddie was being a doctor. Eddie Tompkins went up to seven years when he left being a doctor, University of Iowa. But he got in so much trouble all the time. They suspended him the last year because he would always go down to the school at night and get into the laboratory and get whiskey and stuff for the band. He knocked over something and it started a fire and he got burned while he was in there and they had to get him out. They put him out of the school cause he'd been doing it all along. But they'd go to school and as soon as school was out, they'd tear to Buffalo and join Lunceford's band. They say, 'Lunceford, we got a trombone man with us'. Quite naturally when we play anything we had our own routines. We could come in a band and the brass would take over a couple of the choruses. And that's how I got in Lunceford's band.

He was playing the Apollo and I went down and heard the band and I thought the band was fantastic, it was a show band. So I say, 'I think I'll come in' and Lunceford pays me $35 a week. The music wasn't all that great, but they just had a variety of a novelty. They had a dancing chorus. Six of the guys come out and do the dance, a whole routine. Time they get back they had a glee club and then they had a trio with Sy. So then I was the guy that could really voice that six-part harmony for myself cause they didn't have but five horns, and they weren't writing for six horns. So that's why the repertoire was short of my part when Trummy Young went in my place. Lunceford told me

70

'you have to teach him - 3 weeks and you can leave the band'. I didn't know you could just leave anyway. Cause there wasn't that much music.

They didn't do that much solo work, they didn't have to worry too much, cause see the guys wasn't writing good harmony in those days, not six-part. So I had to kinda get in there and work with Wilcox and Sy and all of them with the six-part harmony business. And the reason I left Lunceford 'cause he never did give me no more than $65 a week. And I joined Basie for $150.

See, when he went out to Larchmont Casino he made $4000-$5000 in one night. See he had a co-op operation and when he went out to Larchmont, he hit the top from that air, he went on the air. Then he said, 'There ain't no more co-op operation'. He dissolved it. Guys say, 'When we 'gon get credit?' He said, 'We can't have it no more, ain't got it no more'. That was his answer, so I say, 'Well you ain't 'gon have me no more'.

They played a date and John Hammond comes out and saw me and say, 'Basie's short' ... they only got 12 arrangements and they're your numbers. They're in the Roseland and they need more stuff like that - ain't got nobody to write it. So I said, 'Well I'll come over for a year." So I gave Lunceford Notice. I made "Harlem Shout," "Lunceford's Special," "Bird of Paradise" [Duke] with Eddie Wilcox, "Running A Temperature," "Oh Boy!," "Hittin' The Bottle," "Avalon," "Oh! Eddie," "Swingin on C." But I was taking up a lot of time in trying to help the guys in voicing that six-part. Then I wrote a lot of things where I use the five saxes, but I used Dan Grissom on the sax. I did "Honey Keep Your Mind On Me." If you notice closely, he's playing sax on that, the singer. It was a novelty section, and the powerhouse was Willie Smith so that made it different from other bands 'cause he was so strong. He played saxophone so loud that we never did write him in the background at no time with the reeds. He was loud as the whole brass section. Whenever the reeds were playing those harmonies Smith was holding his horn, we didn't write him no part cause you couldn't never get him down low - he'd be strong, let him rest and be strong when he come in. ...Crawford had a lot to do with that band, cause he had his own style on the drum, a two-beat thing and all that helped Lunceford's band. Mose wasn't what you'd say a real great bass player, he was just a two-beat man so I guess that helped, so he just rode on top of Crawford - [so it was like] Crawford played first drums in the band."⁹⁷

Eddie recalled: "Sy Oliver and Eddie Wilcox were writing for Lunceford, but they'd had only three trumpets, two trombones, and four saxes before. They hadn't had much experience with wider arrangements, and few of the bands had more instruments than that... I stepped it up to five saxes. I showed Wilcox how to voice that way, and coached him with the sax section. I was also teaching Willie Smith how to voice for the instrumentation we had, and he was even willing to pay me. Now we could have six brass, too, and I could handle that without any trouble. ... I wrote a part for myself, sometimes in the bass and sometimes above, but either way to get that extra note. I had a good range and could play it, but it was hard to set some of their earlier arrangements in six-part harmony...

When we were at the Larchmont Casino, there was a moving stand that used to excite people. ...News got to the papers that I was on Notice, so they booked a battle of music between Basie and Lunceford in Hartford, the night my Notice expired. The radio stations were talking about this man who had been with Basie, then with Lunceford and was now going back with Basie. ...That night, when we packed up, the valet switched my stuff to Basie's band. We went to the Ritz Carlton in Boston..."⁹⁸

Eddie recalled: "...I liked that show business angle. I think a band should be able to entertain and the Lunceford band did a lot of different things. He had a trio that sang real nice, and different guys in the band sang – Dan Grissom and Sy Oliver both sang with the band. Then he had the Shim-Sham-Shimmy Boys; they were named after the dance, but they were just guys in the band. First, they'd play and then about six guys would come out, dance around, then jump offstage and run all around and tear up the house. As soon as that's over, there was a glee club. The whole band was in that. Then Willie Smith would sing "Rhythm Is Our Business," and we all did things behind him while he was singing. The band also did imitations of people who were hot; sometimes we did it with the curtain closed in front of us...

I made a lot of arrangements for that band. ... I've seen times when they had six or seven bands at the Savoy, big names. You couldn't get two bands

72

in the Renaissance, and when Lunceford would play there, he'd just pack 'em in. You couldn't get in the place and he probably cleaned up since he was getting a percentage, but he never passed any of that along to his band. The most I ever made was seventy dollars a week, and I only made ten dollars on the arrangements. I'd call him on this, but he'd always say we were crazy, that he was paying us enough – and that was his biggest mistake. I began to get tired of the band and decided to leave. I'd been playing and arranging a lot, plus I was teaching Sy] and Eddie. You see, Sy was a fine writer; he had good ideas But at that time he didn't know how to voice any further than maybe five-part harmony, so I helped him with lessons.

I was still only making $75 a week and Lunceford was bringing in enough to do better than that even if he did have to pay people off. ...About this time John Hammond came by where we're playing, up in Larchmont, New York, and asked Lunceford if he could 'borrow me for a week to write some arrangements for Count Basie'. ...Not too much later, John Hammond came around and offered me $125 a week to go with the band. About the same time, Lunceford sees what's happening and begins to give a few raises – Wilcox to ninety dollars, Willie up to seventy dollars-and he tells Sy that he'll pay more for arrangements. ...When I gave him [Lunceford] the notice, some promoters set up a battle of music in Hartford, Connecticut, with Lunceford and Basie, side by side. Then about three days after I'd given my notice, Lunceford came over to where I was staying and started complaining to me that I'd started a mutiny in his band. I asked, 'Who's leaving?' And he said, 'Almost all of them... They're going to come to see you, and they're going to ask you why you are leaving the band. Please don't tell them you're leaving because of the money; tell them you just want to play with Basie.' Then he started to try and use psychology on me and said, 'You don't want to break up the band. Don't you love this band?' I looked at him and said, 'Yeah, I love this band. I just don't enjoy being with it anymore.'

Lunceford didn't really seem to care what I thought, he could have offered me more money right then, but he didn't do it. So I left the band up in Hartford. I played the first set with Lunceford and when it was over the guys in the band *helped me pick up all my stuff and move it over to the Basie band, right in front of the audience.*"[99]

"*"Harlem Shout," recorded by Jimmie Lunceford in 1936, contains the germ about 2/3 of the way through of "Swingin' On C," recorded by Lunceford, Earl Hines and several other bands in 1940. It's a fact that Basie wanted his band to sound more like Lunceford by just about that time, 1940, and Eddie would have been a prime source of the connection.*"[100]

Eddie recalled: "Like in Lunceford's Band I wrote the baritone with the bass but you wouldn't know it, saxes going another way, not distinctive, just solely bass all the time. Sustain it. Gives it a heavy reed tone in the brass section. The baritone carries heavy volume. It didn't bother the quad sax section. Like "Running A Temperature." If you listen close, the baritone is going out in a direction away from the other saxes altogether. But if they put a mic up to it, that would be too broad and make it bounce too big. Rock'n Roll came in there with that electric bass and you could hear it and I think that's how it took over from Jazz. I figured that the rhythm sections was too little for a 16 or 17 piece band. Conga drums always seemed a bad idea to me, too much muddling and too much execution. I like the music to be danceable, I like to hear the band play music that you can pat your foot and clap your hands when you hear it.[101] With the rhythm section in Lunceford, the (riser) stand swayed front to back, you could hardly stand up. In the Basie Band, it swayed side to side. In the Lunceford Band, I choreographed so that the trombones picked up their trombones and we breathed in unison. Lunceford's band was forced to go into half-way seven ...and I don't know why he wanted that, but I make it anyway just 'cause it was Lunceford. I did the "Bird of Paradise" and that was a classical, I broke it down; and "Rhapsody Junior." I think the Publishers paid Lunceford to do them. Whatever Lunceford say, we try 'em.[102]

Lunceford was crazy about the resonator. Therefore, I was writing guitar solos into the arrangements as well as trombone trios.

Lunceford dissolved the corporation and the guys said, "Man, we ain't going to get cut, we can't handle it no more, ain't got it no more." I gave Lunceford notice and he gave me $75 for playing and $75 for arranging.

In Hartford, Connecticut and they had me up there a day before the concert. They interviewed me on the Radio that day, said: "We got the man here that was with Basie three years ago, been with Lunceford and he's going back to Basie, and he's going to tell you what he thinks about how this battle is going to come out".. The battle of the bands was between Basie and Lunceford! So I made both bands the greatest bands in the world on each style. Place was packed!"[103]

<u>Jimmie Lunceford And His Harlem Express Orchestra</u> (L-R) Sy Oliver, Paul Webster, Russell Bowles, Eddie Tompkins, Eddie Durham, Elmer Crumbley, Eddie Wilcox (piano), Jimmie Lunceford, Jimmy Crawford (drums), Willie Smith, Laforest Dent, Al Norris, Joe Thomas, Moses Allen (bass fiddle), and Earl Caruthers.

"Gorgeous Alice Dixon, who has returned to Broadway after a two-year layoff and is winning new laurels as the featured singer in the show at the Kit Kat club, where Jimmie Lunceford and his boys ladle out the swing. Featured in her repertoire are "Heart and Soul," a beautiful number arranged by Henry Wells with Andy Kirk, and "What Do You Know About Love?" Arranged by Eddie Durham. *The Pittsburgh Courier,* Newspaper (Nov. 12, 1938).

Eddie Durham *publicly* departed from the Jimmie Lunceford Orchestra April 30, 1937 not long after returning in mid-March from their one-month Scandinavian. But on March 20th he performed with Basie. Apparently, Billie Holiday was in the band.

Eddie recalled: *"Lunceford played a date - and Benny Goodman's brother-in-law, John Hammond [Sr.], came and saw me and said: "Basie's short, only got 12 numbers and they're in Roseland, they need more stuff but they got nobody to write it." But Basie's booking agent was Music Corp of America (MCA) and they was worried about their investment. So I promised to **come back** [to Basie] for a year, if he ran short. So I went as a trombonist and we opened at The Apollo, March [20,] 1937."*

Count Basie A Sensation In N. Jersey

NEW YORK CITY, Oct. 28 — The fascinating and unusual swing music of Count Basie and his new sensational orchestra blazed the trail again for other colored orchestras to follow when this week they became the featured attraction at the famous Meadow Brook nitery in Cedar Grove, N. J.

Moving into the spot for a two weeks' engagement after his theatrical success in Baltimore, the "Count of Swing" becomes the first colored attraction to ever play the nite club in question. During his two weeks' stay in the Mosquito State, the famed pianologist will be fed musically throughout the country through the channels of the C.B.S. extensive radio chain.

Following in the steps of Noble Sissle, Basie and his orchestra, through the aid of good management, have broken down the color bar in countless nite clubs and hotels in the country. His most recent engagement being four weeks at the Ritz Carlton Hotel in Boston, at which time he became the first race attraction to play there in the past year.

Notwithstanding the sensation he created with his music when first discovered by Benny Goodman a few seasons back, Basie today is heading a much improved aggregation. Just recently it was added to greatly by the talent of Benny Moten and Eddie Durham. Another outstanding feature of the Basie group is Billie Holliday, a lovely lady who ranks high among the present-day crop of top-notch swing singers.

Always an ardent admirer of the band, Benny Goodman, white

The Pittsburgh Courier (Pittsburgh, Pennsylvania) Sat, Oct 30, 1937 - Page 20

"King of Swing," paid it and its leader another tribute via the radio last week, when, on three different occasions he gave time to their latest tune, "One O'Clock Jump," a supreme effort in swing music composed by Basie himself.

SAY YOU SAW IT IN THE PITTSBURGH COURIER

The Pittsburgh Courier-Sat, Feb 20, 1937.
M. & M. Smith, Courier photographers, broke into the MS. factory to get the above glimpses of proceedings just before Jimmie Lunceford sailed for Norway Saturday night. Kneeling, left to right: Mr. and Mrs. E. A. Brown, Edwin Wilcox, Bernice Smith (peeping through), Annabelle Wilson, Al Morris, Taxie Calvin, Pack, Billie Woodson and Eddie Durham.

APOLLO 125TH ST. NEAR 8TH AVE.

HARLEM'S HIGH SPOT FOR SHOWS!
ONE WEEK BEGINNING TODAY—CONTINUOUS PERF.

COUNT BASIE AND ORCH.
BILLIE HOLIDAY Sepia Record Star
Hollywood's Dancing Favorite **JENI LE GON**
AND A BIG, FAST REVUE CAST

EVE. PRICES 25¢ & 40¢

MIDNIGHT SHOW TOMORROW! RESERVED SEATS PHONE UN 4-4490

New York Daily News - 19 March 1937. Fri - Page 247

"The resonator was a piece of aluminum in the form of a shell, like a loud-speaker, that fitted in the center hole of the instrument under the strings. Durham explained, "You had to have an instrument with a hole the size of a 45-rpm record." Oliver added, "…probably our best jazz arranger at the time.

…When someone, at rehearsals, made an error in playing the chart, Eddie would just sit there fooling with that gismo [the aluminum resonator]…It was up to me to straighten out the guy who made the mistake."[104]

Eddie was not a traditionally 'school trained' educator as Jimmie was. However, as you will ascertain from the experiences restated herein, Eddie effectively taught new techniques discreetly, intuitively and sometimes humorously, by actions only and without saying a word. He worked with enough top musicians to ascertain their unique learning ability and adapt his teaching method to a specific person without causing friction. Lunceford obviously observed Eddie, as Sy did. But undoubtedly, Lunceford a mentor and former professor whose star students comprised his orchestra, would instead recognize Eddies' preoccupation - as an additional talent, a cherry on top of Eddie's writing and arranging skills, as something uniquely marketable. Jimmie promoted Eddie by recording Eddie's invention, with his orchestra. This resulted in the groundbreaking guitar solos on, among Eddie's other prominent contributions, "Honey, Keep Your Mind On Me," "Hittin' The Bottle" and "Avalon".

"As a guitarist, Eddie was indeed a terrific improviser and technician, and Jimmie Lunceford should be credited for allowing Eddie so many wonderful solo guitar spots on the band's recording sessions, especially considering the experimental nature of featuring such a new kind of sound and instrument."[105] *John Colianni*

As a father, when dad wanted us to clean our rooms, he had a saying, *"ya know, a roach will walk a mile for a crumb."* He never had to hit us as was very common in that era, he knew what example to give so we'd think about the situation. My mother being decades younger and raising five children, did not take kindly or intellectually to our disobedience. Well, in that era somebody had to be the corporal disciplinarian. But she couldn't actually hit us when he was home. So, when we inevitably did, or didn't do something, and we knew we were overdue to go fetch that switch from the tree in our backyard, we'd hang on his leg whenever he had to go out, begging him not to leave! He never knew why. It wasn't funny then, but we all still laugh about that today!

"He would reveal a great deal if you paid attention. He was often putting it in front of you and letting you find out whether you recognize it. There were other times when he would really spoon feed you the real mccoy. I am fortunate that I was so spoon fed. Certainly among the better educators, even in an indirect, informal fashion, I can attest to that." *Phil Schaap*

Phil Schaap (who Eddie referred to as *"Computer Man"*) responds to Eddie's answer to a question on the air. "Your first arrangements for Lunceford are very obscure Ellington compositions, "Rhapsody Junior" and "Bird of Paradise." I really am touched though because I asked, '*What classical pieces did you arrange for Lunceford',* and of course the next composer mentioned by Eddie Durham, one of our musical figures, is of course, *"Duke Ellington"*! That's who was a classical composer, and I couldn't agree with you more, "Bird of Paradise" and "Rhapsody Junior," your two arrangements for Lunceford".106

(Eddie / Lunceford recordings: see "Appendix "A")

Robert Lockwood, Jr.

"Lockwood's music shows the influence of not only his stepfather, Robert Johnson but also that of jazz guitarists Charlie Christian and **Eddie Durham**. By the mid-50's he found himself in the enviable position of being the studio guitar player in Chicago. He can be heard on classic blues songs like "Little Walter's "My Babe" and "Boom, Boom, Out Go The Lights"; Sonny Boy Williamson's "Nine Below Zero" and "Eyesight To The Blind." He also recorded with Muddy Waters, Otis Spann, Eddie Boyd, Willie Mabon, Sunnyland Slim, Roosevelt Sykes, and others. (Hear: "Steady Rollin Man" DLM 630)." ***Peter "Cornbread" Cohen***, *CBP* 107

"Now when I used to ask the other guitarists who came in why they reacted with their mouths dropped, was it because Eddie was so great, they would say, "Well it's not just that, it's the way that he fingers the chords, the way he actually makes them happen." First of all, he used to put his hands over the neck, over the top and he had the damnedest ways that he would put his hands and it was totally unique and guitar players that used to play with Benny Goodman all kinds of people and friends of mine used to come to watch him

because his approach was totally original. Which is why you could really never imitate the way that Eddie Durham played the guitar. Totally unique if you listen to those 1938 Kansas City Five records, and Kansas City Six with Lester Young added. You can't even talk about it in terms of guitar playing like you would talk about Charlie Christian or Jim Hall or the standard way that people play the guitar. I mean, he invented a new way of playing it, the chords, the way that he moved things, the voicing was totally unique. He had big hands, 'cause he used to show me things on the piano. He used to show me the introduction that he wrote to "Time Out" and I mean he could stretch unbelievable with these huge hands. But I think he also did that on the guitar."
Loren Schoenberg

"Eddie's music, however, has remained an inspiring influence on me as both a pianist and arranger. I truly admire the way Eddie was able to convey that joyous, driving, powerful yet light and fleet sense of swing into his orchestrations that I've heard. Some recordings that I can mention include "Oh, Boy!," which he wrote for the Lunceford orchestra. Amazing arrangement and performance! And the band recorded many more of his charts on the *Decca* and *Vocalion* labels in the 30s-40s. "Harlem Shout" is another inspired swinger, and I can imagine how the dancers at a venue of the day like the Savoy Ballroom would go crazy for this kind of piece. "It's Time To Jump And Shout" is another great chart, also for Lunceford, and I discussed this one with the trumpet star Snooky Young, who has a solo on this, and who was with Lunceford for a few years. Many others to name - "Swinging On C," "Running A Temperature," "Pigeon Walk".

...But next, let me talk about an amazing pair of compositions by Duke Ellington which were done up into a couple of the most interesting arrangements I've ever heard - "Rhapsody Jr" and "Bird Of Paradise." The Lunceford band's pianist, also a great arranger, Eddie Wilcox, collaborated with Eddie on these renditions. Amazingly enough, it appears that Duke didn't write and record these numbers for his own band, but appears to have gifted them to Lunceford, whose band recorded both. Among other fascinating aspects, there's a section on one of these where the instruments are orchestrated as to simulate a solo stride pianist. These two recordings -

combining as they do the compositional and arranging talents of Ellington, Durham, and Wilcox, must surely represent one of the most unheralded of great collaborations in the world of Jazz." *John Colianni*

Andy Kirk, Mary Lou Williams

"Durham helped me quite a bit with sounds. He'd arrange a popular tune giving all the instruments different notes, extending a seventh chord to an eleventh or thirteenth. All of the arrangers knew by heart each note an instrument should make and when there was a mistake." 108 *Mary Lou Williams, Jazz pianist, recording artist, Bandleader, composer (Duke, Goodman, Monk, Parker, Miles, Dizzy).*

Eddie recalled: "Terrance Holder was the leader before Andy. I came in the band a couple weeks and he run off and left the Band, some members went with him. So Andy Kirk took over the Band, Andy Kirk's Twelve Clouds of Joy. The song, "Until the Real Thing Comes Along" got created because see Pha Terrell was a dancer in a dance team with a little fella they called 'Van', but Van deceased. But they came to my house at 3 AM, "Man, we got a song here..., listen." So, I went down to the riverbank with my old guitar. I wrote out the lead sheet and he took it. Later they corrected the words and eliminated stuff like 'I worked for you, slaved for you, fingers to the bone for you, I'll moan for you, groan for you'. Pha was singing in Andy Kirk's band. Andy must've helped it along, or maybe Mary Lou Williams made the arrangement. Ten years later in KC, my first wife's grandmother said, "you left this thing up in the attic" and it was that original piece of paper I wrote. But that's not my composition - and I don't claim nothing I didn't do - I never did 'cause that's a racket I don't like, it's dishonest. I could've been on that song. They had a big hit though. They couldn't write though, they hummed it to me and I wrote it down."[109]

"[Sammy] Can (sic) and [Saul] Chaplin, those songwriters, they were little old boys hanging around us," said John Williams. "Sammy Cahn was up there in the studio every day; he would run errands for us. 'The Real Thing' put us on big time," and that's when we began to make a steady salary. it was on the Hit Parade for two weeks. That was the big thing in New York. Your band

80

made the *Hit Parade*, whoever wrote the number had it made. Cahn and Chaplin idolized us after we made that, because we really made them. Can ended up a millionaire." But no one else associated with the tune did. John Williams ended as a hotel porter and factory worker. Andy Kirk took a clerk's job for the Musicians Union in New York..."110

"After that, Kapp didn't want us to play no more swing music," said [Mary Lou] Williams. "We had to play all ballads... The band was now traveling regularly, in demand because of "Real Thing".111

"As Gunther Schuller observes about "Until the Real Thing Comes Along," "By 1937 and thereafter, as a result of an immensely popular recording by the band's singer, Pha Terrell, its jazz playing days, while not exactly numbered, were certainly threatened."112

Jazz editor Barry Ulanov says,... "One of the difficulties about jazz is that it's very hard to notate it, but Duke Ellington could and so could Mary [Lou Williams]. Very few other people have been able to put on paper the feeling of jazz. There are always technical problems, and the rhythm is the most serious: you have to have such a tricky system of dots after notes in order to get the slight changes between values of ordinary eighth, quarter and sixteenth notes"113

In the rare four minutes of salvaged silent newsreel footage, Eddie Durham is briefly seen twice, performing on trombone with *The Count Basie Orchest*ra. Historically, *Carnival of Swing* was the first outdoor "Jazz Fest." It predated Woodstock (1969), The Cavalcade of Dixieland Jazz Festival (1951), and Producer/Impresario George Wein's popular, annual Newport Jazz (founded 1954) and Newport Folk (founded 1959) Festivals. At some point, the recordings of *Carnival of Swing* were unearthed, restored by Doug Pomeroy, and released in 2010 as "*The [Bill] Savory Collection*" (*Mosaic Records* MD6-266). *(Eddie's performances, arrangements, compositions / The Savory Collection: see "Appendix "A")*

Count Basie

Eddie recalled: Tommy Dorsey came to me after I'd left - this was before he hired Sy. He said, "I see where you left Basie, and I didn't think anybody ever left that band."[114]

"Constructed with the flavor of a music that de-emphasizes theme and uses background as foreground, and emphasizes a solo in a small group feel, with a distinct rhythm inflection."[115] *Phil Schaap*

In the dead of New York's winter, January 16, 1938, several significant events overlap. *The Benny Goodman Orchestra* debuted at Carnegie Hall to a sold-out crowd. 1.This was the first Jazz/Swing concert held in a Symphony Hall; 2.Basie, Jo Jones, Freddie Green, Walter Page, Buck Clayton, and Lester Young, jammed on stage at Carnegie with Goodman before rushing up to the *Savoy* in *Harlem* where; 3.*Count Basie and his Orchestra* battled the *Savoy Ballroom* resident band - *Chick Webb's Orchestra*. When Goodman's concert ended at Carnegie, some of his men also headed up to the Savoy because Webb's Orchestra gave them a whaling a year earlier. Basie relied on the wave of Eddie Durham's back-to-back swing dance arrangements. Phil Schaap said: *"Basie called a rehearsal for Durham to bring in new material and the piece Eddie brought in was Swinging the Blues. Basie told Durham and the band, don't tell anybody about this piece, don't even whistle it. We will rehearse in secret and spring it on the Webb band in a month. So they put it aside to use it as a blockbuster."* An announcement at midnight on NBC by Martin Block proclaimed Chick Webb won. But that decision is still hotly debated by attendees, including dancers Norma Miller and Frankie Manning, who said until the day they died: *"it was the greatest thing that ever happened!."*

However, on May 29, 1938, another trailblazing event. 23,400 fans paid 50c admission to see 25 live swing bands at New York Municipal Stadium *Randall's Island* for a benefit concert titled *Carnival of Swing,* broadcasted by WNEW. It was racially integrated. Benny Goodman was not there.

Most clubs would shut down during Summer months due to a lack of air conditioning. Two months after the *Carnival of Swing Festival,* impresario John Hammond had air conditioning installed at *The Famous Door* (66 W.

52nd St.) in exchange for a four-month residency for the *Count Basie Orchestra* to rehearse and perform from July 11-November 12, 1938, and this included nightly broadcasts on the CBS network. In 1937, Benny Goodman's band debuted onto the airwaves. Eddie Durham does not perform on these broadcasted recordings, but his compositions and arrangements are showcased. *(Eddie's arrangements, compositions / CBS-The Famous Door: see "Appendix "A")*

"The band had recently hit town and was playing the *Roseland Ballroom*, and most of its members were staying at the *Woodside*, which achieved a kind of immortality with Basie's hit "Jumpin' at the Woodside." Drummer Hal Austin remembered Ella at the *Woodside*: "When she was living in the *Woodside Hotel*, *"Jumpin' at the Woodside"*! Eddie Durham wrote that tune. That was a good-time building! "[116]

"Eddie told me he stayed at the *Woodside Hotel* with the Basie Band." ***Albert Vollmer***, Founder & Manager of *The Harlem Blues & Jazz Band*

"We rehearsed at the *Woodside* for our first job in New York City, downtown at the *Roseland Ballroom*. We were scheduled to play opposite Woody Herman. I remember the night we opened; Woody and all of his guys stood around and listened to us and then they played. They really messed us up and washed us away that night, it really wasn't even close. We were a bit under-rehearsed and some of our guys had to be replaced. We got a lot better very quickly, but it was a bad start. I thought John Hammond could die that first night when we played so badly."[117] ***Buck Clayton,*** Jazz trumpeter, Swing era (1911-1991)

After Eddie left the Basie orchestra for Lunceford's, Hammond wanting to edify his investment, realized that Eddie is the quaesitum to the failing Basie orchestra. He personally petitions Eddie to leave Lunceford and return to Basie for one year, with the lure of doubling his pay. Basie was endlessly exhausting the use of Eddie's charts, which were inherited from the *Bennie Moten Orchestra*. Eddie's name had been removed or inflicted with moiety and he perhaps thought he could rectify this somewhat, by returning. Eddie did his friend a favor and returned for a contractual year. It certainly benefited Basie who as bandleader received the customary, well-deserved co-writer credit. But Basie like others, needed Eddie to make it all cohesive. It is because Basie knows of Eddie's ability to score "proof-perfect" charts, with no mistakes. This is the reason why the genre he developed, labeled "swing," can be replicated a century later. In that one year, distinctly it's Eddie who is responsible for the hits and creating the archetype for danceable swing-music.

"Basie really began to get a book together when Ed Durham was in the band. After Durham left, Basie began to buy different arrangements from outside...I don't think the Basie band had anything new except the idea of the two tenors. After all, Fletcher had swung just about everything that could be swung. Maybe Fletcher's things were a bit more polished, but Basie had those tempos like had. …. Ed Durham contributed a lot, too. He didn't write too complicated and he voiced so open, like Jimmy Mundy, and I think it caught the dancers better… Basie's two battling tenors were two of the best… I think that started the tenor sax duet within a band.[118] **William "Dicky" Wells**, Jazz trombonist, Swing era (1907-1985)

Eddie recalled: *"With Basie, less is more. Basie was a lazy pianist, so he got in nobody's way. He liked to play in C & F which didn't fit the horns. He would play his key in front and, was known to make the shortest modulation, 1 measure, 2 beats, perfect. Ram Ramirez says nobody else can do that, like in One O'Clock Jump. Basie was tenor crazy, gave all music to Lester and Herschel. Jack Washington didn't get his share because of this, a baritone in a double tenor action. Basie would not go against me, and he made tenor history."* [119]

"Music Corp of America (MCA), Basie's booking office, had become worried about the band's lukewarm reception, and it was rumored that MCA had hired Durham to build up the Basie band. When questioned about the circumstances of his hiring, Durham merely said, *"I'm just going to work for my old friend Bill Basie."* The first Basie recording date using a Durham arrangement was made in July at the session that produced the famed *One O'Clock Jump*. Durham's contribution to the date was *John's Idea*, a tribute to John Hammond for bringing the band to New York."[120]

"The first place that we played was the *Apollo Theater* and we not only played as a band but we played for the shows. … Of all the bands we played against at the *Savoy*, our only problem was with Chick Webb because he had

84

such a following. He had been playing at the *Savoy* since the 1920s and had a lot of fans. The first time we played against him in 1937, I thought we won, but there were so many of his fans there. I think he got the nod that night. …The main bands we played against in addition to Chick Webb were Benny Goodman and Duke Ellington, and these were my two favorite bands."[121]
Buck Clayton

Eddie recalled: "I came back to help [Basie] with the repertoire. Dicky Wells replaced me a year later. Cause when they were playing Shady Rest in Newark, NJ, it opened 9 PM and I got there 9:30. I put my uniform on and Wells come up with his book under his arm and his uniform on. I said, 'Here's your new trombone player." Then I left. …Basie wasn't being business enough, he wanted to have a good time with me, not to write. Tried to convince me it was both of ours band. If anybody brought arrangements around that was a little odd, he didn't want it. Buck Clayton was writing nice, but Basie would play it until I'd say 'play these two numbers Buck did yesterday and only then would Buck's numbers get in, I had to instigate. Moving too slow for me 'cause I was out to write and play. Basie always wanted me to take it easy, party-minded, he said that 'I shouldn't work hard, I could hire somebody to write; Ed you meet them in Albany, NY'. When I got there they were rehearsing at the park. So I got the Pullman Car overnight and met the band.

I had agreed to go with Basie for a year, and I guess I could have stayed longer, but I had really been with Lunceford too long. He was a college man, a different kind of leader, nearly all in the band were college men, and I never heard a word of profane language with them. But Basie's was a regular type of band like all the others, and it got to the point where I couldn't stand much of the radical stuff.

The only guy I knew to come near Lunceford was Glenn Miller. Tommy Dorsey was rough, rougher than Basie. [122] Basie only had about six arrangements then, and he'd told John [Hammond] I'd written some of them. Now here is Hammond talking to Jimmy [Lunceford] and I'm standing right there - - nobody asked me what I thought. But he told Hammond he couldn't get along without me. Then I said to Lunceford that he should let me go for a while; I'd go help Basie and if I wasn't successful I'd come back and stay for *a year. I went down and checked out the Basie band. They were at Roseland and they had some problems and I thought I could help them with some arrangements. Not too much later, John Hammond came around and offered me $125 a week to go with the band. I've got to give John credit. He always felt the band could be something, and it was at a time when nobody else was paying them any attention. ...When Basie first came to New York, he was pretty ragged. I wrote some things for them that helped them; "Good Morning Blues," "Time Out," "Topsy"... I only stayed about a year and put maybe twenty-five numbers in the book."*

Ironically, a half-century later as these compositions fell into the ambit of the *"[Sonny Bono] Copyright Term Extension Act (CTEA) of 1998"*,[123] where the one-year Contract was finagled to infer that the music written under that contract as "works for hire." This translated into Eddie collecting royalties as co-composer, but his heirs losing the legal right to *recapture* publishing income, after works fall into Public Domain. However at the time, Eddie's consistent barrage of hits spearheaded a reign of publicity, which titled Eddie Durham "the hit maker." This was priceless to his career in the 1940s.

Public Domain retires the income to the copyright owner but not to the publisher or record company. This prevents heirs from recapturing inherited rights (to renegotiate, shop, or self-publish). The necessity for an entertainment agent and lawyer prevails upon any artist. Otherwise, the artist will most likely fall prey to the many rampant vultures.

Eddie's publicity reign was of great benefit when most of the other musicians were drafted for WWII. Eddie, instead, was handpicked to lead national fundraisers as Musical Director via USO tours, coaching the various musicians in the all-girl orchestras. They were supplied with buses, unlimited fuel during a gas ration, and no shortage of government funding.

Jimmy Rushing

It is also noteworthy the combination of Jimmy Rushing's lyrics and vocals being annexed to the charts which Eddie Durham wrote for Basie, is pivotal to Rushing's momentous career as vocalist. Rushing and Durham performed together in *Walter Page's Blue Devils* and *The Bennie Moten Orchestra's,* in the 1920s.

"One of the things I loved about him, and why he was a role model for me, first of all, he was a meticulous man. But I think he was one of those people who, evidently he had a complex mind or he couldn't have accomplished all of this. But most people who have complex minds are not accessible to other people. My point is, he could take a complex thing, and explain it to you simply. Most people explain simple things in a complex style. But I think that is really a virtue when somebody who has a mind that amazing can still make you understand what they're talking about. I know my mind was nowhere near his in complexity but every time he talked to me I felt like, although I was, I wasn't talking to a scientist, I wasn't really talking to this brilliant mind, I was talking to a person. Just like he knew what to say to me, he knew what to do in almost all circumstances. He knew what to write for Jimmy Rushing, Glenn Miller, Count Basie, Benny Goodman, Jimmie Lunceford, Kaye Starr, Jan Savitt, or The Ink Spots."[124] ***Benny Powell,*** Educator, Jazz trombonist (1930-2010)

"Regarding a Memorial for Dicky Wells at St. Peter's - the First Church of Jazz, in New York City in December 1985 (The Rev. John Gensel, associate pastor), with performances by Jimmy Butts, Buck Clayton, Eddie Durham, Charlie Frazier, Al Graves, Max Lucas, Al Sears, Boss Townsend and singer Laurel Watson,[125] the trombonist Grey, Al recalls: "He really hit me in the heart, when we went to a mutual dear friend Dicky Wells' memorial. This particular day they had a memorial and we didn't have nobody from Count Basie's band in the place except Eddie Durham - and he had his trombone because he had played earlier on the [same] program. We went in the back and he pulled out his horn. I said "Eddie, I don't know about (using) this mouthpiece" and he said, "*ah, you can play anything.*" I played "My Buddy" and then after that, we chatted and he thought that he could write a tune for me. He would pick up his guitar to find out what direction he wanted to go in writing tunes."[126] ***Al Grey,*** Trombonist (Benny Carter, Lucky Millinder, Clark Terry, Dizzy Gillespie, Count Basie, Bandleader (1925-2000)

"Oh Eddie" is a subtle number composed by Durham…and recorded in Kansas City when RCA bought its recording equipment from Chicago and rented a local studio."[127] *The Gazette*

Eddie recalled: "I wrote a song called "Swingin On C," but that wasn't made for a band, that was written for drums. And they would have to tune their tom-tom and the bass and the drums could play the one-note melody. Cozy and Gene Krupa kept on asking about me because I say I had a special number made where they gotta tune their drums, but I didn't see 'em, but they were waiting for it. But they run into Battle, and Battle say, 'Yeah I got that number!'. Cause I was in California. So that's why I turn around and let him have credit 'cause he did promote it that way. And they got "Topsy" and Cozy played "Topsy," but Gene wasn't with him. But "Swingin on C" was the number they was supposed to do. So I let it alone. The melody is one note in that tune. So Earl Hines played it and the trumpet did something else and called it "Swingin On Hi C" so I let it alone. But I still let them know that it can be done on the drums, but you gotta tune the drums and tune them tom-toms, and you'll get the note. The drums will play the melody and when the horns play it, you will hear the melody."

Swinging The Blues

Eddie recalled: "I liked it with lyrics [by Lambert Hendricks & Ross]. I went down and caught the Broadway Show, it never did leave Broadway. It was a big show with a lot of chorus girls & dancers. But the guy who was producing it at the Broadway Theatre, he said if he couldn't get in Hollywood and he couldn't make Las Vegas, he was gon' drop the show. So he spent up somebody's money and I went down there and they had the chorus girls all singing it, and they picked up their mics, they backed up to the stage and they had their mics laying on the stage. And I liked the singing version but that's just 'cause I like to hear some of the lyrics to some of the numbers."[128]

"Good Morning Blues" (The title of Basie's Biography)

"Time Out": When Count Basie's band made its first splash in 1937, many swing bands were in danger of becoming over-arranged and mechanistic. Eddie Durham's "Time Out" is a wonderful example of the band's flowing and bluesy feel. After a brief statement from tenor saxophonist Herschel Evans, the band's main soloist, tenor man Lester Young launches into a zen-like solo that makes a perfect complement to the spare backgrounds allowed him. Composer Durham plays the electric guitar solo (one of the first in Jazz)."[129] <u>(Eddie / Basie recordings: see "Appendix "A")</u>

Durham's Base Four

"Commodore Records was founded in 1938 and "was essentially the creation of one remarkable man, Milt Gabler who… was the CEO, the producer of virtually the entire catalog, and frequently his own shipping clerk… Incredibly, Gabler was simultaneously active as head of recording, for one of the most prolific pop (and jazz) labels of the period - Decca Records.[130]"

John Hammond, Sr., initially produced *The Kansas City Five* for the Brunswick Label on March 16, 1938. This recording session in New York was originally intended to be released as *"Eddie Durham and His Band,"* to showcase Eddie's electrically amplified guitar sound without Basie's piano. These are some of the very first electric jazz guitar solos. Eddie used a Gibson ES-150. For this reason, among others, these recordings are historic and a collector's dream. Eddie hired Buck Clayton on trumpet and 3/4 of the All American Rhythm Section, Freddie Green, Jo Jones, and Walter Page - with Eddie on trombone and guitar.

Kansas City 5 & 6

Although Eddie arranged, coached, composed, and choreographed for an array of bandleaders, these successful albeit brief collaborations were not published in an indelible fashion. In fact, the sweeping exclusions are questionable, as though ascribing broad credit to him could negate the eminence of the bandleader. Eddie's tenures are stamped with his charts and recording dates but sometimes his arrangements or length of tenure are debated. Stanley Dance called it *"scandalous"*.[131]

Even the treasured, famed recordings *"Eddie Durham and His Base Four"* featuring Eddie's pioneering work on the electric guitar, were renamed *"The Kansas City Six,"* to honor Lester Young.

"During Durham's electrically amplified guitar solos, especially noteworthy on "I Know That You Know" and "Way Down Yonder In New Orleans," were the first of their kind on record."[132]

Eddie recalled: "I am the only electric guitar. Billie Holiday was at every session, right at the mic, mouthing encouragement as Freddie Green sang. I'm playing the guitar, but it's the voicing of the strings. That's why that guitar can play with Freddie, 'cause I was in one position and he was in another. And that's why you ain't never heard two guitar players sound like Freddie Green and myself. We could play rhythm together and it would still be two different guitars. Freddie Green is the greatest rhythm guitar player in the world.

I'm featured on electric guitar, interchanging with Freddie Green, Walter Page and Jo Jones. It's a unique voicing of bass carrying one melody and the clarinet carrying a lick melody, with the voicing all spread apart for clarinet, trombone, and trumpet. Then I switch to electric guitar and added some voicing behind Buck Clayton's solo and then switched back to trombone for the out-course. You can hear my trombone in the alternate take when I slide off."

"The *Kansas City Sessions*, …electric guitarist and trombonist Eddie Durham was the first composer/arranger to capture the flow and spontaneity of Kansas City Jazz on paper."[133]

"Some of the greatest records made are The Kansas City Five and The Kansas City Six. The KC6 has almost from the beginning, always come out under Lester Young's name. These are very famous records. But the truth is that anybody who knows these records and the KC5 recordings, knows that these were originally Eddie Durham record dates. He wrote the arrangements, he played the trombone and guitar, and even beyond that, they've got the Eddie Durham feeling if you know his music. It's his vibration. KC5 was done early 1938 for The American Record Company, produced by John Hammond, Sr. They made four tunes listed as "Eddie Durham and His Band" [aka Base

Four]. They lost one of the records but Hammond knew that these were great, great records and so he took them to an independent record label owned by Milt Gabler, called Commodore. So they recorded the rest of the tunes in late 1938 and added Lester Young.

So I got to write the liner notes for one of the issues and Eddie told me about the session and the vocals by Freddie Green, singing "Them There Eyes." Billie Holiday and Freddie were dating at the time. Billie did not record "Them There Eyes" until early 1939 and this is late 1938. But if you listen to the record, you hear Freddie Green sing it exactly like the Billie Holiday version, every little inflection.

Eddie also said that Hammond came down, but Lester, Billie, and a few others had gone into the bathroom to smoke marijuana and it was all over the place and that Hammond and the recording company wanted to shut down the session and kick them all out; *'you can't do this in our studio'." Loren Schoenberg*

"I just played rhythm on the date, with a group called the Kansas City Five. The electric guitar -the first I'd ever seen- was played by Eddie Durham. I never tried electric myself; the sound would interfere with the acoustic rhythm thing we had going."[134] ***Freddie Green*** (1911-1987)

"A musician who was to take a major role in jazz-guitar amplification, Eddie Durham, played a resonator guitar in Bennie Moten's band from 1929 and recorded with one in Jimmie Lunceford's band on "Hittin' The Bottle" (1935). After taking up the electric guitar, he made historic recordings in New York in March 1938 with The Kansas City Five that feature loud electric solos in which his volume level easily matches Buck Clayton's trumpet. "Laughing At Life" features background electric chords played with staccato, and blues and Hawaiian-style slides. Two bright linear solo breaks have a bouncy rhythmic style with liquid runs and touches of partial chords. "Good Mornin' Blues" starts with single lines, moving into a skillful and attractive chord solo with partial voicings, and "I Know That You Know" has an infectious, nimble solo. "Love Me Or Leave Me" opens with broken chords and the tune is played as a chord melody before Durham plays a solo using a wide register with single notes, then adds broken chords and a chord solo. Subsequently, with tenorist Lester Young added to make *The Kansas City Six*, Durham's more flowing solo style can be heard on "Way Down Yonder In New Orleans",… "Countless Blues" opens with the type of riffs that later made the guitar preeminent in other genres. Durham was at the forefront of a revolution that established the guitar as a major ensemble instrument for melodies, soloing, and chords. This opened up possibilities in jazz for the guitar to develop stylistically."135

These priceless sessions not only capture seminal recordings of electric guitar, but also include rhythm guitarist Freddie Green's only recording as a vocalist, and Lester Young recording on clarinet. *(Eddie & His Base Four; KC6 Lester recordings: see "Appendix "A")*

*"You didn't play one tenor sax right after another tenor. Herschel Evans and Lester Young started playing solos, in each number, one after the other. That was Basie's idea; now people think that's the thing you've got to do. I put it in the arrangements. Basie couldn't write music but he could create. If I could hold him down long enough, I'd get something. We wrote about 3,000 songs. If he didn't help me on some, they put his name on anyway. We didn't care."*136 Eddie Durham. *Latrobe Bulletin*, Newspaper.

John Hammond

Eddie recalled: "When we was rehearsing the song "John's Idea" I named it after him when he was sitting in the audience. When he was on the radio and they asked him how did it get its title, he said, "Well, it was a little thing that they just called 'John's Idea' for some reason." He never did say it was my tune and plenty guys called me up about it the next day. I could never put a title on the tune and I told Basie, let's call it "John's Idea." I just told them guys, 'maybe he forgot it'. But it was right there on the music, it's not Jimmy Mundy's. Charlie Christian and Floyd Smith, they never mentioned me either.

"Hammond was a controversial person during the swing era because he was opinionated, on occasion was guilty of conflicts of interest (he produced records, and then wrote reviews of the records he had produced), was arrogant, and could be pushy. On the other hand, he was independently wealthy (a member of the Vanderbilt family), and never took financial advantage of any artist. Indeed, he never charged any artist a management

92

fee, even though he was directly responsible for many musicians getting excellent gigs. This made him unique because the business of the swing era was dominated by assertive vulgarians who had little regard for such niceties as ethics or respect for other human beings. Their concern was singular – money. They saw the musicians they interacted with as naive children who rarely cared enough about their business to know what was going on, much less to check-up on their managers. Consequently, abuses of artists were rampant."[137]

These abuses still persist today.

Herschel Evans & Lester Young

"Earle Warren emphasized the good feelings between the star soloists, maintaining that "little things that happened between Evans and Young were of no great consequence." Dicky Wells observed that they were "the best of friends" regardless of whether or not they were speaking to each other. Jo Jones was convinced that "there was no real friction" between the two... Durham accounted for Young's relaxed or "lag-along" style-and unwittingly provided a possible explanation for the title of Young's most famous composition by saying, *"That's why he used to play after [the] beat. You hit something, he heard it...he'd leap in...then and fast."*

Durham maintained that Herschel Evans did much the same thing. ...Durham gave Young a specific place in the reed-section arrangements that he wrote for Basie and outlined the reed section's arrangements...[138]

"In Well's opinion, the presence of the two tenors was a "distinguishing feature of the Basie orchestra, and such an integral part of the first band that duplication in later years was impossible." While praising the quality of Buddy Tate's playing, Wells argued, "It's pretty hard to duplicate the original, especially when the original is perfect.""[139]

"Several Basieites downplayed the alleged bad blood between the rival tenor stylists and occasionally tried to explain the real nature of their relationship. Buck Clayton stressed, "I know that they respected each other even though they didn't talk to each other very much," adding that when they sat "back to back in the reed section, it wasn't any kind of an indication that they didn't respect each other."[140]

Dicky Wells noted that Evans "had a first tenor sound that made a real contrast with Lester's," and Buck Clayton recalled that he "was intensely proud of being a tenor sax man from Texas." Wells insisted that both Evans's conception and his playing were highly original: "Herschel was playing that way before he ever heard Hawk in person." Jo Jones, not one known for lavishing praise, believed that Evans "was a natural. He had a sound on the tenor that perhaps you will never hear again" -in fact, in Jones's view, he played the way it was supposed to be played."[141]

"Topsy" and "Time Out," as well as "John's Idea," "Moten Swing," "One O'Clock Jump," "Good Morning Blues," et. al., are arranged and [co-]written by Eddie Durham, who also performed on these recordings. The incredible performance of these Basie sessions are of specific monumental credit to the genius of Eddie Durham who arranged precisely for each musician according to their talents and particular, sometimes peculiar sound, as he did for the

94

many other bandleaders, vocalists, band members and soloists mentioned in this book.

Lester Young

"One of the reasons that I was so thrilled to play with Eddie Durham was because he was so tight with Lester Young. Not just tight as a friend, but tight on a musical level. I was getting to know someone who knew my idol, Lester Young, who died when I was about a month old, so I never got to hear him in person. But I did get to know Jo Jones and Eddie and through them, I would ask questions. But I became totally obsessed. Lester Young never played better than on those 1938 Kansas City Six recordings with Eddie Durham. Those are absolutely unique. Eddie told me that Lester Young had great ears and he could hear any chord and any harmony. He may not have known the name for the chord, but Eddie used to rehearse with Lester and he would pick up the guitar, with his big hands and unique chords and that Lester would pick up the sax and play the exact chord back! Eddie said he never could get over that and he talked about that all the time." *Loren Schoenberg*

Eddie recalled: "*Lester n*amed me "Poundcake," called me that everywhere; the same time he named Billie "Lady Day." And I never did know why. Funny cat. Used to say "All the physicians come to hear the musicians." I was teaching him the name of chords. Once I hit the chords, he could run them all back immediately. Great memory. Lester studied with me more than Herschel.

Lester on Clarinet

Lester was a saxophonist but occasionally played clarinet. He had soul in his clarinet tone and never played too many notes, just enough for you to keep up with him. He played less notes than anybody and he doesn't sound like nobody else on clarinet. He didn't execute a lot, he didn't believe in that. So much soul. Something out of the ordinary, some sort of soul spirit in there, some kinda way. But I met people who thought Lester was the greatest clarinet player in the world. I tried to figure out, where'd they get that from. We'd be backstage, say in Germany, place is packed. The boss comes over and tell me, "there's three people standing around trying to get an autograph from you because you played with Lester"! So I autograph and ask them, "you wanna stay to hear one number" and they say, "Well, is Lester on there?"

"Pagin The Devil" they run me down about that in England, they come in from other countries and stop for ten minutes and say, "I just come by to get an autograph. They'd hold the record so tight like I was gonna take it... The bass fiddle is playing the melody and Lester's playing that next counter-melody, which is below the trombone in that low register and that's the other lead. So it's got two melodies. It's the voicing, but I don't know if anybody else can play it like Lester's clarinet. He blends right with that bass and that trombone in the low register, they don't even know the trombone is playing. Nobody know whose got the lead. That's the $64M question. Buck Clayton's playing and I'm playing and Lester. They hear it, but they can't tell you what the melody is. Every musician can't get the right tone out of it. ("Pagin The Devil" Kansas City album for Dave Dexter - Decca Records Nov. 11, 1940) Horns are in E flat. Sometimes the brass section's in one key and the rhythm in another key, minors against majors. But only Duke knew about this, 'cause I went to him and we'd laugh about it.

Herschel Evans

Eddie left Basie in 1938.

"Herschel Evans had a heart condition. About six months later Eddie went to the Savoy to hear the band. He said that he walked into the ballroom, the band was playing and he heard this sound coming from the bandstand. But he didn't know what it was, it sounded like a voice. He knew it wasn't Jimmy Rushing or Helen Humes singing. And he walked up and it was this voice and it was Herschel. He said that he knew that when he heard Herschel playing that sound, that he wasn't going to live long. But it wasn't that it was like a sick sound. It was like before people die, something happens and some kind of humanity is pouring out of the sax. He would tear up when he told that story because he loved Herschel so much." ***Loren Schoenberg***

"On Herschel Evans' very last recorded solos, which were with *The Lionel Hampton Orchestra Jam Session* on December 28, 1938 "*The Bill Savory Collection* gave us an incredible treasure of music from the late thirties,

96

including many of the jazz greats. However, I believe that the Herschel Evans discoveries possibly could be the most valuable of all, considering how little we have of this magnificent tenor sax player! This discovery is unique, it represents his last farewell, only a few weeks before he passed away of a fatal heart attack. He plays two rather modest blues choruses on "*Blues*," and does his best to swing "*Rosetta*" and "*Dinah*" in up-tempo. It is obvious that he has problems with breathing, his usually big sound is much thinner than usual. Not that this matter very much, as we are most taken in by the historical occasion.

Finally, however, we have one of the Bill Savory collection's greatest and most important findings, a full version of "*Stardust*," nobody to interfere, except from some soft ensemble backing at the end. This treasure shows what this great saxophone player could do with a ballad, and there is nothing like this with Basie, "...*Sentimental*" included." He plays so sadly that one is deeply moved, listen to how he starts the second chorus, as crying for help. Without trying to be after-wise, it seems that he knew his days were numbered. "*Stardust*" is a great performance, one of the greatest treasures of jazz tenor saxophone of the vintage era, and a worthy goodbye from one of its greatest performers."[142] On Evans' July 7, 1937 recordings with the *Count Basie Orchestra*, "A very fine 'duet' with the band on "*Topsy*," plus an intro of maximum inspiration on "*Time Out*," where he lays out to Lester Young. The remarkably effortless transition demonstrates how much the two tenor saxophonists had in common in spite of many differences, for instance their sound. Naturally they had to be influenced by each other, sitting side by side for years. ...However, it is "*Doggin'*..." which makes the strongest impression on the listener, a sparkling solo which probably is his best recorded one in a fast tempo. Let me even say he outdistances Lester Young by far!"[143]

Allen Durham

Picture & credit Wilbur "Buck" Clayton Collection Digitizing agency: University of Missouri--Kansas City. Library. Dr. Kenneth J. LaBudde Special Collections.

https://dl.mospace.umsystem.edu/islandora/object/umkc%3A9770 Side 2 of 2-sided photo-album panel.

Buck Clayton standing with members of his band at the Cotton Club in Culver City, California (left to right): Kid Lips Hackett, Teddy Buckner, Arcima Taylor, Ike Bell, Red Callender, Bert Johnson, **Herschel Evans** *(wearing eyeglasses)*, <u>Allen Durham</u> *(on steps, behind Buck)*, Bumps Myers, Frank Pasley, Winslow Allen, Caughey Roberts, Eddie Beal.

New York "December 1, 1937 recordings: "The two recording sessions with *Harry James* are very valuable. Not only does *Evans* solo well but the presence of several alternate takes gives another dimension to his playing. Certainly Evans was an improviser of high status, both brief and long soli show a lot of differences to the listener's pleasure. One tune in particular deserves attention, ...[When We're] *"Alone,"* whose second take contains a masterpiece of a brief solo in a pleasant medium tempo fitting Evans very well. Truly one of his best recorded soli ever."[144]

Eddie Durham recorded with his cousin Herschel, on this date.

"That was in the summer of 1941. It was around that time that Herschel Evans joined the band - he played tenor saxophone. He was up from Texas, and he had a whole lot of soul in his horn. He had a unique way of playing. He had a great big body on his horn, and when he started playing, he swung like mad. To me, he was one of the greatest men who ever played the horn. …I could see the tenor saxophone coming into prominence. I said, That's the horn that people are gonna be listening to," and they did. Johnny Hodges with Duke, Willie Smith with Jimmie Lunceford. A lot of them made big names for themselves. After Herschel left, I started talking a lot of young guys into playing tenor sax - including Dexter Gordon and Illinois Jacquet. I think it was that summer that we first played Michigan State Fair. And then we went into the Graystone Ballroom in Detroit."[145] ***Lionel Hampton,*** Vibraphonist, pianist, bandleader.

Drummers

"I saw Jo Jones set up his drums and I started to hear the sock cymbal and I couldn't see it even though I was standing right in front of the band. Freddie Green was playing acoustic guitar, but I was disappointed that Eddie wasn't there at that time, 'cause I had heard quite a bit about him. I guess because he was moving around, you know, playing two instruments and being such a great arranger naturally everybody wanted him. But, I kept hearing boom chip boom chip. I wanted to know where was that "chip" sound coming from. So it was a 7' high sock cymbal and that was the first time I'd ever seen a sock cymbal. It was Jo Jones and he showed it to me on the intermission. It was on the floor." ***Illinois Jacquet,*** saxophonist/bandleader

Eddie recalled: *"Jimmy Butch is one of the greatest rhythm drummers, for dancing, I ever heard in my life. Drummer Willie Jones played with Thelonious Monk, Lester Young and Charlie Mingus. Another guy I liked was pianist Dick Wellstood. He went with us to Canada and I had Eddie Barefield with me, Dick Vance and I think that was Jimmy Crawford's last date. We was so surprised that he could sit in a little band and swing that band. I'd say, 'Jimmy I didn't know you could swing with a little band!' and he said, "I do!." And that's all he said.*

Now where Jo Jones' playing was different from Crawford, you see what made them both successful and also Gene Krupa, those guys believed in tuning those instruments, just like you tune any other instrument. Today these drummers don't believe the drums supposed to be tuned. So they don't need no stage on there to tune 'em, 'cause they don't wanna use 'em . So the drums ain't tuned-up right today. Buddy Rich tuned his drums, I don't believe he'd play 'em if they couldn't tune 'em. All those fellas back then tuned those drums. Sonny Greer, Chick Webb. I used to go to the rehearsal hall, and Jo Jones and Big Page would go, we didn't never carry Basie, but the rest of the rhythm would go - and I would lay down on the floor and put my head on the stage and let the rhythm play and you can tell when them drums are tuned, if you tune that drum right, you will hear that bass note, in the drum. See them Drummers don't tell the secrets too much. And I stayed with Willie Bryant and Cozy Cole and every morning he was up training, and I don't see how guys don't get music out of a drum and don't never practice and don't tune the drums... but that's important. The rhythm section play in tune and it will go into that drum, piano, and everything and they hit the note on the piano and I see Jo Jones tune the drum up to A or B or some other note and I'd say 'there it is right there!."

"When Jo Jones came to Kansas City, I used to take my guitar and trombone and jam with him from four in the morning till eight or nine. He was playing that modern stuff and it sounded good. He was sharp on it and he was really creating a style. I don't know where he got it from. He hadn't been east – he hadn't been any place. But he was something else! It was natural with him, and maybe he doesn't get enough credit for it now."[146]

"However, the role of the saxophone or horn section has retained its basic presence as the cornerstone of rhythm and blues. The single string runs of the electric guitar solos often follow the saxophone riffs and emulate the horn sounds."[147] ***Al Govenar***

Eddie was a pioneer in another aspect in that he sometimes used his valve trombone as trumpet, which came from the 101 Circus and his guitar like a clarinet. Now, music stores sell pedals, effects and Apps to produce the sound from one instrument of another instrument.

"Eddie Durham did more to influence the big band era than anyone alive. The beat, feeling was special. He left room for unparalleled soloists in the Basie band to expand and heretofore, these things were not heard of in other big bands. Eddie freed up the drums through Papa Jo Jones (not just boom boom) but with broken rhythms; this was a precursor to contemporary drumming." **Maxwell L. Roach**, Bebop/Jazz Drummer, *DownBeat* Hall of Fame, *Modern Drummer* Hall of Fame, Educator (1924-2007)

Trombone Tricks

Eddie Durham played both valve and slide trombone, sometimes with a plunger mute, ranging from the pedal register as far up to a *high F* - and he played this range until he died at 80 years old! His range was never limited because a technique (he invented or mastered) of non-pressure playing, sustained and preserved his lips unscarred and unmarked. Scarring is an injury and hence inhibits hitting high notes due to the pain of applying pressure on the blister, sort of like walking in tight shoes after you've already developed a callous. Eddie's trombone performances were exciting because he was able to completely focus on choreography and trombone humor. And oh yes, he had some trombone tricks! Eddie plays slide trombone on One O'Clock Jump (Basie).

"On most releases of The Kansas City Five recordings, they don't list Eddie Durham on trombone. He plays the trombone in such a subtle way you don't hear it. I knew these records before and I never heard the trombone. But if you listen carefully, you can hear that he plays the trombone like he's in the other room. You can hear a hint of trombone. What's that? It's mysterious and it's Eddie on the trombone. Genius!" *Loren Schoenberg*

Eddie recalled: "I taught a lot of tricks to the other trombones in the [Lunceford] band, Russell [Bowles] and Elmer [Crumbley]. Sometimes when the band was playing, Russell and I would jump out of our chairs and get in a sword fight with our trombones. I'd pretend to cut him and then jump off the stage while the band was playing. We were a regular clown outfit, but then the band could go back and blow you away."[148]

Eddie recalled: "I always liked the trombone sound in the circus band. And I liked the instrument because a guy could make it sound like he was crying. I just liked trombone players from the start -Charlie "Big" Green, Jimmy Harrison, J.C. Higginbotham, Joe Nanton with Duke, and later on because he was sweeter, Lawrence Brown. Then I got crazy about Tommy Dorsey ...Trummy Young ...Dicky Wells. I liked all these guys, but I didn't copy any of them.[149]

They always tried to hold the trombone back by trying to make an obbligato instrument out of it, like a tailgate, which is the tail along, slow. But trombone players are fast. I can just about play anything on my trombone you can play on an alto. It's a way to do it. When they write, they don't never write nothing for trombone where they gotta stretch out. There's a lot in trombone that's never been brought out, cause it's a hard instrument. Don Redman started into that and then I started with that "Slip Horn Jive" trick stuff, but I knew it was a lot more could be done.

Duke didn't go too far with it either, because in order to do something with it, you should be a trombone player that's far advanced on it. I give Duke a lot of credit because he started out with so many different effects. They have dropped all those ideas. They got all those mutes sitting up on the shelf and the guys come out with no mutes.

I know there are 14 positions on it instead of 7 - officially 7 at three inches apart. I play a 1½ inch apart, perfectly, solo work and you can execute. But you gotta have somebody with pretty good range. With one or two guys with a good range, you can do anything that you can do with anything else, there's a lot of effects. That's how you can get so many things on it that the trombone players don't know. The big round one is a wha wha mute. There's also a solo-tone, we call them anything. Jack Teagarden, he used the plunger sometimes, but he was an open horn man. I used all types of mutes and plungers.

102

Benny Morten was an open horn stylist. Tricky Sam [Joe Nanton] was definitely an innovator with the plunger. The mutes was just a section of the deal for brass. Tommy Dorsey set that style for sweet music, I mean you couldn't get around it. That guy didn't have no trombone tone, he had a tone, he play like a fiddle. But he didn't play much Jazz cause it would've spoil his lip, he couldn't do 'em both. J.C. Higginbotham had a good style. Trummy Young was a flash man executor, play like alto saxes, he had another style altogether, top of the horn. He's not given enough credit. He was supporting Louis Armstrong, but he could've raised way up.

When I was with those bands I was busy writing for other guys and nobody even knew I could play horn, but I knew plenty horn then. I'd write for the other guys, tryna push the band and I didn't play. Now they think this and that, but you can't play like that in a big band, and if you are the arranger, you don't write too much for yourself, you gotta push the band over.

With Bennie Moten I played valve trombone, in that 1929 picture that's a valve trombone. I didn't do any solos, I could have, but I thought that the man whose supposed to solo, let him solo. Valve is cutting the notes instead of the horn moving. Only thing cut a note on a slide is your lip and lifting from one position up to another position with your lip. Cause that horn runs down in degrees and to get that over again you go back down and you start and you come up high and you come up again and as you move up you can sound... A trombone is made for slurring and legato movements. If you ever heard a brass band, they starting at 7th position and they in rhythm, they all the way up here and that's what made kids like trombone, they like that ahhhAHHHH, that's what attracted people's attention, but they don't do too much of it.

I would use three B flat trombones, no bass, it'll get in the way it's too low - and here's the difference - four trombones are great when you're sustaining and you're not moving fast. But three trombones moving can sound just as great as six sustaining. Three can move easy cause you gotta use certain positions, certain keys. You don't let 'em break them slurs and that's hard to do, you gotta know the horn. A musician ain't gonna know that until I write it and then I marks the position. You got six different F's on that horn. They would say, 'I knew two'.

103

Just like fiddles are better when they don't break. When you've got three violins ones gotta come down, the others got a short long note, and he's gotta go back up while they coming down - you can tell it. That's why they all gotta bow the same way. Dicky Wells can play the music, he's got a big tone, he can play it. I can break him down, he'd understand it. He would know what you're after, he picks up quick. Before I'd hire anybody they would have to audition on the music. You gotta get down to earth. Ain't nobody can play that tone like Tommy Dorsey."[150]

"Someone once told me that Eddie Durham was dubbed the most violent trombone player, the way he threw that slide and caught it just before it flew off!"[151] **Chris Flory**, Jazz Guitarist, Bandleader

"Eddie had a way of throwing that trombone out there. It was always that one sound he had. It was clear, creamy, crystal. Talk about genius', he was a giant genius or a genius giant." ***Rudi Sheriff Lawless***

"Eddie Durham used to do some hilarious tricks with the slide of the trombone. He'd flail the trombone up and down, playing the same note continuously, in two different positions! People would look at him "WOW, how's he doing that!." Cause he's moving the slide up and down, but the one note is coming out. He could play very fast and what trombone players call "the positions," there are 7 positions and he could play very high notes on the trombone. Another Texan trombonist, Jack Teagarden was also a master of this, using different positions for one note.

Well, one night at The *Orange Inn*, thankfully it was kind of quiet, Eddie gets up to solo and does some of this stuff, and guess what! The slide went out like a spear, I mean flying 30' across the room! I thought, 'oh my god, there's going to be somebody with a trombone slide sticking out of his head and they're gonna sue 'em!' Well, thank God it was a slow night and nobody got hit! But it was funny and he couldn't stop laughing. But I saw him do that particular trick literally hundreds of times, so his average was absolutely wonderful. Maybe he did it on purpose, I don't know. You can see his doing this trick on the film footage with the Jimmie Lunceford Band.

All that showmanship stuff and all those tricks that they do, a lot of that came from Eddie Durham. Other people like Sy Oliver, talked about it so I know this for a fact. That whole comedy routine that they do while they're playing, Eddie choreographed. Eddie brought that to the Artie Shaw Band and to the Glenn Miller Band. And when you look in all the movies of the Glenn Miller Band and they're doing all of the tricks, and the trombones are going up in the air and they're looking around, and the trumpets are waving, a lot of that is Eddie Durham. That's part of what made Miller such a big hit. Eddie was in great demand because he didn't just write the arrangements, he used to coach the band in showmanship. When I see those movies, immediately I say, there's Eddie Durham! He made the bands look like they were having a great time." *Loren Schoenburg*

Benny Powell/ Grey, Al

The following interviews of prominent Jazz trombonists and recording artists Benny Powell (1930-2010) with Al Grey took place the afternoon of May 31, 1999, at the home of Al Grey (1925-2000) in New York:

Benny Powell*:* "Swinging The Blues" that's Eddie's tune. I still use it in teaching now because it's a simple tune and it was a perfect vehicle for playing. I usually teach my students, the blues is a 12-bar tune, but it has to have a framework and this is one of the most perfect frameworks, and you can teach kids in fifth grade with this.

Al Grey*:* Because "Swinging the Blues" is very melodic. That's the first thing about Eddie, he wrote his music so you didn't have anything intricate to play. He would just swing the blues. He had Basie's band and he was a very big contributor. Very big. He knew how to write for Count Basie's Orchestra. When I was in Basie's band, we used to get many, many arrangements, but it was up to the band to say whether you would use the arrangement or not; many arrangements were thrown away because it just did not fit Basie's band, or it was too intricate to play or it just didn't swing. I have met a lot of the biggest writers at that time. I remember Nelson Riddle brought in some charts for the band and some we did use, but most we did not. And one was a hit tune "Lena & Lenny" a tune we played for Lena Horne.

Benny: The difference between an arranger who would write intricate stuff, because I was part of Basie's later band too and you're right, if it got too intricate Basie thought that the guys would have to work too hard just to make the challenge of reading it, but if it was simple, you could add something to it and that's how Eddie wrote - less is more.

Al: Eddie's charts were written to swing. We're back in the era now where Swing is back. "Swinging the Blues" was one of the main tunes that we had in Basie's book. We played this a long time before I even knew that Eddie had wrote it.

Benny: I just found out recently that he wrote "Every Tub." That's a strange title, but you know, those guys were visionaries - it meant every tub sits on its own bottom, you know, everybody's responsible for themselves. Nowadays they're studying all this metaphysical stuff, these guys were doing it long ago.

Al: "Good Morning Blues" was a tune that I had the pleasure of doing on a recording with Dakota Staton, a tune that had a lot of feeling to it.

Benny: Basie's band was sometimes based on blues singers. Jimmy Rushing was a blues singer when Eddie was there. An excellent story… *Good Morning Blues, Blues How Do You Do?*… and it repeats. It was really a story. Jimmy sang it simply and the band played it simply so the arrangement was perfect for both and it worked perfectly for Basie. Eddie knew what to write for everybody.

Al: Back in those days a lot of the musicians just had the feeling but could not read the music. Eddie was one that could and he knew how to simplify the music for those who were slow in reading music. That was another one of his greatest accomplishments because he knew what to write for them. I have played "Glen Island Special" with Basie's band. I was in Basie's band quite a few years later and some of the arrangements was sent to the stockpile as Basie kept entering new music all the time. He really believed in trying to do new things.

Benny: There was a very famous venue at that time *Glenn Island Casino*, that many of the famous white bands used to play in. Eddie was unique in the fact that not only did he write for Basie, but as you discover all of his music, you see that he wrote for many of the white bands as well.

Al: We used to play "I Don't Want To Set The World On Fire" nightly. We used to say FIRE! It was a tune that was loved by every one of that period. I used to make fills on "Sent For You Yesterday, Here You Come Today" with Count Basie for Joe Williams. It was needed to fill in those gaps. A flag-waver is one of Eddie's real fast numbers, like "Lafayette," it would be closing the set or the evening. Automatic for Eddie because he knew how to write for all of these different categories. His work was noticed by the singers. When he came on playing trombone, that's when we became very close to each other. We met when he was playing with Basie and I was playing with Dizzy. He had wrote up charts that I would be in the studio that would be his arrangements. Eddie Durham was a person that was very quiet and very professional and he didn't have to say anything because he was always immaculate and he was just a great artist.

Benny: So far of the tunes we have talked about, this shows his versatility. Not anybody can write for *The Ink Spots*, balladeers, as well as write for Jimmy Rushing, a stone blues singer because they're completely different. "Sent For You Yesterday…" is very much like "Good Morning Blues," it's a story. A blues tune is very repetitious for the most part, the same lines repeat themselves.

Al: The song "Topsy" I always thought that Cozy Cole wrote the tune, but Eddie wrote that? We used to play it nightly as well. My partner at that time was Buddy Tate. And Buddy and Eddie were very close. I recorded this tune. We used to do "Wham Rebop Boom Bam" nightly too. The *feeling* makes a swing band. If you don't do that it's just another tune, it's not rewarding. Eddie had such *feeling* in writing, until you couldn't help but learn the tune. Very melodic and simple.

Benny: So many people have heard Eddie's work and not even realize that he had input. In a sense, he was co-writing it. But at that time arrangers didn't get credit. But arrangers were writers too because that's what they did.

When I came back in 1980 I went down to *Sweet Basil's* to jam one Saturday with Eddie Chamblee. Chamblee was very gracious with his stage, he let guys he knew come down and sit it. I'm sitting on one side of the room and I see this older gentleman, whom I didn't know, sitting on the other. Actually, he was so humble that I thought he was dead. He didn't blow his own horn, he didn't have publicists. Anyway, he took out his horn and I took mine out. Chamblee invited us both us to play. So he counted off a tune. Now, I'm a nice young kid and in deference to my elder, and when he started playing, I looked at him in shock! Because I knew his trombone playing but I had never seen him. It was very unusual because Prez and Sweets who had been with the Basie band would come around often, and maybe Eddie Durham did also, but he was such a humble, quiet man. But once he played four notes, I knew who he was. So after that, I had a chance to play with him just the two trombones and rhythm section, up at The *West End*. In fact, he was very gracious to me. Every time I saw him, he was trying to give me something, a gig, or some connection. So I got a chance to meet him later in life but I didn't know him when he was doing all of this writing for bands.

I guess when he brought arrangements there he just gave them to Basie and maybe he sat in the back of the room. Most guys wanna come up where they can be seen "Oh that's my arrangement," "Oh that goes in letter B" but, NONE of that about Eddie Durham. In the four bars I knew it was him because he had a distinctive way of phrasing, it didn't sound like anything else. I had heard it many times on records. He was economical in his solos just as he was in his writing. It was a different way of phrasing. If you're a trombone player you can see the difference in the uniqueness.

But it was like somebody turning on the light switch for me, it was like WOW, I've heard this before! Who is this man? Then I found out who he was later. Soon as we got off the bandstand, it was like we knew each other for a long time. He was very gracious, we talked and exchanged numbers and we talked often. In fact, Phil Schaap hired him for this gig up at The West End, he asked if I would like to play with him and I said, of course I would!

Non-Pressure Technique

Benny: When we speak of a non-pressure system, it's actually not applying pressure on your lips. The natural feeling when you want to play a higher note is to squeeze it against your lip and use pressure. What Eddie Durham did was, he was able to really play without tightening up on your lip. To me he was an inventor. That's how he was able to do all this stuff. He invented new ways to do things, new ways to write things. So as with everything else, he invented a way to play trombone that would allow your lips to last a long time. That is, not pressing it up against your mouth, it's sort of pulling it away from your lips but still getting the same result. That's, I think how he maintained his range, playing high notes long into times when most guys his age, couldn't do that anymore. If Eddie Durham was here right now he could play higher than I could now, because of the system he used. I haven't really developed that non-pressure system. I use it minimally, but he had it down to where he could use it all of the time. So does Al, 'cause he plays some fantastically high notes.

Al: In Jimmie Lunceford's band when I took Trummy Young's place, Trummy had a lot of high notes he used to play. And Jimmie Lunceford wanted you to play any solo *like Eddie Durham* and anyone who played that on record he wanted it played the same way. I used to play "Margie" and it was so high and Eddie told me, "*you can hit these high notes, but you're straining yourself when you do it.*" He would breathe opposite to the way you would normally do it. So Eddie would say "*put it in the diaphragm*" (breathe in) and then you control it up on the lips and then you can keep that pressure off because the air that's in the diaphragm you're pushing it out, thus pushing away the mouthpiece from the horn. That way you can keep the pressure off. And that was his invention right there. And you can hit one note and stay on it pretty long, with no pressure. And from that, you can hit high notes. Nowadays, they took that what he was doing and they have developed it into circular breathing, where they keep going, rotating that air. They didn't know anything about non-pressure and Eddie Durham exploited that. Like Louis Armstrong, everything was jammed up, and that's why Louis had such a big gash along his lips. I never saw Eddie with that.

Again, Eddie Durham has been a person to have give the music world so much in learning, so much in he was a melodic writer. See now since we're into the books so much, we out there playing so many notes. Basie told me one time "Don't try to play all you know in one number," meaning that coming from Dizzy Gillespie's band we used to try to play everything. Like Benny Powell was saying, *it didn't mean that much*. Feeling - like he would swing, he had the feeling to give to you, so it would make you think about it. Like that "Topsy"... I have recorded that.

I'm very proud to say that I knew him and very thankful that he was a willing person to show you. I'm blessed. Why? Because it has helped me. I'm moving on with it. I can play pretty high, yes I can. Eddie gave it free. For instance Tricky Sam, he knew how to do the plunger, but he wouldn't show no one, he wouldn't tell you how he did it. But I was up 'n coming with a different phrase in what he was doing. He would say yahhh, yahhh, and I would say, wah. Another fella told me one day that it was different. This is playing with originality, of doing something that someone else was doing. Benny Powell and I, we are very thankful to have any moment to speak with or about Eddie Durham.

Benny: By the grace of God and with a flashlight, you can find a note on the trombone! 152

Eddie recalled: *"I can play higher or lower on trombone than any of them. I developed that. If you notice I ain't got no scars on my lips, I plays "non-pressure" and that's why if you look at my lips you can't tell that I ever had a horn up there. For the real high notes, I drawback - I don't play toward the horn, I play that drawback. Just like Paul Webster and Eddie Tompkins. I don't know who else plays like that."* [153]

Eddie had a style of playing that you could always remember him. There was always certain notes that he would hit on the trombone, he used a plunger, he would cut off the top of the plunger and used that as his mute. Everybody else would have a particular type of mute, but he always used a plunger. He clowned around a lot on stage. He was a fun person. He had long stories all the time." ***Lillian Durham***

Eddie recalled: "I have a picture of me with Bennie Moten, with a valve trombone, but I played slide too. Now the valve solos come out different than slide because it's the valves cutting the notes, instead of the horn moving. In Be-bop they 'lip it up' from one position, so it sounds like a valve. They always held the trombone back by trying to make an obbligato instrument out of it, like a tailgate, which is supposed to tail along slow. But trombone players are fast 'cause I guess I could play just about anything on it that you can execute on an alto, there's a way to do it. Cause if you ever heard a brass band, those trombones start in that seven position and they are in rhythm, all the way up. But it's a hard instrument, so when they write, they don't write for the trombone where you have to stretch out, they play it back cheap.

There's a lot of trombone never been brought out. Don Redman started into that trick stuff a bit on "Slip Horn Jive." You should be a trombone player to do it because that's advanced. Supposed to be seven positions, three inches apart, but I know fourteen positions on it because I play inch and a half apart with solo work and everything else that had notes. But you got to have a couple guys with pretty good range, then you can do it. Can't have guys coming out with no mutes. I use a plunger, cut it off the bathroom plunger. See, I'd use three B-flat trombones, there used to be tenor trombones. Four trombones are great when you sustain it and not move it fast - you can hear it. The Tijuana Brass band came along and they made great success with the horns they had, so it can be done.

On trombone, I use 14 positions to play, but I never did just go into that to perfect it. But that's why I play high, because 8 positions starts after B flat. You gotta play all down in the horn to get 14 positions, the positions are thronged apart, inch and a half. They come between the positions, inch and 3/4 apart instead of 3 inches. You gotta play in between all them positions, ain't no notes normally when you down... But when you up high, you can probably play inch and a half apart and anything you can make in the first position, you can make all over the horn when you get up high enough. But you gotta have a lot of range. You gotta have a six-octave range and it becomes to be a violin.

111

But I didn't stick to trombone all the way like that, I went on to other things. Well, I could be tops on either one I wanted to play, but it's easier to write than it is to play 'cause you might not hold up with your lips. Look at my lips you'd swear I don't play no instrument, never see a mark on 'em, I play non-pressure when I get up there. But why teach all that when they can't understand what the guys are playing in the other positions. I started teaching to Bennie Green, but he left right away. Part of it was in the Glenn Miller Band, but they didn't know it."[154]

Eddie was scheduled to teach a college course the year he died. Nevertheless, herein are his foundational and advanced principles and advice.

Music 101

Eddie recalled: "They preferred sousaphone in a dancehall because you could hear it better. Without amplification, a lot of guys weren't strong enough on bass fiddle. But Walter Page you could hear! He was like a house with a note. He didn't have the best ear, but he worked hard, and the string bass was in demand. How was his sound produced? I think it's in the coordination of the stroke in the head. The bass is one of the greatest things in the world for rhythm, but instead of writing a two-beat bass on the fifth and tonic, I kept it moving on chromatics to the chord. It sounded good, but when they saw it on paper, musicians said, 'This has gotta be out of tune!' Walter Page is the guy that created that walkin', walkin'… I wrote it long, but I couldn't control and master that swinging motion till I'd been in the band a long time."[155]

Riffs/Tempos

Eddie recalled: "The difference in the Kansas City riff and other places was it carried a melody that you could write a song from. Like Lester Young with "Jumping With Symphony Sid", that was a riff but it made a melody. Like "Moten Swing" was a riff, just made up for an ensemble to go along with "Driving Me Crazy," then we made a melody out of it. Kansas City Jazz generally they style a certain tempo that seemed to fit the public, not too fast or slow. That was one of the secrets about the band when Basie got it, he's genius at setting tempo that'll charm. Jo Jones was responsible for a lot of that too. Many bands made "One O'Clock Jump" but I've never heard a band with the exact tempo that the Moten band recorded and Basie would go along with it and learn those tempos from Jo Jones. I wanted to make Blues danceable. Today they do a lot of presentation concerts, where you're not dancing, so you can play those things but get away with faster tempos. But when it was a dance, it was a groove thing, like my "Swinging the Blues" and "Blues In The Groove." But "Moten Swing" could capture an audience either way. It hits the person - and when it hits one it hits millions, when it's just exactly the perfect tempo. Get the right tempo, get the hit. Harlan Leonard did "I Don't Want To Set The World On Fire" in a tempo different than Tommy Tucker. Jay McShann has that western idea of getting the tempo, not over-executing and the riffs he sets you can write songs from. Tempo is a gift in itself."

See that's what kills hits. That was the success of Count Basie, tempos. 200 bands made "One O'Clock Jump" and there's not one band that's got the exact tempo that Basie had and that's something seem like it would be very important to capture the people – is the right tempo. Cause we didn't allow Basie to start it off, 'cause he didn't have the right tempo sometimes.

Only Jo Jones knew that tempo. Jo Jones was responsible for all tempos over there. But Jo could get it, stop, play it over – he'd stop you and say, that ain't it. That was the secret to that band with "One O'Clock Jump." A lot of bands get close as they can, and so you get close enough, it don't have to be the exact, people would accept it.

Lunceford did my number called "Swingin on C," but he played it too fast, way too fast. I just made it over last night, 'cause I'm gonna record it with the Kansas City Six but it's gotta be well-rehearsed.

"Swingin on C" was a number created for the melody to be played on drums, the drums could play that one note, it's a one-note melody. I made it for Cozy Cole and Gene Krupa, I told them about the number, but they never did hear it. I took off to California and Cozy run into Edgar Battle.

Edgar had "Topsy" in his Cosmopolitan Publishing Company and everything you give him, he put his name on it as co-writer. So they say,

113

"Where's Eddie Durham, he had a number for us to record, the two drums."
Battle say, "Don't worry, I got the number." He carried "Topsy" to them and
they didn't know the difference. And that's how that got involved and I never
did do that number for anybody else."[156] Alan Hartwell's Love Records
released Cozy Cole's version of "Topsy Part I" and "Topsy Part II" in 1958.

Arranging

Eddie recalled: "When you're the arranger, you don't write things too
much for yourself. You got to arrange for everybody and get that band off."

"Buck Clayton (from Kansas) said that the reason why the Southwestern
Jazz was so different is because of the blend of the African and Native
American." Oscar Pettiford felt that way.

"The music is brimming with genius. There's so many aspects of it. There's
compositional genius. He wrote some astoundingly great pieces in blues song
form, in over typical American popular songbook forms - and once in a blue
moon and outside both those idioms, and his arranging of it is clearly a
designer's miracle. He's as important an arranger in Jazz as can be named…
this is a dominant aspect of his musical value in the long-term. The one aspect
of it that's troubling is of course that these arrangements in the original
manuscript, largely don't exist. Taking off the records is fool's gold, in other
words you think you heard all the notes on the record, but you didn't. One of
the reasons I know this is because what Eddie Durham told me himself and
what Earle Warren told me about the performance of "Topsy." Eddie
Durham's getting notes from places that don't actually exist. If you listen to
the home stretch of that, there aren't enough notes to account for all the *F clef*
or *bass clef* playing. One of the secrets is that Earle is doubling alto and
baritone sax - and jumping. Jack Washington is doing much more of that -
he's playing alto in the section, but a dominant part, he's also the key soloist,
he takes a full course solo on baritone sax. But if you listen to it all the way to
the end of the record, you run out of notes if you stay in the reeds. The extra
baritone sax note in "Topsy" is played by a trombone, played by Eddie the
composer and arranger. He's out of musicians and out of the ability to
exchange instruments. No one is equipped to hear these things perfectly - the
music manuscript is the proof of the pudding and in Eddie's case, these

114

manuscripts largely, almost entirely don't exist. So there's a tragedy there. So the arrangements primarily exist as the recordings. …If it's a five-part sax harmony, can I hear five notes? Now there are only 12 pitches …but what exactly Eddie did on that note on [the reeds on] "Toby," recorded December 13, 1932, I'd go so far as to say, is unknowable without [Eddie or] the actual musical manuscript. But the record sounds the way it does because Eddie stacked the notes a certain way and insisted on certain timbres. Even in the Bennie Moten material, he's got people switching sections and doing all kinds of wacky stuff."[157] ***Phil Schaap***

"Arrangers got no notice whatsoever. You took this chart into the band and it was never, ever announced that this is an arrangement by say, Eddie Durham. So consequently it kept many arrangers and composers, it held them back. I know this very strongly from Benny Carter. He wrote "Peyton Place." He never received any credit and that also enters into where they did not want you to be known. Don Redman and Eddie was together a lot. But they had the race records and they only wanted black folks to hear this music. But it was swinging, so until the white kids would be in the basement and their parents would be upstairs and the sound would be slipping out and they got outspoken, Ut Oh! We love this music! But then they found out that it was very important to change it so that they could make the money. And that's when it got from Race music to Rhythm & Blues. Eddie Durham was a big part." ***Al Grey***

Melody

Eddie recalled: "Harold Austin, Budd Johnson, Buster Smith, Paul Quinichette, Jay McShann, Claude Williams-fiddle. I programmed a little show for them so they could have something organized, typed it on paper. House was packed. We played eight bars of this, make harmony. We were all over with the whole thing and with the curtain closed, they come off, Paul Quinichette walked through the curtain and played a number by himself. In the last number, four of us would come up under the curtain and join in. I say'd that to say this, I followed him, I went out and I played "Georgia" (slow) because I didn't want to do over two numbers. The rest of them could do three, four. I'd say, "You don't need to bring anything out on me at all" and I did it with a plunger and I didn't put one extra note in it, everything I did was a melody deal, no running at all, but something heavy. The house come down, the kids jump back, they want to come up and see that plunger. They say that's what a melody will do, a chorus and a half, that's all. I went back out for my encore and I played "Danny Boy," another slow tune. [Frank Haywood] Henry came out one weekend on his vacation but he really wanted to play. So he sat in and played "Misty" on his soprano, then he played "Sophisticated Lady" on his baritone, same deal, nothing but melody. He didn't put an extra note in and he got a standing ovation. So they gave him a suite and all he want to eat, got his picture in a few papers, a whole page. You ought to see his write-ups. Louis Armstrong say 'Stay close to that melody as you can, and the public will get with you'. The musicians may not like it. You got to have a sweet taste with it, to just play melody - it's how you phrase it, got to play it like you sing it. Johnny Hodges look like he's coming, a mile before he hit the note - and then he run a few little extras. He played for the public. Charlie Parker is playing -- ain't nothing but showmanship, he can't remember a note he played.[158]

Harry James

Eddie Durham also arranged for trumpeter Harry James December 1937-January 1938. James was still with the *Benny Goodman Orchestra*, who incidentally, Durham had also arranged for. Durham arranged all of the four tracks for Harry's first recording session as a bandleader and performed as a trombonist. He brought with him the a*ll American rhythm section.* "Texas Chatter" was a song Durham recalled "*I left Harry an original, "Texas Chatter," which was recorded at a later time without me.*" "Texas Chatter" [and "One O'Clock Jump"] were recorded on January 5, 1938, where trombonist Vernon Brown replaced Eddie. Eddie received no copyright credit.

"Along with seven other Basieites plus Jess Stacy on piano, Durham participated in trumpeter Harry James' first recording under his own name. Durham did the arrangements and played trombone."[159] *(Eddie's arrangements/ H. James recordings: see "Appendix A")*.

Eddie recalled: "Harry came to me and say'd, "I want to record. I want some Texas boys. You get some of the black boys and I'll get some of the

116

others. I'd like to have Herschel, and Jo Jones." And he got Jess Stacy. But see they was finishing up a job with Benny Goodman and they laid off that week. He went and rented a studio and paid in advance for it. Benny come around two days later and went to the Union. The Union say'd, 'He's entitled to two weeks' notice'. And that messed up the week. So he say'd, "Well you go down to my house and I left a couple a numbers there for you to fix. You can make a brand new Texas Shuffle. I say, 'alright'. He say, "You can take 'em home with you. I'll be in town in the morning a week from now after I finish this week - and don't never mention Jess Stacy." Cause he was with Benny's band and while he was off, he was gon' record with Harry.

That's when I found out how good a musician Harry was. You write for a guy, you can learn [him]. So I made him some things and I shortcut 'em. If you know anything about music you got four bars out, you supposed to write all of that stuff out. Well, I skipped over them bars. And when I get to the end, instead of writing a half-rest and an eighth-rest and a quarter, so you can push the note in, I leave that out and I push the note in just by itself. He read all that stuff by sight and some high notes. I say, 'This guy is a real musician'. I say, 'Let me tell you about them notes here you gotta count out - I didn't write all that - he say, "Awe that's all right, let's go down it" First time he played and he pushed the note in; that's that short end stuff. So that's what happened with his band. I did one session with him on trombone and then I was gone and he was still recording. Jess Stacy he sneaked in and recorded 'cause he didn't want nobody to know 'cause of Benny Goodman. I didn't try to judge Jessy out but he had to be alright."[160]

Artie Shaw-Billie Holiday

"Billie Holiday - She'll sing swing…with Artie Shaw, whose orchestra will play the fox trot, collegiate shag and Lindy hop at the ball. Her lilting vocals jibe beautifully with the Shaw style and if anyone in the Harvest Moon Ball audience has been wondering what swing is all about, he'll know after he hears Billie and Shaw together. The engagement of Miss Holiday by the Harvest Moon Ball dance committee rounds out an extraordinarily interesting entertainment program. Artie Shaw and Nano Rodrigo each will do an especially composed concert piece. Shaw's is yet unnamed and rehearsals

117

have been secret - but word has leaked out that it will make his famous "Fe Fi Fo Fum" sound paled by comparison." *Daily News* (New York) Mon, Aug 29, 1938 p.27.

Eddie recalled: "Billie Holiday and I were with Artie Shaw together [1938]. Some of the first numbers I made with Artie Shaw was "Them There Eyes" for Billie Holiday. She came to Artie with me, but I only stayed a month. I also charted "My Blue Heaven," "On The Sunny Side of the Street," "I've Got The World On A String." Only "My Blue Heaven" is available [RCA Victor album of air checks from the Hotel Pennsylvania broadcasts]. Laren's[Loren Schoenberg] got one of the arrangements. "It's Time To Jump And Shout" we never did put on the market. The lyrics was 'It's time to jump and shout, Let's drive these devils out'. Artie had a lot of trouble with that because he was under a contract that said anything that he played they was gonna record it. They couldn't release it, got a lawsuit 'cause they wanted the song. Helen Forrest was there for about a week after I come into the band. We went all through Connecticut and Boston.

We had a lot of fun 'cause I had to hang around with Artie and I thought he was crazy and I told him. I say, 'when your top go, you'll be alright'. He say, "Yeah?" I'd say, 'yeah, it's gon go in about 3 weeks'. I was a little simple at that time. He still running around puttin it on me, "You think I'm going crazy?" and I'd say, 'Nah, you already crazy'. We used to ride in the car to some of the dates, some of the Band. It would be Artie driving, the piano player, me and two others. And they was always laughin. He'd pull up to the train station at somewhere to one of the jobs and say, "When is this train coming, 'cause I'm gon put Billie on this train, I don't want her in the car with me no more." Cause they was laughin'. Course he didn't know what they was laughin about. But they was laughin 'bout him. And so she said, 'Look at him sittin up there, he thinks he's Jesus Christ. He say, "What they laughin about" and so he say, "I'm a put her out." He didn't want her ridin' in the car no more. So somebody say to Billie, "What you think about Benny Goodman?" and she'd say, "He thinks he's god. That's another big laugh, Artie don't know what you talking 'bout".[161]

118

Billie Holiday's last recording with Artie Shaw was "Any Old Time" recorded the end of July, 1938. By the end of that year, she left.

"The noted fugitive from swing, Artie Shaw, is returning to the band-leading profession with reservations. He will start with a new band on the Burns and Allen NBC radio program…Last year, Shaw…renounced band-leading… He expressed himself, in effect, as fatigued by acrobatics of wild-eyed young men and bare-legged, short-pantied girls. He was depressed by their limited contrapuntal horizon. Thus to Mexico he fled for a time to the more composed philosophical climate of the Ancient Aztecs. …Shaw also is the husband of film actress Lana Turner…"[162] *Elizabethton Star,* Newspaper (Tennessee 1940). (Eddie arrangements / Artie Shaw: see "Appendix A")

Benny Goodman

"…About our competing with male bands, a couple of weeks ago three of us were interviewed for NPR, and when I heard the interview about ten days ago, they had inserted a track from Benny Goodman's band and we had the same chart in our music and the interviewer said, 'I challenge anybody to decide which one is the girls band and which one was the Benny Goodman band.' It was amazing because he put the two tracks side by side, and even I couldn't tell."[163] Rosalind "Roz" Cron.

Eddie recalled: "Goodman did some things of mine. He did a real good job on "Sent For You Yesterday Here You Come Today," but it was never released over here. He did "Topsy" [Nov. 10, 1938, Lionel Hampton on drums] right after Basie. If I could've done a special for him, he would've got a hit. Cause I would've made it a little different. Benny is so far out now, he's got his own office and 'Laren' who played saxophone with me is managing the office. So, Benny cares for nothing looks like, because Frank Sinatra called in, they was tryna get him to play the Inauguration Ball. He don't want no part of nothing. He don't wanna do nothing no more than he don't wanna do, maybe at Carnegie and he don't care to do that too much. He turns down everything. He let a lot happen to his arrangements. He let Laren have some of his arrangements, and Laren's band could help him, but I don't know where he gonna play it."[164]

Actually, it was released with vocal by Johnny Mercer. *(Eddie / Benny Goodman arrangements: see "Appendix A")*

Glenn Miller

"Instrumental to the success of Glenn Miller during 1939 was the collaboration of the African-American composer and arranger, Eddie Durham, who wrote and arranged many famous and memorable key "swing" instrumentals for Miller's band, including probably "In The Mood", which was recorded for RCA Bluebird on August 1, 1939. Durham was employed by the famous and powerful black bandleader, Jimmie Lunceford, and Lunceford had agreed to loan Eddie to Glenn. The working relationship and friendship between Miller and Lunceford has been somewhat unappreciated by the jazz and popular music experts. Most have commented that Miller's band played and performed in a style that sometimes resembled Lunceford. Durham may have been the reason. Miller (RCA Victor-Bluebird) and Lunceford (Decca-Columbia) did duplicate some of the same tunes for their respective record labels to an interesting degree."[165]

Glenn Miller on Swing in an interview with Leonard Feather:.. "Duke Ellington is still the champ with me, as a composer, arranger and bandleader. In Duke's band you can see where all the rest of them sprang from. But a large part of Duke's success has to be credited to the great individuals in the band. Incidentally, I think Eddie Durham is one of the best colored arrangers I know. He did Slip Horn Jive for me, Wham, and several others. He's a talented guy who really knows plenty of music." "One quibble is that [George T. Simon] did not interview, does not even mention, Eddie Durham, the band's only black arranger, who made substantial contributions to the library ("Glen Island Special," "Wham," "Slip Horn Jive" etc.) Durham might have shed a special light on the man."166 **Leonard Feather**. *The Miami Herald*, Aug 18, 1974 p142

"That fall [1939], the Miller band appeared for its first engagement at New York's Paramount Theatre, a mecca for the young audience of the day. Jitterbugs had danced in the aisles to Benny Goodman and they were ready to "dig" the newly popular Miller band. Their hopes were not dashed. The Miller band appeared with the newly popular black vocal group, The Ink Spots. Miller took a chance as a white bandleader appearing with the group due to the social prejudices of the day. There was no need to worry. The pairing of the Miller band and the Ink Spots was wildly popular with the Paramount audience. Miller directed Eddie Durham to write several dozen arrangements for the Ink Spots at no charge, which helped the group blend compatibly with the Miller band. The grateful Ink Spots gave Glenn a diamond-studded gold watch at the end of the engagement, which helped them to solidify their popularity. The stage had been set for even greater achievements and fame. Glenn Miller was poised for greatness."[167]

Durham's copyright date of "I Don't Want To Set The World On Fire" is in January 1941. It was released by the Ink Spots that same year.

"Bebop was a listening music. But that's where Eddie fit in so perfectly because he wrote music that did Swing. It was because it was accessible first, but it was intelligent on top of that. You can just write quarter notes, there's nothing to that. For instance the song "In The Mood." By itself it's a dumb tune. What made it famous was Eddie's 1939 arrangement of it. If you don't believe it, just listen to some previous versions of it. This version of it that he arranged is one that defined the whole era. Whenever you see a picture that depicts the War in the 1940s, you hear it in the background and since the music is used, what's going on visually, you just subliminally hear this." ***Benny Powell***

"Eddie Durham was a key arranger for Glenn's band beginning June 1939, having penned Glen Island Special' and 'Wham, ReBop Boom Bam' as well as others. It was also at the urging and professional suggestion of Eddie Durham that Glenn and ensemble play at the famed Savoy Ballroom (April 28, 1940). Although Miller made his mark earlier at the Glen Island Casino for the 1939 summer season, Durham urged him to perform at the Savoy to 'settle' the question that he and band had, indeed, 'made it'. The litmus test was, if the patrons at the Savoy took to his band then, yes, according to Eddie Durham's learned and wise view, he had – and, his popularity was legit! He was and it was! Miller respected Durham."

Mr. Durham was most gracious and a real gentleman and allowed me to tape our 1981 Ohio to New York telephone conversation.

Next, an exclusive interview by **Mr. Glenn D. Mittler** with Eddie Durham debuts, strictly regarding Eddie's tenure with Glenn Miller's Orchestra:

Eddie recalled: "I was upstate there in Connecticut I had a 14-15 piece band myself... and (Fats Rhythm and Mr. Lear Kramer) one of the Presidents of the Union come over and stop me and they told me about Glenn Miller's band over in Glen Island Casino, 'cause they had heard of it and say'd I had the type of stuff that would help him, I'd do better over there with him because it was gonna be tough for me with this band by myself, right off. It really wouldn't have been tough, but we didn't know. See 'cause I had a lot of stars in the band, Bon Bon was up there with us from Jan Savitt's band. I went on and got my own band, so that's why I wasn't there. And that's how I got involved with Glenn Miller, they told me he needed some of the stuff I had.

So I went to his band and I carried in part of the "Saint Louis Blues" and changed around his band some..., carried it in like it was, so he made that and that was a good number, but that was arranged by one of the saxophone players. ...I did about ten numbers over there and I arranged all of them myself. He had a funny way of working with his reeds though, he didn't want

122

me to change the flow. I did my own voicings for the Jazz numbers you see...but he didn't want me to interfere with their way of playing.

Anyway, they had a little secret with the reed section that the rest of them ain't got right now, they don't know 'bout it. One was the caliber of men he had, I never did get acquainted with all of them. The way he phrased, like I used to write arrangements and I used to mark red lines for the band to breathe because it's very important if all guys can turn their breath a'loose at the same time for certain passages to complete those passages. You play and one guy breathes before he finish the passage, that conflicts with the passage of the second. A lot of them can do it, but it doesn't come out. And this way you get the basic swing. We did quite a bit of that with the Lunceford's band. But Glenn Miller insisted I could do anything I wanted to do with his reed section, but don't let them take their mouth off the mouthpieces. Those guys used to say "I'm so tired of holding these notes" but he say "I'm specifically interested in the sweet flow" ...cause they wanted to get a strong force on the reed section and swing like Basie or Lunceford, but I say in order to do that the saxophone player has to take their mouth off of the mouthpiece in order to run into that... When he turn his back, walk away and go get him a coke or something, even in a rehearsal, they would open their mouth 'cause they know what to do to get that punch. Oh man, he'd have a fit. He'd come back to the band "I heard it, it's no way you could've got that strong punch in the reed section less you take your mouth off..."

I don't know if the new band knows about that or not, 'cause it would help them...cause they kinda like students in that band like Lunceford's band. Glen Island Special wasn't released under my year, but it's paying off pretty heavy in the royalties right now... I [also] made the arrangements on "Saint Louis Blues," "Tuxedo Junction," "In The Mood," and a few other things... well for Marion Hutton "Wham" and "I Want To Be Happy"...

I had a home out in Kearny, New Jersey, it's right on the Passaic River. He outsmarted me there. I wouldn't show up to some of the rehearsals sometime, and I had a minimum to do a number, haha, I bring in one this week, I wouldn't show up the next week and then I'd show up with two more. He'd tell the Manager he say, "Pay this man, I don't need but one [hit], if he bring

123

in another one like this…" And that man was so right about that. You don't need but one. Cozy Cole, he got "Topsy." He didn't need but the one. Basie got a quite a few of my arrangements. Seems like to me it's always one number that's it, except Nat Cole, he'd make a hit with anything. Miller got me the place in Kearny, that was to keep me quiet, keep me from running around downtown and not showing up. That's where I wrote "Harlem Shout" and maybe "I Don't Want To Set The World On Fire" – I was working with Bennie Benjamin. He went to see Count and ask Count about me, and Count told him say, 'Man he come when he want to'. He said, 'well what about a Contract' they told him "man, this cat, he don't care nothing about no Contract." One of them told him 'Get him out of town so he can write some songs'. Cause writers and musicians most times back in those days could do what they want to, they was half crazy.

Publisher Mort Brown he gave me the lead sheet to "In The Mood," 'cause I was working for him. In them days you get $50 a week, come in, write what you want. Joe Garland made the stock arrangement for Mort Brown, I'm pretty sure he did and Mort give it to me. And then quite naturally I had to revoice and restyle. It had three or four-part harmony, they made it for three horns in them days. I didn't look at Joe's arrangement, 'cause the bands didn't consider no stock arrangements in those days, at all. The only stock I know that anybody did like it, was Benny Goodman did "Topsy," a special I made on it for bass, and then we made a stock, you know, a special. He got that from Mort Brown and he went on and record it like it was. Cause it had the four parts for the sax, that's all they had. Glenn Miller had a big band and I don't know if Joe Garland did anything for Glenn at all. Anybody did anything for Miller had to be after me, 'cause I was with him about a year and a half and nobody was around him but me.

He'd audition outside arrangers for one hour. All his rehearsals was two hours. The last hour belong to the staff arranger. They'd start at 1 o'clock and he'd tell all the guys to bring the arrangements. He'd play 'em down and I'd come in at 2 'cause I wouldn't let nobody hear no arrangement that I was making in that rehearsal, I didn't want nobody in there at all, not even Glenn. I'd walk away and Glenn get in front of the band and I interpret. See if you

124

had one mistake he'd stop it, Glen would pick it up and give it back. Pick it up, bring it back some other time. And that was the only thing I couldn't take too well. He'd go over about ten arrangements in that hour. Sy Oliver came out and brought one once, he's a good arranger and it was one mistake in it and Glenn pick it up and give it back, so he must've give back a lot of good stuff. He wouldn't allow anybody to bring nothing in there that wasn't copied in ink and he wanted to know whether it was proofed and whether it was correct. Sy was underestimated. I was willing to work with him and help him with his harmony, I helped all of them with harmony. Because they wasn't used to nothing but four saxes and five brass.

When I went in it was six brass and Dan Grisson came in and he played the sixth saxophone. I worked with all of 'em.

So I used to be a little hot on him with them musicians and I say, 'I'm a fix him'. So I made a number called "Wham ReBop Boom Bam" and I brought it out in pencil, and when he was away I passed it out, in pencil and we played it. So he walked away 'cause I didn't like how he stand in front of the band when I was rehearsing. Cause the trombone players all resented him standing, say that he's looking right down their throat, "How am I gon' play?" So I tell him to stay away from in front of them. So he'd go on off somewhere and when he come back I'd turn the band on over to him and say now you do what you wanna do. "Wham" was a swingin' thang for that band 'cause I know how to listen to a band and fit that band. So what he did, he came back and say, "What was that!" This was for Marion Hutton so I say, 'bring a piano in so he can teach her all this stuff'. He went and rented a piano, I put it down and went down there and looked at it once and I never did go back down there anymore. I didn't need to go down there. I was waiting for him to take it up and when it was over, I say 'I gotta take this now and he said, 'Nah, you don't take this, gimmie that music, you don't take that away from here'. He take all the music from the guys. Everybody laughed you know. He liked that number 'cause it was good for Marion Hutton.

I was way out like Sy Oliver, I say, Glenn, this girl can't sing. Cause I had been around a lot of the others, like Billie Holiday, I was with Artie Shaw when she was there. Not only her. Glenn say, 'I don't care, you ever look at her?' I say, 'Yeah'. He say, 'She's a good looking blonde, she's attractive, what do you think the kids will think about her?' I say, "Oh they'll be crazy about her'. Play a chorus with the band and then bring her in and then come back with the band and play like hell. That's the reason she always sang the second chorus to the lyrics, 'cause I never did feature her on top. I went along right with him, I didn't push it. You know you can make an arrangement that'll put a song and a singer over too. It's the arrangement. You could put a singer over, any kind of singer if you wanna go through that. And a lot of people out there got hits but couldn't sing, it was the arrangement put them over.

Miller was working on his theme song ["Moonlight Serenade"], but I never did see him writing anything. I think he arranged stuff for Tommy Dorsey, ...so he must'a write.

Back in those days, these bands like Artie Shaw, Woody Herman, Les Brown and Lunceford and them bands was really kicking. See he was very afraid of things like that. I don't know why. You know I never did see that man smile. And I was around him 'cause I went with him to get his apartment, he and his wife in the car when he was looking for it, out there. I didn't go in, just sit in the car. And I was with him when he opened his bank account. He got the money himself. You know a lot of the bands let the manager down at the office issue the money when they get it, but he wouldn't let nobody to handle his money. I think that was smart of him. I never did see him say nothing much to the band. He always come in and I never would be able to catch him when he first speak or nothing. He'd listen and he'd go off to the bar when I'm rehearsing and when he'd come back and I'd give him the music and say, 'You got it, what you wanna do with it'? He was pretty good in interpreting. When he come, he know what to cut out, he'd listen.

I never did over-write the band see. He and I had a system like this. I would never jump no more than a third with any horn. Maybe jump up a fifth or seventh or sixth or something like that, but not even an octave – that was out of the question. And I never did write nothing over a high C. In order to make the high C sound hi, and after I left they got another trumpet player and they was able, I think, to go up that last note, an "E" I think, on "In The Mood."

126

Then they put another one on it and went a little further. He added that last parts on to it after I left. He added an 'extra tag' we call it.

When I was there he didn't allow the trumpet players to go over high C. But anyway we never did jump over a third with that band either, commercial wise, not in the swing stuff. And that's very important, that makes the band be able to reach the notes easier and you don't have one guy jumping over the other. I don't think people never heard nothing like his reed section. Then again, he had some pretty good kicking arrangements there. He wanted to get over the hump, he played the Savoy for me 'cause he needed his band to be on top. He said, 'Fellas in a year from today, this band will be great musically like I want it'. I said, 'Glenn, this band ain't 'gon be no greater a year from today, than it is right now and I been with a thousand of 'em and I know. Where they're at is at its peak right now'. I meant that and I believed it too. I say, 'You want me to prove it to you?' He said, 'Yeah'. I said, 'Go book the Savoy and see what them guys say and if they accept you, you made'. Cause that's where you go to get the stamp 'cause right there at the Savoy people will let you know if you can play or not. He went and book the Savoy! They couldn't pay him, and they guaranteed him a thousand dollars advance and he took six percent of the door [Savoy Ballroom 140th Street & Lenox Avenue, Harlem, New York City]. And I was about an hour late and they started before I got there and he didn't play one of my arrangements. I walked in the door and that place was packed [over 4,000 people] and he stopped the band cold. And he turned around and went to the mic and said, 'Our Arranger is here, Eddie Durham - and he stopped the band - say, "'cause now we gonna play a set of his stuff." That's right, he did that, right there. My neck went back a little bit, ha ha. That fella, the third partner who owned the Savoy, Charlie Buchannan, he can verify that. When I walked in he was playing something, floating along a little bit, he was stalling I think for me, I think he wanted to make the impression to me. Because he had played an hour and he hadn't played anything of mine.

See when you walked in the Savoy if you've ever been up there, you could see from that high stage anybody who walked in. They go around two ways and come in. And when I walked in Marion Hutton got up and told all the

127

band say, 'Hey, there's Eddie'. Glenn stopped the band and they all stood up and he introduced me to the people. Somebody put me up on the stand but I didn't know what he had played. Glenn said, 'And now we gonna play a set of his arrangements'. It's a lot different in an arrangement, see you can make an arrangement for stage presentation and have that sound-man, but it doesn't record too good sometimes. Things you can leave open and they can put that showmanship on, and even in the music you've got room to have some flexibility playing.

I wrote some numbers for the hats. One called "Echoes of Reeds and Brass" and the melody would be played with nothing but hats, in intermits in brass – everybody hit one note and when they finished, that melody. He opened up with I think "Tuxedo Junction" and he played "The Saint Louis Blues" and ...broke up their house! They eat him up, they couldn't get enough. He didn't smile about it. I never did see him smile!

The next week he said, "I'm going to do my Camel hour audition." He went and made an audition for the Camel hour cigarette program for the commercial. Before the year was up, man they was going to Europe. He's talking about waiting another year. Cause he came in once or twice and he wanted to fire the rhythm section. He told me, 'I'm gonna fire this piano player and this drummer. Look for somebody.' So my statement to him was just like it was to Basie or anybody else I was around, I said, 'Listen, I worked with this drummer and worked with the piano player damn near a year and I got my arrangements here, so now when you find another rhythm section you be sure and to find somebody to take my place, 'cause I won't be around. I won't go through this with no band, no more, ever'. That was the end of it 'cause I got very salty about that. Somebody told him, 'You'll look up and that guy'll be gone for good'. I meant what I said. I say.

I asked him, 'Did you go down and hear Basie's band last week?' I'd heard that he'd been down there. He'd say, 'Yeah, yeah.' I say, You forget about Basie's rhythm section and do your thing here, ain't nobody gon never sound like Basie's rhythm section, you don't need it in here no way. Get a Glenn Miller creation. If you let these guys go, I'm going too 'cause I ain't going through this no more. You ain't gonna find nobody no better than these guys right here.' I didn't rub no elbows with them but I liked the guys.

When I was with Glenn the first year, all of his rehearsals was at the Glen Island Casino in the day. A sight reading Band. I bring the arrangements in, not to rehearsal, at 9:00, give it to him, no mistakes, it had to be proofed, pass it out, let 'em played it while they got the crowd and that's the way he did my numbers. Everything was played on the show before they rehearse it 'cause they could read it. Then I'd come back to rehearsal and clean it up.

Cause one of them numbers I made they had hats and plungers. Now I went downtown and bought all of them for him. That's when they first got to use 'em. And I let 'em lay around quite a bit and they was playing the numbers and the guys come off and the drummer said, 'Well I'm gonna ask him'. He said, "The rest of them didn't wanna ask you for three days, When are we gonna wear these hats?" They thought it was some Halloween affair. I say you gon play these hats in some of the tunes, the doo-wah stuff. I was amazed over how quick they learned it.

One day in rehearsal, I showed 'em how to use it, 'cause there's a trick in writing it too. Most all of that stuff was in B flat, 1st, 2nd & 3rd trombone. I write everything where they never have to move from the position, surrounded with your arrangement see - make a fan easy. One man had to go to the fourth position and I told him how to lay it on his left hand and hold it and showed him how to do it right there. Next night I come back and they was fanning away! All that come from me 'cause I was doing it with Lunceford, they were experts in that – the timing and the precision.

All these other arrangements come after I left. He didn't have nobody over there when I was there. But he must've had some good arrangers after I left I guess. He only have about 12 or 15 numbers from me, but they were good flag wavers and he used 'em right off. In one day I taught 'em how to use those hats. The only thing you gotta watch out about is, once an arranger come in and do something it can be copied and impersonated on the other arrangements.

As a trombone player, Glenn Miller wasn't a hot man but he was a stable, professional trombone player. But you couldn't tell him that, 'cause he didn't believe it. On Slip Horn Jive I had to play that on the record, in order for him to be satisfied in what he played. He didn't know the difference in which record was played. He thought he was all off. He didn't allow me to give the trombone players no solo, he didn't want nobody to take no solo in the band except... and the trumpet player. Some number we did and I wrote the solo out for the 2nd tenor man. I forgot about "Slip Horn Jive." Mort Brown of Lewis Music [Publishing] made a stock on it, they put it in a stock form. I don't know who did it. They may have changed it around a little but they kept the same trombone parts. And every time I'd walk in, the trombonists would say 'let's get our gun and shoot him'. They didn't wanna play that.

Glenn was a heck of a leader and a creator and he knew how to interpret what he wanted. Cause I could turn the arrangements over when I finished and he would go in them and he would turn them back to me and I'd polish them up some more to perfection. He'd say, 'Go over that "Saint Louis Blues" again with the guys and straighten them out'. Lunceford was like that too. That band could read and was the only band that I know that was a sight-reading band all the way down. Cause we pass my numbers out in advance. "Wham" was played the night before, 'cause most times I wouldn't make rehearsal. I'd show up at night 'round about 9:00 when they was ready to start, 'cause I would say he gonna wait and play it anyway. And he'd say, 'What's the tempo on this "Slip Horn Jive"?' I'd start it off and I'd say, 'but you can play it a little slower tonight' and he'd say, 'Nah, we gonna play it the same tempo'. He come down with that and the guys didn't like that so well.

Here's another thing, that reed section paid me $2 a piece that's $10 a week, and that was money in them days. They paid me that in order to discourage him about a baritone sax, 'cause don't any of them wanna carry no baritone around. He'd bring up that baritone and I'd say, 'Man you don't wanna fool with no baritone and spoil the guys – forget about that baritone'. He'd say, 'Well I'd like to have a little of that Lunceford swing' and I'd say, 'That'll come anyway'. But that wasn't me - that was the reed section – all of them! They said, 'Cause he'll ask anybody, "You play baritone" – I don't *wanna carry no baritone around'. I wouldn't even argue with him, I'd just say, 'Naw man forget that right now, later on, later on – don't spoil your band with that. That was the end of it.*

Sometimes I'd had to go down to the studio and I'd have to take my mouthpiece in his horn and if it was recorded, I'd say, make this over again, and I would play his part. I would record his part, I was a good imitator in them days and I could make myself sound like him. Then he make it and I would make a tape. Then, later on, I tell the guy I mixed 'em up, Now play each one of 'em and I say, Now which one of 'em are you on Glenn? He say, "Nah, that ain't me, that's you!." I'd say, 'That's the one you made'. He always had an inferiority complex that he wasn't playing right. He could play. Cause I made some recordings with the band. I made it to prove it that he couldn't tell the difference between me and him. He would say, "That was you" and I'd say, 'No, that was you'. He was worried about Tommy Dorsey and all them guys.

See the manager told me that in front when I went over there when they hired me to write. He told me "You gotta give him credit as an arranger, 'cause he don't wanna be credited the trombone player on account of Tommy Dorsey." But I think them guys put that in his head too. So I went along with that 'cause they say, "You'll get credit all along 'cause the critics will pick up on your style anyway", which was true. And he had interest in most of the songs that I wrote, originals, but he insisted he didn't want his name on 'em, like other leaders. But he wanted some of the song, haha. He collect through Agreement. He said, "No, I put my name on there as a writer of the song and later on everybody in the country gonna recognize his style, if they don't, the musicians will all know it and they'll tell everybody." [168]

Eddie's arrangement of "In The Mood" and his composition and arrangement of "Wham ReBop Boom Bam" were recorded on August 1, 1939 at Victor Studios, New York. His compositions for Miller such as "Wham ReBop Boom Bam", "Slip Horn Jive" and his *arrangements* of "St. Louis Blues," "Hold Tight," "Tiger Rag," "Farewell Blues," "I Want to Be Happy," "Tuxedo Junction" and "In The Mood," remain popular standards of

American music." Eddie Durham earns not one cent from songs written by others, which were immortalized solely by his *arrangement* of those songs.

The quaesitum of the arrangement of "Tuxedo Junction" might become clear after some reflection on various Newspapers reporting in that time period. If their reporting's were repeatedly anomalous in stating Eddie Durham as the arranger – it seems to me it would have been noticed and thereafter been corrected by any of either, the publisher, publicist, record company, band leader (Glenn Miller died December 1944), or other person claiming to have arranged it:

"In 1940 he arranged for the famous Glenn Miller band for eight months and turned out such original hits as "Glen Island Special," "Wham," "Slip Horn Jive," "In The Mood" and "Tuxedo Junction." The last four months of 1940 he was with Jan Savitt as arranger." The Bristol Herald Courier, Oct. 24, 1943.[169]

"Eddie Durham and His All-Star Girl Band," featuring the four Durhamettes...While Eddie Durham and His Orchestra are not known in this region, he is best remembered for the original tune hits turned out in 1940: "Glen Island Special," "Slip Horn Jive," and "Tuxedo Junction," while arranger for Glenn Miller and His Orchestra." Republican and Herald Newspaper, May 14, 1943.[170]

"In 1940, he arranged for the famous Glen Miller band for eight months and turned out such original hits as "Glen Island Special", "Wham", "Slip Horn Jive", "In The Mood" and "Tuxedo Junction" The last four months of 1940 he was with Jan Savitt as arranger. In 1941, he organized his own band with Bon Bon under the Durham name, but it was short-lived because of the draft." The New York Age, Newspaper (Dec. 18, 1943).

"Eddie Durham, musical arranger responsible for such swing hits as "In The Mood" and "Tuxedo Junction," will bring his all-girl Negro band to Edmonton's Barn for two nights, May 31 and June 1, it was announced this week by Tom Hayes, manager." Edmonton Journal May 6, 1944.[171]

"Durham turned out some tuneful hits, too, during 1940 when in between, he arranged for Glenn Miller's band for eight months, "Glen Island Special,"

"Wham," "Slip Horn Jive," "In The Mood," and "Tuxedo Junction" are all from Durham's musical pen." The Detroit Tribune, Oct 16, 1944.[172]

"The leader, Eddie Durham, has for years been well known as a guitarist and trombonist as well as an arranger for such big name orchestras as Benny Moten, Jimmy Lunceford and Count Basie. He arranged for the famous Glenn Miller Band for eight months and turned out such hits as "Tuxedo Junction" and "In The Mood." Star-Phoenix, May 19, 1944.[173]

Eddie Recalled: I always was blinded by liking the real leader, creator. I was a fanatic for that and I thought Glenn was a creator. He knew how to handle his band. He was a businessman. I only seen one or two good businessmen in the business and that was Glenn and Jimmie Lunceford. I was pretty well upset when the man disappeared. I get pretty deep with men who create and do things with music and Glenn Miller was one of the finest and all I was interested in was he had one of the greatest bands. He didn't bother nobody. I never did see him bother anybody. He wasn't too friendly with them but he wasn't mean with them either, he wasn't hostile. I don't know what was on his mind. But in them days sometimes it pays not to be too close. Lunceford didn't bother around with his band in any kind of way either.

I didn't know Artie Shaw made it ["In The Mood"] too, a lot slower, but could be the wrong tempo.

"Let me also make mention of a really fabulous piece he arranged and composed for Glenn Miller, "Glen Island Special," which was a hit when Miller recorded it for *RCA*. When they were called upon to play in a hard-swinging mode, Glenn Miller's band - well known for a repertoire somewhat more on the commercial and sweet side - could also easily hold their own (and then some) with the more Jazz oriented bands from Harlem. And in this arrangement, their version of "Glen Island Special," which thanks to Eddie's brilliant arrangement, supports that statement very excitingly." *John Colliani*

"In The Mood" as played by Glenn Miller, continues to be, to this day, THE most iconic tune of the Swing Era, no doubt about it. I don't care who's on the dance floor, what club it is - when you play that arrangement people start dancing, even people who don't know anything about big-band or Jazz music.

Many times I've asked myself why. Why not "Swingin the Blues" which is a better piece of music, or "One O'Clock Jump"? Something about that melody captures people's imagination. Eddie used to talk about it all the time but I frankly wasn't sure, but I knew he had something to do with it. I asked him some questions but the story became pretty clear when you dig deeper into it. The story is that it's nothing but a triad and you'll find those three notes in Beethoven, Bach - nobody invented those three notes. But putting those notes together as a Blues tune, it goes way back to the 1920s…it was just a little riff.

A great composer, arranger named Joe Garland, took this riff and wrote "In The Mood" and nobody cared about this song. Then the tune caught Eddie's ear and he re-arranged it. Eddie arranged for all these bandleaders even some he didn't perform with. So for Glenn Miller's band one of the things Eddie was doing was taking arrangements that other people wrote and changing them, moving things around, polishing them, recomposing them like a piece of clay, and he definitely had a hand in "In The Mood." Because if you listen to Eddie's arrangements, it was a long history of a certain kind of dynamics, voicing's and musical effects that were distinctly Eddie Durham.

Historians and people around the world who are really into Jazz, they know about Eddie Durham, he was that kind of figure. And if you know his music that well, when you listen to "In The Mood" you will hear in there some of Eddie's things. In 1983, The *National Academy of Recording Arts and Sciences (N.A.R.A.S.)* finally awarded him Hall of Fame credit for the arrangement [thanks to Phil Schaap]." *Loren Schoenburg*

Glenn Miller chose Eddie Durham to move him into the forefront of the Swing era bands, leaving behind his Dixieland sound prior to 1939. *Dan Weinstein*

The December 4, 1940 issue of *Variety* magazine ran the article "Untangle 'In The Mood'" where it mentions: "In The Mood," as recorded by Glenn Miller, is one of the records generally credited with helping to shove that band to the top last year…"

Noteworthy is that both of the Miller and Shaw versions begin with a twelve-bar sax riff, played twice. Eddie Durham was the arranging thread for Shaw (1938), Miller (1939), Lunceford (1935-40; who was admittedly admired by Miller), and Basie (1936-37).

Eddie recalled: "I actually had two styles. I could swing or play sweet as any white band. That band was so good that when we played Pleasure Beach, all Connecticut State was trying to get in the park, and we were hurting the business of the big names they hired. But in the end, I let them talk me out of it. I was having trouble, so I let the band go and carried my book to Glenn Miller.[174]

"I came here from my own band at The Oak Grove Casino, into Glenn Miller's band, Summer of 1939, to the Glen Island Casino where Miller ended up staying for maybe three or four months. My contract with Miller called for two arrangements per week but when I went in with "Saint Louis Blues," when I come back to rehearsal I could always improve it. I'd give them gimmicks and rehearse them for a month. They were the greatest sight-reading band I ever worked with. I'd proof with no mistakes and all of my arrangements were passed out at night at the Glen Island Casino, in front of a big crowd. They read the tempo flawless! Glenn was a big fan of the showmanship of the Jimmie Lunceford Orchestra, so when we rehearsed "In The Mood" I had to go down to Manny's and buy the derbies and hats. I taught the brass section all those fans and waves. For Glenn, I arranged "Tuxedo Junction" and "Glenn Island Special."

Now on "Wham ReBop Boom Bam" Glenn Miller came to me and say, "I don't want the horns jumping like that, them cats gonna miss that and ain't gonna sound level, ...dot DEE dot, dot DEE dot" - that's nothing for a horn today. So I say, 'I'll straighten that'. The trombone hit the low note, trumpet hit the high note - two horns are making that. Cause he was always worried about the horn playing up high and down low and then up. And he didn't want the music no more than about a third apart. He could have been right, but I never checked that out - and he wanted everything to perfection. I stayed a year and a half until he went overseas, I didn't want to go overseas even though they offered me a captain's rating. But we didn't tell the band I wasn't going until they got ready to leave. Marion Hutton was there at that time.

When I met Marion Hutton, singer, Glenn say, "I got a girl to sing" and I'm going to rent a piano and I'll put it right here in this room and I want you to teach her. I heard her sing one song, well I was like Sy Oliver then, I say Glenn "this girl can't sing." Cause I'm looking for an Ella Fitzgerald or a Billie Holiday, or Helen Forrest or somebody. He say, "NO but this is what I want." So, I had to go back and take my hat off to him after she did it. He said, "she's a blonde and the kids will like her. What you do, you write the arrangement, make the intro and if you don't think she can make it, you let the band play, bring her in let her sing a little and you go out like hell with the Band," and sho nuff I did that, and on some other numbers I made for him. And it come out just like he say and I had to take my hat off to him. Kids had a fit over it. He say, "What do they know about who can't sing?," I say alright, you want that?, You a smart man."

One thing I liked about the Glenn Miller Band, they were sight readers. Everything Glenn Miller ever played of mine was passed out in the ballroom before we rehearsed. I come out the night before and say, "here it is," and like a number like Slip Horn Jive, some of the guys can't play it now (1985). I say "Glenn, don't play it in that tempo." That's why he demand there be no mistakes in my arrangements & scores, not nothing, it was perfectly proofed. Pass it out, stomp it off before a big crowd, I give them the tempo and the Band would play it. After they play it, then I come back and then I rehearse. That saved me too, when I come back I didn't have to write another arrangement, I'd say, "we gonna rehearse this." Then they learn how to get fire. Get fire. But he had one of the most beautifulest bands I ever heard. Perfect intonation. The only thing was now I needed to teach them how to get fire.

See the black musicians ... they was strong to start with, that's why they don't play sweet music too good. But they can attack the note, like in Lunceford's band, five, six, or seven different ways. But the white boys was thoroughly trained, and only use two ways to attack the note and that's why most of the white band's sound alike. There was no way to bring Glenn

136

Miller's reed section into a fiery deal, 'cause he knew and he'd say, "Do anything you wanna do with the Band, don't let 'em play sweet" and they couldn't take their mouth off the mouthpiece for a 4 bar rest, had to breathe through the corner of their mouth. They all come off rubbing their lips. And I went down to hear the bands and Buddy Franco at Roseland, four nights straight to hear all the Bands. I said, "Let them boys alone, the public don't know the difference, all that little stuff you think that Glenn had, see they gonna make it with this. They ain't gon play that, they'll walk off the stage if you try to tell 'em what to do. And if one of those guys took his horn out of his mouth when he come back on the note, wherever Glenn was he could come back and he could tell that he took his mouth off, and he'd say, "Well you must of told him" and I'd say, "No I didn't bother with it" and they say, "That's the only way you can get that punch, is to open your mouth like Earle Warren, Willie Smith and then run into the note and you go way down to the Bar, they watching and give the signal. And they would open their mouth and run into a note, and he'd come right back say, "Ah Ha, I heard you do it! "Don't bother with that, do anything you wanna do, don't destroy my sweet music." He didn't want me to make 'em punch.

"Baby Me"

Eddie recalled: "Kaye Starr, [sang] my arrangement "Baby Me." Not just Glenn Miller, but ALL the Bands, the minute I walk into a band, they'd say, "Man we got a battle somewhere," or, "We gotta open here, we want some of your flag wavers"...they called 'em 'flag-wavers'. And I never did give 'em real sweet music. I knew the money was gonna be in the Ballads." (Durham / Miller See Appendix "A")

NINETEEN 40's
ASCAP/BMI/Mutual Music

The American Society of Composers, Authors & Publishers had political problems in 1941.

"ASCAP and the radio networks had been unable to agree on rates for the use of songs copyrighted by the society's publishers. The networks banned all ASCAP music from their broadcasts effective January 1, 1941, and formed their own music licensing and collection agency, Broadcast Music, Inc. Bandleaders had to scramble. Glenn could not play ASCAP-licensed hits such as "In The Mood", "Tuxedo Junction", "Pennsylvania Six-Five Thousand", and even his own theme, "Moonlight Serenade", so he used a new theme, "Slumber Song", written by "Mac" MacGregor and assigned it to Glenn's BMI publishing firm, Mutual Music, Inc."[175]

Today, you cannot be a member of both ASCAP and BMI, however for a short time "I Don't Want To Set The World On Fire" did, because it was copywritten in 1940.

To date, "I Don't Want To Set The World On Fire" remains the biggest income producing song in Eddie Durham's catalog, with "Topsy" a close second.

"For him to be able to write for a blues singer who's just nothing but emotion, going from there to writing for a balladeer "I Don't Want To Set The World On Fire" and for him to be able to write a flag-waver that's a dynamic tune, a tune used to close the show and by the time you get finished, well Al Grey can tell you about standing ovations, he calls them 'standing O's', if you do a flag-waver you can almost be sure to close the show dynamically. But that was his versatility, he could go from gentle to bombastic and have it ALL make sense. He never had any notes out of place and you never felt like anything was superfluous." *Benny Powell*

In April 1939 Eddie wedded Earsie Bell Hiller. She is a trombonist who is later a member of his *Eddie Durham All-Stars Orchestra*. She is with him before his tenure with Glenn Miller, and throughout the USO Tours - at least until Mabel Ruth is born, Eddie's first, and their only child together.

Eddie's mother died in 1945. She had the joy of several grandchildren. His first mentor and eldest brother, Joe Jr. died in 1947. Both saw Eddie reach his pinnacle of fame and for that time period, fortune of liquidity.

Harlan Leonard

Harlan Leonard and his Rockets - Harlan "Mike" Leonard played alto saxophone, occasionally tenor. He was with Eddie in the Bennie Moten

138

orchestra in 1929. "Desperate for fresh material, Leonard contacted his old friends Buster Smith and Eddie Durham… Durham supplied Leonard with an arrangement of a new popular tune, "I Don't Want to Set the World on Fire," originally scored for publication as a ballad, the tempo intended by the composers. The producer for the session, however, insisted that the band give it an up-tempo treatment to appeal to jitterbugs. Durham's loose hard-swinging arrangement lifted the band to new heights, and the song's catchy melody and novel lyrics perfectly suited Myra Taylor's personality and playful style. …Inspired by Ella Fitzgerald's hit "A-Tisket A-Tasket," Eddie Durham's arrangement of the novelty "My Pop Gave Me a Nickel" featured Myra Taylor's playful vocal style and bubbling personality.

Bluebird released Leonard's lone hope for a hit, "I Don't Want to Set the World on Fire," in late November [1940]… Registered with BMI, assuring airplay, "I Don't Want to Set the World on Fire" failed to click with the record-buying public. In the end, the up-tempo swing treatment of the ballad, at the producer's insistence, robbed Leonard of the hit that could have catapulted the Rockets to the top, much like what "Until the Real Thing Comes Along" did for the Kirk band."[176]

Due to WWII draft, the band broke up in 1944. Leonard abandoned the music business and eventually became the chief of the Cashiers' Section at the *Los Angeles Internal Revenue Service*. Eddie is the composer/arranger, but he does not perform on Leonard's recordings. *E Durham/H Leonard - See "Appendix A"*

"...Did you know that former Secretary of the Navy "Edison" once wrote and published a song? It's titled "Don't Ask Nothin' of Me" and will be aided for the first time by Eddie Durham's band from the Chatterbox in New Jersey over WOR."[177] *Daily News* (New York) June 6, 1940

"Bandleader Eddie Durham has a letter of thanks from Secretary of the Navy Edison for launching the latter's song, "Don't Ask Nuthin' of Me," on the airwaves..."[178] *Daily News* (New York) June 19, 1940

The 46th Secretary of the Navy (born in 1890), Charles Edison was commonly known as "Lord Edison", he was the son of Mina and Thomas. He also served as New Jersey's 42nd Governor. Ironically, his father, inventor Thomas Edison, developed the phonograph (patented 1878) while working on two other inventions, the telephone and the telegraph, a machine that would transcribe telegraphic messages through indentations on paper tape, which could later be sent over the telegraph repeatedly.

Edison's inventions enabled the critical, immediate national communication essential to conducting the business and enjoyment of music and its varied productions.

Eddie Durham & His Band

Eddie Durham Rehearses

—Ray Levitt Photos

New York—Early rehearsal shots of the new Eddie Durham band catch the saxes grooving one. Left to right—Eddie Williams, tenor; Buster Smith, alto & baritone; Bill White, alto; Ben Smith, alto; Stan Payne, tenor. Below, Durham, the former trombonist - guitarist with Bennie Moten, Lunceford and Basie, gets off on electric box. Eddie, also a great arranger, has big plans for his new combo.

"Down Beat" magazine - June 15, 1940

141

June 15, 1940 - Ray Levitt photos

Full band personnel ➤

Eddie Durham's Band Features a Guitar Like a Clarinet

Ace Arranger Uses Electric Strings for Miller Style Purposes

Eddie Durham, ace arranger, trombonist and guitarist, whose writing, blowing and strumming have been featured with Jimmie Lunceford and Count Basie, now adds band-leading to his list of attributes.

The new outfit will be like most colored groups in that it features swing, and as such will be best suited for ballrooms and theatres. However, Durham intends to play good sweet also, and therein lies the identifying feature of his outfit.

All sweet arrangements will be specials; there will be no dull renditions of stocks. Towards this end, Durham has evolved a style that features his electric guitar. It will be played an octave above the sax quintet, the result being a sound somewhat similar to Glenn Miller's reed section.

Durham will also feature his guitar on the jazz—ditto for his trombone, which he will play singly and to form a trombone trio. Most of the swing arrangements will be specials by Durham, similar to those he made not only for Lunceford and Basie, but also for a host of other white bands, including Miller's.

The personnel consists of saxists (left to right) Eddie Williams, Buster Smith, William White, Ben Smith, Stanley Payne; trumpeters (l. to r.) Joe Keyes, Eddie Roane, Freddie Webster; trombonists John Haughton and Sandy Watson; pianist Conrad Frederick; guitarist Mario Dorcey; bassist Doles Dickens, and drummer Artie Hebert. Webster's trumpet is featured as is a vocal quartet.

The band, still in rehearsal stages, has not yet signed with any office.

142

"Dave Dexter, born in 1915, was raised from an early age in Kansas City, Mo. and was an enthusiastic supporter of jazz musicians (of all races) from his first days as a newspaper reporter in that city, later working for Capitol Records for 32 years and finally for Billboard magazine."[179]

In 1940, Dave Dexter [*Down Beat Magazine writing under the pseudonym of "Barrelhouse Dan"*] produced his first record, the "*Kansas City Jazz*" album for *Decca*:

"Into the studio came a second group headed by the gifted arranger, trombonist, and guitarist Eddie Durham. ...With Durham for my second session were Buster Smith and Willard Brown, alto saxophonists; Lemuel Johnson, tenor; Joe Keyes, trumpet; Conrad Frederick, piano; Averill Pollard, bass; and Arthur Herbert, drums. We encountered no problems in mastering *Moten Swing* and *I Want a Little Girl*. In fact, things went so uneventfully that Bob Stephens left me alone in the studio to manage the date myself." Further: "Count Basie's road manager, Milton K. Ebbins, handed me a test pressing of a leaping Basie instrumental "At the Forrest." 'Review this when you have a chance,' he said straight-faced. 'Eddie Durham composed and arranged it. Basie thinks it's something special.' I placed the disc on a turntable and noticed the title, *Diggin' for Dex*"... Billy May's crack studio band 30 years later (recorded) *Diggin' for Dex*...Durham once composed at least a minor masterpiece and his chart deserved new recognition."[180]

"Coming to the studio prepared, Durham brought an ensemble from his recently formed big band, featuring Buster Smith on alto saxophone and Joe Keyes on trumpet. ...Lips Page closely emulated the style of the Moten Band for his two selections. Working with Eddie Durham, Page sketched a simple head arrangement based on the Moten band's original recording of "South." ...Since issued in 1928, "South" remained popular on jukeboxes, causing Dexter to misjudge its provenance. On the companion side, Page and company recorded "Lafayette," in which they recreated the true sound of the Moten band. ...Unlike Page, Durham had no interest in faithfully reproducing the style of the Moten band. Eight years after composing the original arrangement of "Moten Swing," Durham crafted an updated version specifically for the Kansas City Jazz session. Although Dexter described the new arrangement as

143

a "faithful interpretation," Durham departed from the style of his original, choosing a more laid-back tempo and de-emphasizing the compound riffs that distinguished the earlier Moten version in favor of his floating electric guitar solos and Buster Smith's fluid alto-saxophone work. In a nod to the original, the reed section brightly riffs through the last two choruses, which are accented by Durham's guitar fills. In his liner notes, Dexter explored in great detail the significance of "Moten Swing," while barely mentioning Durham's rendition, indicating his disappointment with the new treatment. Durham's lazy arrangement of McKinney's Cotton Pickers' flag-waver, "I Want a Little Girl," better suited Dexter. This new version is taken at an easy drag expo and features the leader's guitar plucking almost exclusively… Durham's orchestration of this pop tune shows his solid knowledge of scoring, for it comes off the turntable as a soft subtle bit of jazz. The rhythm section can be felt from the down beat and particularly worthy of attention is the ensemble passage in which the saxes and the guitar cleverly 'spread' apart harmonically, achieve an uncommon tonal quality.34 …Durham, having moved beyond the Kansas City tradition, foreshadowed future trends in his contribution to the set."181 *(Eddie / Dave Dexter "KCJazz" recordings: see Appendix "A")*

"In 1940, he formed his own band, with such as trumpeter Joe Keyes, altoist Buster Smith and drummer Arthur Herbert included in the personnel. This band made only two records, both in an anthology titled Kansas City Jazz on Decca. But Durham found it difficult to keep the band together after World War II began."182

Eddie recalled: "I booked my own band up here and we were held over for four months at The Oak Grove Casino in Bridgeport, Connecticut. The recordings are on November 11, 1940. I had guys like Joe Keyes, Buster Smith, Ben Smith, Eddie Williams, Doles Dickens, and Arthur Herbert in it. The president of Local 802 told me it was too smooth for a colored band, and that I'd be more successful if I went with Glenn Miller.[183] The reeds included Willy White, Lemuel Johnson and Don Stovall after he left the Metropol, then Tony Pasco's brother came in to replace Don Stovall. George 'Bon Bon' Tunnell was singing with Stanley Payne, sax; Eddie Roane, tpt (until he left

and went to Louis Jordan), Freddie Webster, John Haughton, Sandy Watson;
trombones and Conrad Frederick, p; Mario Dorcey - g. "

Freddie Webster's presence is notable given his important role as an influential trumpet player in modern jazz. He was a primary influence on Miles Davis.

EDDIE DURHAM AND HIS BAND :
Originaire de San Marcos (Texas) le 19 août 1906, Eddie DURHAM est tout à la fois un tromboniste talentueux, un arrangeur apprécié (singulièrement heureux, ici, dans *I Want A Little Girl* et *Moten's Swing*) et l'un des premiers utilisateurs, en jazz, de la guitare amplifiée. Au sein des grands orchestres de Count Basie et de Jimmie Lunceford (auxquels il confia des partitions remarquables : *Topsy, Out The Window* pour le premier; *Lunceford Special, Pigeon Walk, Harlem Shout* pour le second) il enregistra sur cet instrument des solos sobres, parfaitement construits et pleins de naturel (cf. notamment *Time Out*, avec le «Count» - MCA 510013).

Ses qualités sont bien mises en évidence ici, encore qu'on puisse lui préférer certains des musiciens de son entourage. Le trompettiste Joe Keys, souvent «oublié» dans les dictionnaires était un des musiciens les plus respectés de Kansas-City - l'un des hauts lieux du jazz à l'époque où furent gravées ces faces. Quant à l'altiste Henry «Buster» Smith, que s'arrachèrent les plus prestigieux leaders de cette ville, on le surnommait le «Prof». Les autres altistes lui vouaient un véritable culte, singulièrement le jeune Charlie Parker, qui s'inspira largement de lui pendant ses années de formation. Les deux interventions de Buster dans *Moten's Swing* comptent, d'avis unanime, parmi les plus réussies qu'il ait enregistrées.

ROSE (3'16)

Sélection et supervision : Jacques LUBIN
Collection : M.C.A. Record Library
Maquette : Étienne ROBIAL

mca ➤
DISTRIBUTION CED

EDDIE DURHAM AND HIS BAND

New York, 11 novembre 1940

Joe Keyes, trumpet; Willard Brown, Henry "Buster" Smith, alto-saxes; Lemuel Johnson, tenor-sax; Conrad Frederick, piano; Eddie Durham, guitar; Averil Pollard, bass; Arthur Herbert, drums.

**68.336-A I WANT
A LITTLE GIRL (3'12)**
Arrangeur : Eddie Durham - Solistes : Durham, Johnson, Frederick, Keyes.

68.337-A MOTEN'S SWING (2'38)
Arrangeur : Eddie Durham - Solistes : Smith, Durham, Smith.

**68.338-A FARE THEE, HONEY
FARE THEE WELL (2'50)**
Arrangeur : Eddie Durham - Solistes : Durham, Lemuel Johnson, vocal with Keyes, trumpet : Frederick, Johnson, tenor-sax : Durham.

68.339-A MAGIC CARPET (2'53)
Arrangeur : Eddie Durham - Solistes : Herbert, Durham, Smith, Keyes, Johnson, Durham, Keyes, Smith, Durham, Keyes, Durham.

(Eddie / "Swinging Small Bands 2" recordings: see Appendix "A")

Eddie recalled: "I might write in F minor, like Buster on alto on Moten Swing. I was really intending to play the lead all the way, and that would've gave you the lead at that time, just like Glenn Miller had a lead with his clarinet. If you notice, I did quite a bit of it with the guitar, but the guitar wasn't up to perfection in those days.

That's when Walter Winchell gave me the writeup as the best band of the year (1940). Mrs. Kramer and somebody from the Union come down and told me that "they're not going to let you through, you sound like a white band and you're hurting the bands over there." There was Pleasure Beach two miles away, paying them a lot of money and you couldn't even get on the highway, let alone standing room. I was playing out on the pier too but came one night and all the wires were cut. I went to the D.A. and he made them give me some light on Sunday, and hook up to anything. So the politicians was on me, on one hand trying to hold me there, and the racketeers on the other, wanted me to leave. So I made a deal with the city by Pleasure Beach. They wanted me to bar all the whites on Sunday, because of Harry James band playing the other side. So I put up a sign "SPECIAL PARTY TONIGHT" but the white kids came from New Haven and the black organizations come down on me right away for segregating. So I let the band go and went to Glenn Miller."[184]

I Don't Want To Set The World On Fire

My personal favorite version of "Fire" was recorded in 1960 by vocalist Betty Carter (birthname Lillie Mae Jones). Magnificent!

"The hottest tune along Tin Pan Alley this week is 'I Don't Want To Set The World On Fire'. The sheet music is a sellout and three recordings of the number have been released in the past week. Tommy Tucker and his orchestra, with *Amy Arnell and the Voices Three*, are credited with the first wax work on the number; the second by Horace Heidt, with Larry Cotton, *Donna and her Don Juans*, and the third by the *Charioteers*. Three more platters are to be made within the next week…The tune… was written by four lads, Bennie Benjamin, Eddie Durham, Sol Marcus and Eddie Seiler. … Sol Marcus and Eddie Seiler, white, both hail from New Jersey. The former is Louis Prima's pianist and the latter is a band manager." [185] *The Pittsburgh Courier,* Newspaper (Aug. 1941).

Glenn Miller performed "I Don't Want To Set The World On Fire" on the *Sunset Serenade Broadcast*, November 12, 1941 with Ray Eberle, Marion Hutton, *The Four Modernaires* and Bobby Hackett.

The Frederick Brothers Music Corporation produced a recording of "I Don't Want To Set The World On Fire" for *Bon Bon Tunnell & His Buddies*

(NY July 23, 1941), which is the only version composer Eddie Durham performs on.

Eddie recalled: "I Don't Want To Set The World on Fire, that's the in-between tempo, I wanted to put it in that vein, I wanted to carry it back down slower, so the lyrics could be played and understood, we were writing for the lyrics. But I think Guy Lombardo did the right tempo. Bon Bon's (Decca) would've been the swing version. I made the arrangement for Ella Fitzgerald, I ran up to the Savoy, and Teddy MacRay was rehearsing the Band, but they were packed up, and you know musicians they don't wanna stay no longer. I say, I brought this up here special for Ella, I think it'll be a hit, I had reason to believe it and Ella wanted to do it, but she couldn't get the Band to wait, but she said, "Let me sing it anyway" and she sang it with the piano. Gale's Secretary came running out the office, [she] quit typing saying, "What was that song I heard, that's gone be a hit! Let me hear that again." I said, 'Ella you get it later' and that's how she didn't do it. Mrs. Kramer told me that song is gonna be a hit. Everybody heard that song said it's gonna be a hit."[186]

Bon Bon Tunnell

Bon Bon and His Buddies

Personnel*: George "Bon Bon" Tunnell (vo)*

Eddie Durham – tb (performed on "FIRE," only with Bon Bon)

Jackie Fields (as), Jack Parker (d), Henry "Buster" Smith (cl), Joe "Cornbread" Thomas (t), James Phipps (p), Al Hall (b), Jack Parker (d),

The Pittsburgh Courier (Pennsylvania) - Sat, Dec 7, 1940 - Page 20

BON BON TO TEAM UP WITH EDDIE DURHAM

NEW YORK CITY, Dec. 5—Bon Bon, former vocalist with Jan Savitt's white orchestra, is currently negotiating to take over the leadership of Eddie Durham's band. ★ Durham, former trombonist with Jimmy Lunceford and Count Basie's bands and later arranger for many of the big-time outfits here, has been leading his own band for the last six months in this territory. Recognized as one of the best arrangers in the business, he was recently offered a spot with Lionel Hampton's new band, which fell through when Hampton moved to the coast to organize.

In the event that Bon Bon and Durham come to a working agreement, the band will be called Bon Bon and his orchestra, featuring Eddie Durham. According to the latest developments, there are several complications that have to be ironed out before the merger can be made.

Eddie recalled: "Bon Bon was a singer (he could also play piano). He didn't want the Band in my name, so we put it in his. But he married a wealthy girl and she didn't want him traveling. We played at The Howard Theatre, but then December 1945 he didn't show up at The Apollo Theatre. They sued him, he quit the band, paid everybody off and that broke up the band."

(Eddie / Bon Bon: see "Appendix A") (Bon Bon's Touring Musicians: see "Appendix B")

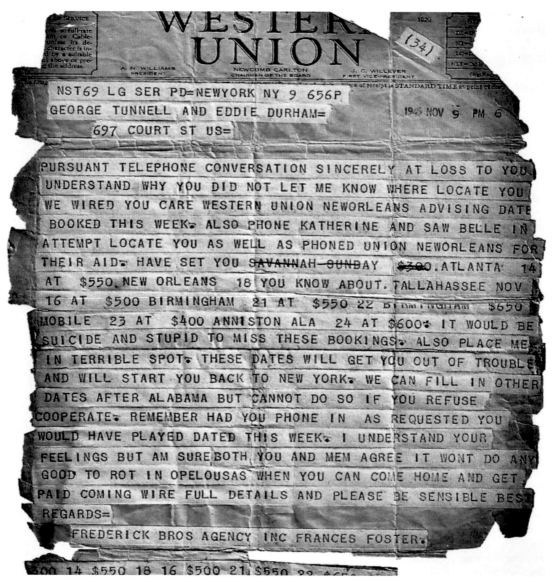

WESTERN UNION

SERVICE

A. N. WILLIAMS
PRESIDENT

NEWCOMB CARLTON
CHAIRMAN OF THE BOARD

J. C. WILLEVER
FIRST VICE-PRESIDENT

(34)

NST69 LG SER PD=NEWYORK NY 9 656P

GEORGE TUNNELL AND EDDIE DURHAM=

1945 NOV 9 PM 6

697 COURT ST US=

PURSUANT TELEPHONE CONVERSATION SINCERELY AT LOSS TO YOU
UNDERSTAND WHY YOU DID NOT LET ME KNOW WHERE LOCATE YOU
WE WIRED YOU CARE WESTERN UNION NEWORLEANS ADVISING DATE
BOOKED THIS WEEK. ALSO PHONE KATHERINE AND SAW BELLE IN
ATTEMPT LOCATE YOU AS WELL AS PHONED UNION NEWORLEANS FOR
THEIR AID. HAVE SET YOU SAVANNAH SUNBAY $300.ATLANTA 14
AT $550.NEW ORLEANS 18 YOU KNOW ABOUT.TALLAHASSEE NOV
16 AT $500 BIRMINGHAM 21 AT $550 22 BIRMINGHAM $650
MOBILE 23 AT $400 ANNISTON ALA 24 AT $600. IT WOULD BE
SUICIDE AND STUPID TO MISS THESE BOOKINGS. ALSO PLACE ME
IN TERRIBLE SPOT. THESE DATES WILL GET YOU OUT OF TROUBLE
AND WILL START YOU BACK TO NEW YORK. WE CAN FILL IN OTHER
DATES AFTER ALABAMA BUT CANNOT DO SO IF YOU REFUSE
COOPERATE. REMEMBER HAD YOU PHONE IN AS REQUESTED YOU
WOULD HAVE PLAYED DATED THIS WEEK. I UNDERSTAND YOUR
FEELINGS BUT AM SURE BOTH YOU AND MEM AGREE IT WONT DO ANY
GOOD TO ROT IN OPELOUSAS WHEN YOU CAN COME HOME AND GET
PAID COMING WIRE FULL DETAILS AND PLEASE BE SENSIBLE BEST
REGARDS=

FREDERICK BROS AGENCY INC FRANCES FOSTER.

00 14 $550 18 16 $500 21 $550 22

"*The Ink Spots* were the biggest group out there. It makes me wonder back in those days did we get correct counts of what was being played, what was being sold. By Eddie Durham writing just that one tune he should have become wealthy on that one tune. Because it was a tune being played all over the world and still being played now. When I was coming along I didn't know about gathering up my own material, publishing it, and making myself named to what I had written." ***Grey, Al*** trombonist

150

Allen Durham

"*Les Hite And Band Returns To Apollo*—After a record smashing run in Chicago, Les Hite and his famous band come to Harlem's 125th Street Apollo Theatre for a week's engagement beginning Friday, February 14th. Les Hite's orchestra has the distinction of being the only sepia band in Hollywood that has appeared in over two hundred feature motion pictures. The band played four consecutive years at Hollywood's Cotton Club. This unusually large and talented group make an annual pilgrimage to Harlem and head a grand revue. The cast includes the Three Chocolatiers, creators of "Peckin'" and the new dance craze known as the "Hickey Rickey".... *The New York Age Newspaper*, February 15, 1941.

(*IMDb.com* credits Hite with one feature movie "*Fools For Scandal*" in 1938 and two movie sound tracks, in 1938/1942. However, he was in several movie shorts and soundies.)

Allen Durham with "Les Hite" (1940-1942)

Allen Durham - trombone (center row, first chair) **Les Hite** Orchestra 1940-42:

Alfred Cobb, **Joe Wilder (top row, center & photo courtesy),** Britt Woodman, Walter Williams, Stumpy Whitlock-tpts; Quedellis Martin, Floyd Turnbon, Rogers Hurd, Sol

Moore-saxes; Oscar Bradley-b; Benny Booker-d; Corey Woodman-p, Frank Pasley-g; Les Hite (standing).

Personnel –New York, circa June 1940 recording of:

"T-Bone Blues"

T-Bone Walker (g/voc), Hite, Floyd Turnham (as), Britt Woodman, Allen Durham (tb)

Paul Campbell, Walter Williams, Forrest Powell (tp), Quedellis Martyn, Roger Hurd (ts), Sol Moore (bs), Nat Walker (p), Frank Pasley (g), Al Morgan (b), Oscar Bradley (d).

Other recordings: March 1941; January 1942 (includes **Jersey Bounce** with Dizzy Gillespie).

Allen Durham with "The Lionel Hampton Orchestra":

"He told us he'd arrange to have Al Durham … join us… Well, Durham didn't arrive on time … and then Durham finally shows up in his old car with six people… I should mention that Prohibition was over by this time, 1933. … So we set out in the early hours of the morning on November 9, 1936. We had a white Chevrolet, and my drums and vibes were in the back. Allen Durham, a trombone player with me, helped us drive."[187]

Personnel, Los Angeles California, October 16, 1944 recordings of:
Million Dollar Smile (L.Hampton/P.Roberts/M.Buckner-Arr.)
Tempo's Boogie (L.Hampton/M.Buckner-Arr.)
The Lamplighter
Overtime

Lionel Hampton (vib), **Allen Durham**, Fred Beckett, Sonny Craven, Andrew Penn, Vernon Porter (tb), Wendell Culley, Joe Morris, Dave Page, Lammar Wright Jr, Snooky Young (tp)

Milton Buckner (p), Charlie Fowlkes (bs), Billy Mackel (g), Fred Radcliffe (dm)

Charles Harris, Ted Sinclair (b)

"My friend Mabel Durham, the trombonist Allen Durham's wife, asked why I didn't go out with the wives anymore. I told her that my husband John [Williams] did not want me around because of their heavy drinking…" But, she added casually, "I was seeking thrills here and there, which was unknown to my husband. My friends and I were daredevils. Mabel Durham and I were quite wild together. John and Allen would say, 'Please don't go out tonight, trouble is expected,' but we'd wait until the guys had gone to work, and down

152

we'd go to the main Negro street to watch the fights and shooting, especially Saturday… John loved gambling, shooting craps. He kept my $75 a week [The Syncopators] and gave me a dollar a day to eat with… That was not enough during that era… Whenever I did receive money, I'd share it with Mabel and Othie [Harrington]."

In November of 1929, Mary was included in *Andy Kirk's Clouds of Joy* recording debut. …Harmonically and rhythmically, she was way ahead of the pack, just as she'd been in her tiny solos two years before with the Syncopators. …By 1937 and thereafter, as a result of an immensely popular recording by the band's singer, Pha Terrell, its jazz playing days, while not exactly numbered, were certainly threatened…

…"Messa Stomp," it was carefully plotted… But much of it, initially, was unplayable – beyond the range of half the instruments.

…I learned more theory from people like the great Don Redman, Edgar Sampson, Milton Orent and Will Bradley.

After their first recording for Decca in March… one can hear how well she had absorbed the interplay of brass and reeds that Don Redman brought to the fore for Fletcher Henderson's band. … Since then, she had also fallen under the influence of Eddie Durham (related to the Clouds' Allen Durham), a trombonist and guitarist and arranger… "Durham helped me quite a bit with sounds… He'd arrange a popular tune giving all the instruments different notes, extending a seventh chord to an eleventh or thirteenth. All of the arrangers knew by heart each note an instrument should make and when there was a mistake."" *Mary Lou Williams*188

"In the manner of the Basie band, [Mary Lou] Williams accentuates the solos with pronounced riffs, climaxing with the full band riffing in the out chorus. …the Clouds of Joy ascended to new heights of swing and originality."[189]

Allen Durham with "The Andy Kirk Orchestra":

Personnel – all recording dates (November 1929-December 1930):

Andy Kirk (brass bass, bass sax), Allen Durham (tb), M.L. Williams (p/arr)

Harry Lawson, Gene Prince, Edgar Battle (tpt), John Harrington (clarinet, alto), Lawrence Freeman (tenor), John Williams (alto & bari sax), Claude Williams (violin), William Dirvin (banjo/g), Edward McNeil (dr), Billy Massey, Dick Roberts (vocals).

(Allen Durham / recordings: see "Appendix A")

154

Allen Durham with the Buddy Banks Sextet: "Banks' Boogie", "Cryin' Blues", "Voo-It! Voo-It!", "I Need It Bad".

Jan Savitt Orchestra

'The Swing Era' music composer and scholar Gunther Schuller notes that: Savitt's band played with such consistently impeccable ensemble and propulsive swing that it kept even its famous shuffle rhythm, constantly energized rhythmically, from becoming a stale cliché. Indeed, the Savitt band had achieved by early 1939 a 4/4 swing amalgam that was an interesting cross between Lunceford and Basie, the shuffle rhythm simply folded into it. *(Eddie's arrangements for J. Savitt: see "Appendix A")*

Eddie recalled: "I got 10 hits in with Jan Savitt's band. I stayed with him not even a year."[190]

"Another dance band was Jan Savitt's Top Hatters, born in Philadelphia who went to New York in 1939. On Decca DL 79243 the music is somewhat reminiscent of Glenn Miller, but laced with good hot solos by Trumpeter Johnny Austin, trombonist Cutty Cutshall and Georgie Auld on tenor. The Savitt trademark was shuffle rhythm, four-four. Tinges of Basie are provided by the arrangements of Eddie Durham and Billy Moore. This record is something of a pleasant surprise."[191] *The Vancouver Sun,* Newspaper.

  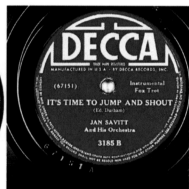

Rebop to Bebop

"A vocal passage in the 1928 jazz song "Four or Five Times" (McKinney's Cotton Pickers/Victor Records) uses the word *bebop*. Washboard [Robert C. Brown] Sam's 1936 recording uses the word *rebop* (Bluebird Records). In 1940, Eddie titles his composition "Wham Rebop Boom Bam," recorded by Jimmie Lunceford, [Lucius A. Tyson] "Doctor Sausage", Andy Kirk, Teddy Wilson, Mildred Bailey/Roy Eldridge, Glenn Miller... this is an Eddie

156

Durham composition and arrangement. He introduced the piece in a record that was at the time slightly just in its initial release, for a couple of weeks, bigger than its session mate. August 1, 1939, is the record date, its session mate is "In The Mood" and both records are by Glenn Miller. They're both Durham arrangements, "In The Mood" and "Wham" but "Wham" is also his composition. He introduces as a secondary theme 'salt peanuts' and this brings us a little bit closer to the bebop tradition... Wham itself, was close to Charlie Parker who performs on its harmony and paraphrases as a member of the ensemble, its melody, on the very first piece he played to his largest audience, the network audience that heard the Savoy broadcast of the Jay McShann Band in February 1942. McShann's band called it the "St. Louis Mood" by this time, but it is a match.[192] *Phil Schaap*

Eddie recalls: Taps [Miller] had the lyrics to Wham. He went to Basie and Basie wouldn't do it because they was all out of meter and he didn't have the meters, he couldn't fit the words with his music. So I listened to it and Taps said, "I need this bad, Basie won't do it." I said, 'I'll fix it up so he will do it'. But Glenn Miller was recording and I said, let me let Glenn play it. Glenn didn't want his name on it because he said, "No, no, because he'd been around too long and they'd pick up on the style." But he took a Writer's share 'cause his name was big. But I told Taps it's better to let him have a share than to have it lay around to today and not ever be known. To get on the chart you got to give up something. But if they can't go write another one they worry about giving up a share on that one song, he's the one who goes nuts. But to be a successful bandleader, you need the cooperation of talent from the band and if their names on it with you, it's good and you pay them, 'cause the leader's name has to carry plenty. Just "Hodges" wouldn't go as well as "Duke and Hodges." It's like pulling a hen's tooth to get a number recorded. You need a front man and in those days you couldn't get past those managers. Wouldn't matter what you had, if you didn't give up, it wasn't going through anyway. Even for the white guys. Miller insisted he wanted his name on nothing I did because he said that my style will cut through later years and the critics will know and he wants his on the cover. ...Salt peanuts, salt peanuts, and Dizzy spoke to me 'bout them two bars, he say, "I just wanna let you know I'm gon use those two bars." I say, Well that ain't nothin, all songs are based on another song - you got it. But he was concerned about them two bars, Salt Peanuts, Salt Peanuts, because he took them from "Wham ReBop Boom Bam," you know, the "dot dee dot, dot dee dot".[193]

"I dig the fact that one of the first recordings Monk can be heard on is a jam (at Minton's) with guitarist Charlie Christian. It's "Charlie's Choice" a.k.a. "Swing to Bop" - actually Eddie Durham's "Topsy" - where Charlie demonstrates why he's one of the most remarkable players ever heard in any genre, with his unique and enchanting flow and his pre-Bird modern conception. Monk's Blue Note albums were titled "Genius of Modern Music," and Charlie was one too."[194]

"Eddie created the elite, like on the live Minton stuff *"Swing to Bop"* are *"Topsy"* changes. Basie's recording of Topsy is my favorite - it's my deepest Jazz roots and I've been playing it for years." Jazz Guitarist **Chris Flory** (recorded with Buck Clayton)

"...An even more striking example is a series of recordings made at Minton's Playhouse, an after-hours club located in the Hotel Cecil at 210 West 118th Street in Harlem by Columbia student Jerry [Jerome Robert] Newman on a portable disk recorder in [May] 1941. Newman captured Christian, accompanied by Joe Guy on trumpet, Kenny Kersey on piano and Kenny Clarke on drums, stretching out far beyond what the confines of the 78 RPM record would allow. His work on "Swing to Bop," a later Esoteric Records company re-title of Eddie Durham's "Topsy," is an example of what Christian was capable of creating off the cuff." May 12, 1941 - Minton's Playhouse, New York City, Minton's House Band, featuring Charlie Christian, Joe Guy (tp), Thelonious Monk, Charlie Christian (g), Nick Fenton (b), Kenny Clarke (d), on 1. "Stompin' at the Savoy" and 2. "Topsy" [aka "Charlie's Choice"].[195]

"Something Eddie Durham in particular began to orchestrate, and then when the real big-band era came along, in the 1930s, it was really for the purpose of dancing. A lot of folks lamented that when the 1940s bebop era came along, wherein Jazz became more of listening music, that was sort of its own downfall because people could no longer dance. Very crude Rock 'n roll, in its early days, was very bad Jazz played by bad musicians, but it had that beat for dance."[196] ***Teddy Wilson, III***, acoustic bassist (son of pianist Teddy Wilson)

Bebop music, harmonically, came directly out of advanced swing era arranging as exemplified by Eddie Durham's charts. ***Dan Weinstein***

Frank Humphries

Eddie recalled: "I recorded three songs with Frank "Fat Man" Humphries Orchestra." This recording is symbolic of Eddie Durham's passing of a baton from his own swing idiom to the dawn of bebop - via Kenny Dorham.

"The first item listed in [the single artist compilations by Bo Raftegard and Claude] Schlouch's discography is a fall 1945 recording session with Frank Humphries and His Orchestra, and here in fact I found Eddie Durham listed on trombone along with Kenny Dorham on trumpet. Not only did I find the two men together, but I discovered that this 1945 session was <u>Kenny Dorham's very first recording</u>. ...as a result of Eddie Durham, the veteran of many a swing-era historic recording session, having joined on this occasion with Dorham, one of the soon-to-be stars of the bebop revolution, this recording represented a meeting of two generations of Texans and of two vital jazz movements."[197]

Frank Humphries and His Band "A Great New Band" performed at:
The Apollo Theatre, Jan. 26 & Nov. 23, 1945; Lincoln Sq. Center, NYC May 6, 1945

Eddie Durham recordings - The Frank "Fat Man" Humphries Orchestra:

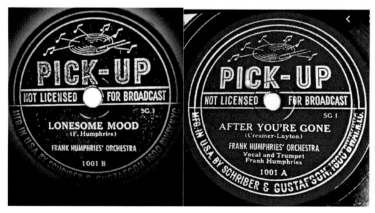

George Williams

Hub Records circa 1945/46

Don Byas (leader), George Williams (vocals), **Eddie Durham** (guitar/solo), unknown (trumpet, bass, drums):[198]

"A Woman Gets Tired of One Man All The Time" (Charles H. Booker) 14002-D

"Don't Care Blues" (Alan Bullard, Perry Bradford)

Discrimination

"When we asked them about segregation and what it was like to be a black musician, Mr. Durham told us about one experience he had with a band where he got a black female singer. *The lady who was head of the band wouldn't allow her in. He said, 'but she's a great girl, listen to these records'. But the lady just broke them and kicked her out. A lot of stuff like that made it difficult.*" *Petoskey News-Review* (Michigan) Apr 24, 1984 p8.[199]

"My name is **Sarah McLawler** and I play B3 organ. I don't remember when I *didn't* play music but I started in the business *seriously*, in the late 1940s, when I was going into the only all-black public school in Indianapolis, which opened in 1927, Crispus Attucks High School, where we were taught art appreciation and where they had a very fine music department. We would go hear the great symphony orchestras at Murat Theatre, hear Marion Anderson, also the Montgomery Brothers used to play at our high school dances. One of the things that always distressed me is the lack of recognition for the excellent women musicians out there. There were other great arrangers besides Mary Lou Williams, who by the way, was mentored by Eddie Durham.

Until her recent death, Dorothy Donegan (1922-1998) was one of the greatest pianists that ever lived but unfortunately, she had to work in Europe to keep busy. You also hear about Hazel Scott. When foreigners come here [to the USA] to visit, the first thing they want to know, where can I go hear Jazz, Blues, Spirituals, Gospel and where can we find cornbread and collard greens. But there's always been integration in the arts. Benny Goodman had Teddy Wilson, Lionel Hampton, Eddie Durham. Bennie would stand his ground. When they said, 'they can't stay here', they would say, 'Well we can't stay here either', Charlie Barnet and Glenn Miller too.

But we paid the price, paved the way and that's why sometimes I feel so sad when I see how the International Sweethearts of Rhythm was so respectful but some of the younger people are not. Use to be a time when you would go to the Studio you couldn't go in through the front door. I don't think many of them today would've survived. Because when we were out on the road, scuffling, we couldn't go to the restaurants. We couldn't go to the bathroom. The only place you could go was to some kind of business in the negro neighborhood, or you went to the YWCA or YMCA - and the code word was 'Phyllis Wheatley'. If it was Phyllis Wheatley over there you knew it was black. When we went out on the road with the big bands, most of the time the road manager was white and had to go into the restaurants and get the food and bring it out to us. A lot of us got our stomachs messed up because we weren't used to eating a lot of restaurant food. I'm not saying you have to live the 1930s and '40s again, but don't throw out the baby with the dishwater. Overseas, those singers got Billie and Ella down pat, and they don't even know what they're saying! American youths need to nurture and hold on to our contributions.

The young people in this country, most don't know their heritage, their music heroes, or that we have brought one of America's greatest exports throughout the world, Blues, Jazz, and add the Swing Music idiom which Eddie Durham invented. You go overseas and those kids over there can tell you the roster of all the great big bands over here. But also, they don't teach it in the schools here. They teach you about classical music history in the USA. Billie Holiday had that unfortunate experience when she was down south with Artie Shaw, and she saw that lynching. She never got over that. That's where that song "Strange Fruit" came from. Billie lived her songs. She was so intense and when she came off stage you'd have to stay away from her. She was pouring sweat after every performance. There are certain [racial] incidences that happen to people and it just tears them apart. Then they run with it or in this case, have to live with it for the rest of their lives.

White kids were sneaking and listening to black music. They couldn't bring it into the house. It was called Rhythm & Blues. So the powers that be had to find imitators. So they called that rock 'n roll or blue-eyed Soul. That was the keyword to let you know that it was whites doing black music. Aretha Franklin was just incorporated into the Rock 'n Roll Hall of Fame and I was very proud but quite shocked at that, 'cause that's a white club. Eddie should be in there because guitar amplification changed the world."200 *Sarah McLawler,* B3 organ pioneer, Pipe organist, Bandleader, Vocalist, Recording Artist (1926-2017)

"My name is **Jean Davis** and I was raised in New Orleans. The funeral procession was a sight to see and I was impressed by that. When I first started playing my family didn't want me to play the trumpet. A girl playing a horn? So I took up drums in high school. I played drums at *The Cotton Club* with Neil Tate's trio and Billie Holiday walked in. She sat down and talked to us, she was very nice. Then my father bought me a trumpet and said that I could play it, but not around him. I ate many a hard rolls with butter to pay for my own trumpet lessons. This was a terrible horn. Then I met Doc Cheatham and he said, *"What kind of horn is this?"* I said, 'I don't know, my father bought it'. He said, *"I never heard of this, a horn from Czechoslovakia, I can't play with you like this. I got two horns coming in which you can choose from. I'll buy it and you can pay me back."* And I paid him back. Doc Cheatham gave me lessons and he made my old horn into a lamp, which I still have.

Later on, when I went to Scandinavia for a year, we were the first black women to play in *Lapland*. They hardly had seen black men but definitely had not seen black women. So they followed us around and we should've gone down in history as being in *Lapland*, they call it 'the midnight sun' because at 2:00 in the morning we would see the sun coming out. Sarah McLawler called it 'Reindeer Land'. When I came back from Sweden I got my own group and played in *Smalls Paradise* and played with Sarah McLawler. Things are not that much better today for women musicians, not that much recognition unless you're a singer.

162

I had an experience where I got hired for a job and my name is Jean so I guess they thought I was a guy. So when I went in, he said, "*So I see you're carrying a trumpet, but where's your old man?*" and I said, 'I'm it for the night'. He said, '*Oh when they recommended you I thought you was a guy, he didn't say you are a woman*'. So I said, 'Does it make a difference long as I can play your music?' He was real outdone and he got on the bandstand and he went through every key he could think of that he thought I couldn't play in. So I said to him, 'Don't hurt yourself because any key you play in I can play in'. So finally he got down to his b flat and what he really plays in. He didn't like it and it was so unnecessary. Certain women get the recognition but it's a rarity."[201], ***Jean Davis,*** Trumpeter

"Another analogy would be Rap music. Nobody had the slightest idea that it would be the big money maker that it is today. Or that its largest audience would be white children. The music itself is so powerful. Eddie Durham made music feel good and he made it accessible to everybody no matter what color they were. Everybody wants to feel good. I'm southern born, born in New Orleans, a cosmopolitan town. But once I left and started traveling through Texas, Mississippi, Oklahoma, many times I've played, even with Lionel Hampton's band, where there was a rope that extended from the bandstand to the end of the hall. Black people stood on one side of the rope and white people on the other side. One of the things I admired about people like Eddie Durham was, they didn't bother with any of that stuff. They were artists and you'll see the movies in the 1920s will have everybody believe that everybody had on sharecroppers stuff. But you can see some pictures of musicians who look like gentleman's quarterly. So there were the people like himself who are really role models to let us know all the little stumbling blocks in front of you, you just go on and do your thing despite that. They did it with such dignity." ***Benny Powell***

"This is the time to let the younger people know what was going on back then. I had a lot of rough times being segregated. We used to have to go around to the back to get our food and then, in Florida one time, they had the rope and they told Lucky Millender, NO autographs. But he couldn't take it, so he gave an autograph anyway and they hit him and we had to pack up the band

and get out of town. So many different occasions we played, one night for whites, or a lot of times at theaters we never could see the black people because they would be up in the third balcony, so we named it 'crow's nest'. When we go off for intermission, they'd say, *'I was looking at you'*, but we couldn't see them. Then I begin to see the change. One night the band was swinging, "Swinging The Blues" in San Anton, and they used to have chairs all down the middle. Blacks on one side and whites on the other. But that night before the dance was over they had moved the chairs and next thing you know they were integrating, dancing. So we could see these things. And now it's almost like everything has to change. Everyone is backing up each other when it comes to being on the other side. I think that perhaps Eddie Durham's music is in that cycle which would come back around. From reminiscing what he did, you don't get to say this until it comes up to be spoken about." ***Grey, Al***

It can occur that abused oppressed people when they later come into a position of authority, will inflict abusive behavior onto subordinates. Eddie, always being scouted, said that he left one bandleader after one week because of the verbal abuse the other band members had to endure.

"Eddie never made me, the audience or the other band members feel like he was frustrated of full of resentment. I never talked to him beyond a certain point, like "Eddie, how do you feel about not getting money from so and so." Never. But he would tell me stories about how they went to Basie and asked him to give back some of the rights to some of the tunes that Eddie and Buster and some of the other guys wrote. That's how he talked. He didn't lecture, he told stories. And then with me, a year or ten or twenty years later, I'd begin to understand what he was telling me. The stuff he did for Bennie Moten "Oh Eddie!"; Jimmie Lunceford, the great explosion of music he wrote and arranged for Basie, "Lafayette" and that great arrangement of "Blue Room" and then for Glenn Miller "In The Mood." He was doing things years before anybody else. But what makes his arrangements unique, he wasn't a conventional arranger. He didn't write in the same simple way others did, he combined instruments, almost like Duke did, they both would do anything in an orchestration.

164

I never lose sight of the fact that Eddie may have come to fame in Kansas City and New York, but he was from Texas and there was a country part to him that he never let leave. He could have because he didn't live in Texas for many decades. But when you talked to him, he was still somebody who came from there. He carried it with him on purpose because somebody with Eddie's skills, if he had wanted to talk like a New Yorker or totally give up all that stuff, he could have. But he was himself, he was proud of where he came from, proud of who he was and his background. When he played the blues and the guitar, you could hear it. You have to understand that Eddie came from near the river and with the Indians. So I think he had a big influence on a whole bunch of different guitar players. I can only assume that T-Bone Walker heard Eddie Durham's records. Eddie was a star back then. There was a certain amount of fascinating myth surrounding the stories about the Indians, the Circus, wild-west people, and all the crazy things that happened in the Texas that he grew up in." ***Loren Schoenberg***

USO Tour-Girl Orchestras

American musicians were already contributing greatly to their country what became America's greatest export to date - Jazz (and Soul) music paired with swing dancing. No one desired to quit performing, especially from a successful working orchestra, and instead go to battle and serve War. In Eddie's case, his acclaimed writeup's, his credentials for being well-traveled, his track record as an ace arranger and choreographer, and his reputation as a gentleman and a professional… distinctively qualified him unparalleled for a specific war-time tailored government assignment.

Eddie recalled: "Now every time I would put a good band together, they'd draft the guys for War. I met an old West Indian guy, a politician, who got me with the Treasury Department's bond drives. …And so long as I gave some service to the U.S.O., the Treasury Department cooperated with whatever agency I was with. I did one day a week for them and six days for myself. I played all the camps and did over four thousand miles in Canada for the Canadian government. For four years during the War [1941-1945] I was the only leader who had a sleeper bus and used gas from the government. That's how I got involved with the International Sweethearts of Rhythm."202

Eddie recalled: "I'd be deferred from the army every six months for the duration of the War. …Its benefits included government-supplied gas coupons and access to a sleeper bus. I was signed up as a bond driver for the Treasury Department with these girls. I used to let some of the bands use our sleeper bus, a big trailer bus with facilities. I'd run into a band like Erskine Hawkins and they wouldn't have nowhere to sleep during the war, in some of them towns."

"You may well ask what Eddie Durham had to do with women in jazz. You can bet your Sunday Reeboks he had more to do with women in jazz than many of the women who were in it… Durham told Sally Placksin in her book "American Women in Jazz" about a gig in Madison Square Garden featuring a dozen of the top bands in the land. Durham finagled a place on the bill just ahead of Basie's, and for Ina Ray's final number he had the band rip off several of Basie's best-known flag-wavers, complete with the original solos.

166

"The girls were waving' their hats like Harry Edison… and they all come out and they didn't believe it… just the same as the boys. They had to. I trained 'em down like that.'" Nels Nelson *Philadelphia Daily News*[203]

"With the war what it is and the draft blowing harder and faster in the male direction, female bands won't be hard to take as time goes into history, especially if they're as good and chockfull of beauty as Eddie Durham's crew." *The Pittsburgh Courier*, (December 12, 1942).

The Durhamettes

In 1939, Eddie Durham got his first knowledge of a girl band, when he signed with the Ina Ray Hutton aggregation…. Durham then joined the All-Girl Sweethearts as arranger, but later conceived the idea of organizing his own all-girl band without the fear of anyone being drafted. Hence, the EDDIE DURHAM'S ALL STAR GIRL BAND. The band got together in January 1942 and rehearsed for eight weeks. The average age of the girls is 19… Most of the girls either double on any instrument or sing and they've all had a musical background. Four are from the *All Girl Sweethearts* Band, five from *Ray's Rhythm* and the remaining five are from musical schools. The band plays from sweet to swing (which includes boogie-woogie) and it features the *Four Durhamettes*. *The New York Age,* (Dec. 18, 1943 p.11).

The **Durhamettes** *Orchestra* opened at the *Howard Theatre* (Washington, D.C. 1942) for the Thomas *"Fats" Waller Orchestra*. The personnel included ***Ersa Bell Hiller, a* champion trumpeter,** Eddie's 2nd wife who birthed their first daughter, Mabel Ruth in 1935. This is Eddie's second child (Eddie, Jr., born in 1928).

"The Paradise Theater will entertain 1,000 deserving boys and girls Wednesday at 4:00 pm at a giant Christmas party, it was announced yesterday by Ben and Lou Cohen, veteran Detroit theater operators… The current attractions at the Paradise include Louis Jordan… and Eddie Durham's all girl orchestra…"[204] *Detroit Free Press* (Michigan) Dec. 22, 1942 *("Durhamettes" full Personnel: see "Appendix A")*

On March 5, 1943 *The Office of Defense Transportation* ruled against the use of privately owned buses. This dealt a deathly blow to some bands.[205]

International Sweethearts

The International Sweethearts of Rhythm included 14-19 year-old girls from different backgrounds from the Piney Wood Orphanage School, White, Black, Indian, Puerto Rican/Latin; Willie Mae Wong on sax was Asian. Pauline Braddy [Williams] on drums, was mentored by Jo Jones. Helen Jones Woods was the daughter of the *Piney Wood School's* founder.

"In 1941, a year after a successful 1940 appearance at New York's Apollo Theatre, the Sweethearts severed their connection with the school. The 'Afro-American' reported in May 1941: "Eight teen girls of Piney Woods School …took the school bus and, pursued by highway police, fled through seven states to Washington and freedom." Their first coach, Eddie Durham recalled: "Not only did the Sweethearts play good music, they also had fabulous gowns, spectacular lighting and great effects." *The Age*, by Valerie Colyer (Melbourne, Victoria, Australia)

In 1941 Anna Mae Winburn became their only bandleader after resigning from her former position leading an all-male band. "Jesse Stone will have replaced Eddie Durham as head scribbler for the Sweethearts of Rhythm by the time you read this while in the head spot for the girl band will be Anna Mae Winburn…" *The Pittsburgh Courier* (May 30, 1942 p20.)

"I remember when I was sixteen, Eddie Durham came to town with his all girl band and I took my saxophone up to the Pla-Mor Ballroom and asked him if I could sit in, and he said, *sure*. I sat in and that was really the first time I had known that girls really play horns and really play real, real music like I hear on the radio and I was just so amazed. I loved it from that moment on, I thought, *this* is what I'm going to do. We had these white girls, they were traveling with us, they would paint their faces dark in order to play, so the police wouldn't come and take them off the stand and be arrested." "It was absolutely necessary that I pass as black… I always looked very freakish and not quite right… and most of the time I just ended up just hiding… We saved ourselves a lot of trouble and headaches by staying on the bus. …" Rosalind "Roz" Cron. "They always took the mulatto to be the white, they'd get 'em all mixed up. We went to the station and we were automatically ushered onto

168

the white car on the train… it was simpler for a lot of blacks who looked white to just go along with the program." "We had the gall to do this in the deep South… it didn't stop us"... "The girls, when we came back from Europe, they fell in love, they got married and started having babies, and it was hard to replace the personnel… "

"International Sweethearts of Rhyth– America's Hottest All-Girl Band", documentary.

"They learned to play - either through school bands or by ear, sitting in on jam sessions the way men did - and formed their own bands, with names like *The Swinging Rays of Rhythm*, the *Darlings of Rhythm*, and the *Prairie View Co-Eds*. The black theater circuit in the North was small, and only the most well-known African-American bands were booked. As a result, many of these black all-girl bands were confined to road trips and mostly one-night engagements in the South and thus encountered Jim Crow laws. Because of the difficulties of public transportation and wartime rationing, tours were impossible for black bands that did not have their own bus. They had to keep moving; both to get to the next gig as well as avoid the inevitable harassment by authorities. …However, separating from the *Piney Woods School* did allow the business to hire professionals. Edna Williams was responsible for the band's early sound, but it was Eddie Durham, …who worked with the strengths of the individual band members to create solos and helped them polish it. …After Durham, Jesse Stone hired more professional musicians and improved the Sweethearts' overall musical technique. Both Stone and Durham knew that the band members weren't being paid what they were worth and were suspicious of the band's finances, and both eventually quit the band over these issues."[206]

"Eddie Durham said the Sweethearts were fleeced by their managers, paid $32 a week - only half of union scale - and told by their backer that their wages were going into a mortgage on a 10-room house. …He gave them that home to live in, but they didn't buy it".[207] *The Age*, Valerie Colyer (Melbourne, Victoria, Australia)

Eddie's contribution to help rectify the situation and perhaps in conjunction with his preparation for departure, sponsored as many female musicians as possible into Musicians' Unions across the country.

Eddie recalled: "The girls played The Apollo and The Buchanan - I wasn't with them. But I went to meet them in D.C. and rehearsed them for about ten days on "St. Louis Blues." Willie Bryant came down and helped the band in dance and sometimes he emceed the show. I traveled around the country with Ina Ray for a year, and we were at the Rose Bowl ten weeks. They had a ten-week run on the radio called "The Choice Hour," coast to coast. Their competition was Bing Crosby on at 10:00. So I went out to write music strictly for that broadcast and Earl [Durham] was there. But then I scored regularly for The International Sweethearts of Rhythm.

I bought a backer to meet [Moe] Gale from D.C., who owned the Arlington Cemetery who kept half a million standing in the band, money was no problem. He had made two All-American sleeper buses. We got Moms [Loretta M. Aiken] Mabley, Ella Fitzgerald and acts like Butterbeans and Susie [Jodie Edwards and Susie Edwards Hawthorne] on the same programs. The leaders all quit playing when I started writing, they were afraid of the arrangements. Ina sang, but her clarinet playing wasn't fast enough. I'd rehearse them, pick the openings most times, just like a manager with the Giants, pick songs according to the audience because Ina couldn't do that. I took the Chinese girl off alto and put her on baritone. It got to be a very good band but I had to handpick the musicians. I sent to the Conservatory in London, England for the first trumpet player because none of them could reach a high C or a good F with volume. They sent a pianist from Zanesville, Ohio. We used five saxes, four trumpets, three trombones. She had Vi Burnside, Lilly Labourtney, Anna Mae Winburn came in and took over the band. We were on, at Madison Square Garden right in front of Basie. I gave the girls "One O'Clock Jump," note for note. They could read what they see and I knew the arrangements. They were playing much more than they thought they were going to play.

Ina wanted to swing like Basie. Ina was hard to handle, but they could play! She hung around The Marx Brothers. Blond, Alice Wills on trombone (duo with the Dorsey band) could play 26 instruments perfectly! Then at the Aragon Ballroom, Dick Jergens wanted to have a battle with Ina's band. So I wrote Ina's few arrangements and I said 'Give me one of yours Dick" and I took

170

Ina's arrangements and made another part of each part. I said, 'Now I want the reed section to sit like this, boy, girl, boy, girl, but the boys sit back a little. Let's use Dick's drummer but a girl on bass drum'. We called that a double band. I had them fanning hats and I'd teach them to really swing like the boy bands. Nora Lane was on the program, MGM was there and after opening for two days, when they closed that theatre, they come out with the second band and opened in the Paramount Theatre in Newark, N.J. I didn't like that because I said, There ain't NO bands can go open out of rehearsal with a new band and go to the Paramount! Basie hadn't. So they did favor them because they were girls.

But Nola called up Paul Whiteman and let him listen and asked "Who do you think this is?" Paul said, "I don't know, it's Great!" She said, "Girls." He said, "I don't believe it, but I'll be down there." Then he called up W.C. Handy and, same thing, he said, "I'll be there with my trumpet during the opening." But the musicians came backstage and demanded to see this boys' band 'behind the curtains'. But it was the gimmicks and the tricks, and knowing how to make those girls intonation where they could play. We got some write-ups. I took most of these girls to my own band, when I'd run out of black girls, I'd use a lot of white ones, from everywhere. Down South I'd use the black girls, I kept them separated, so while the Sweethearts was in the Philippines, the other band was in Canada."

Apollo Theatre

"Eddie Durham is going places with his all-girl band. They opened an extended engagement at the *Tic Toc* in Boston last week and will soon come to the *Apollo Theater*." *The Pittsburgh Courier (*Jan. 30, 1943 p20)

Ella Fitzgerald and the *Four Keys* will be the outstanding attractions, then will come Eddie Durham's sensational all-girl band to provide a brand of music which has been the wonder of the whole theatrical season. Durham has earned for himself the title of the "sepia Phil Spitalny." Two colored all-girl bands are touring the country-the *Sweethearts of Rhythm* and Eddie Durham's outfit." *The New York Age*, Feb. 27, 1943 p.10.

"*Thus, it is my belief that girl orchestras possessing versatility, ability and new ideas will be acclaimed tops in both name and monetary capacities,* Durham avowed. The tricky arrangements, the unique ability of the feminine members of the aggregation to execute same with the utmost skill, the suave manner of presentation in solo work, knowledge of showmanship by every all-star girl, plus that desire to attain the heights of success in their chosen field, makes Eddie Durham's all-star girls the front-runners for "name bands" honors." By Ted Wilson, *The Weekly Review,* Newspaper (Alabama, May 22, 1943).

They performed Dayton's Coliseum in Ohio to a crowd of 10,000 on July 24, 1943, and the Governor of Indiana attended their War Bonds campaign performance at *Victory Field* on July 25th in Indianapolis.

"Direct from Broadway, Eddie Durham and his all-star negro girl band will stop at Hangar 9 Monday night for an 8:10 PM concert before continuing their tour to Hollywood where they will be featured in an MGM movie... The aggregation, which is fast winning acclaim as the finest girl band in the nation, was featured in the Broadway extravaganza, *"Du Barry Brown"* and *"Blackbirds."* They also have their own NBC radio show. Singing stars of the review are the *Four Durhamettes* who won fame at the *Cotton Club*, and the *Ubangi and Plantation*, in New York." *Barksdale's Bark,* Newspaper (Louisiana) (Aug 7, 1943).[208]

"The Apollo Theatre's shows this season have been, more than ever, the talk of New York... Ella Fitzgerald, well-known swing stylist; will be the featured attraction at the Apollo Theatre this week. She will be surrounded with such entertainers as Eddie Durham's All-Girl Band, and a cast of outstanding personalities... Ella's incomparable singing and the "solid" music of the seventeen girls provide ideal musical entertainment... Ella Fitzgerald and the Four Keys and Eddie Durham's All-Girl Band will combine to give patrons of the *Apollo Theatre* a delightful stage revue next week. Yielding to the advice of motion picture and radio experts, she [Ella] no longer heads her own band, although these same experts have induced her to appear on the same programs with Eddie Durham's All Girl Band. The combination is truly "terrific"....Little Jean Starr heads a group of seven new girls-all cornetists

172

and saxophonists who joined Eddie Durham's all-girl orchestra about four months ago. Tim Moore, the Whirlwinds and Peckin Joe will be included in the list of headliners combined for the stage show at the Apollo..." *The New York Age,* Newspaper (June 19 and Oct 16, 1943).[209]

"It took just about ten minutes after the audition for Opal to know that soon she would be singing with Eddie Durham's All-Girl Band. Currently playing the Royal Theatre in Baltimore the stock of Durham's Orchestra has now been 'upped' with this new addition. Opal Spencer hails from Indianapolis, Indiana and is but 19." *The New York Age* (Nov 27, 1943).

"In the first of a series of twelve concerts…Newest singing sensation is Mattie Vernon with Eddie Durham's All-Star Girl Band now on a dance tour."[210] *Ted Yates-The Weekly Review* (Feb. 19, 1944).

Darlings of Rhythm

"There was another group formed who were darker and they didn't get the recognition and publicity that *The Sweethearts* did. This was The *Darlings of Rhythm*, who Eddie arranged for and traveled with. It included excellent musicians such as tenor & alto saxophonist Lula Roberts, who worked with me until she died. There was also Margaret Backstrom who came out of *The Harlem Playgirls* from back in the 1930s; Alto saxophonist Josephine Boyd who left to work at *Club DeLisa* (Chicago) with the *Red Saunders band*; Jessie Turner, a trombonist, she worked with Grey, Al a lot. Another fantastic trombonist, dancer, and singer was Sammy Lee Jett. She was a great showman, she would throw that slide out and catch it and Eddie taught them all that showmanship as he had with all the bands he was with. *(You can see Eddie do this trick in footage with Lunceford on YouTube.)* But you would only see or hear about them at their live shows, the big dances, the theaters. Tiny Davis had a great group with quite a few women from co-eds from Prairie View, Texas like Vernetta Davis. Melba Liston was a good friend of Eddie's, and there was great respect there. She was a great trombone player and arranger and she wrote arrangements for Dizzy, and all the big bands; a multitude of work. But they only bring this out after you die.

But Eddie was the thread through all of that. He knew all the girls and he would write and arrange for them. Vi Wilson and Maxine Knepper also worked with Eddie's bands. Max Roach's love was Jean Starr. One time at the *Apollo*, she hit Max over the head with her cornet and he just kept on playing the drums. When that curtain went down, he knocked her clear off the stage into a trunk! For a little girl, she raised so much hell. She would say, 'Oh so and so was so great, but… have you heard me?', with her hand on her hip. Sometimes it's been rewarding and sometimes it didn't seem rewarding." *Sarah McLawler*[211]

"I wasn't with the original Sweethearts, I worked with Anna Mae Winburn's band, but she called it The Sweethearts of Rhythm. I was just starting out, had never been on the road, didn't know all the songs, but I learned the book. Willeen Barton was in the band. Jean Starr and I look alike but she was shorter. So whenever we'd go into a small town, I'd tell them right away 'I'm not Jean Starr'. Cause we had the same first name and we both played trumpet, and we looked alike, but she raised so much hell everywhere she went." Trumpeter, *Eugenia "Jean" Davis*

"Eddie's other brother Earl, played sax. Very serious man. He did a lot of work with Eddie, he put a small group together for Eddie, all women. That part was with Carline Ray, Willeen Barton, trumpeter Gene Davis and a drummer Dolly [Dottie]. They came into the *Apollo* several times." *Rudi Sheriff Lawless*

Mary McLeod Bethune, founder of the National Council of Negro Women, obtained sponsorship from none other than Eleanor Roosevelt, for the ***Eddie Durham All-Stars*** girl orchestra, on a United Service Organization (U.S.O.) tour with a sleeper bus, sleeping 21 women, traveling 7 days a week, during WWII. "The road was virtually dead, with gas rationing, and bans on pleasure driving (which also included the buses carrying the bands). For the black male bands, unless they were the big names, …there were few opportunities for theater or location work since that went to the often inferior white male bands. *Eddie Durham's All-Stars*, however, had a sleeper bus and permission to ride all over with it, using it for their commercial jobs six days a week and giving the armed forces one day. …*That come through from Mrs.*

174

Bethune. You could drive it on the Capitol grounds... The band toured seventy-two army camps in Canada and Durham kept it going for the duration of the war." "When Eddie Durham hit the road with his African American all-girl band in 1943, he was often billed as '*the Sepia Phil Spitalny*,' to capitalize on the more famous leader's name recognition, even though Durham's band played swing hits of the day rather than the light classical fare, hymns, and patriotic hoopla favored by the 'Hour of Charm'.[212].

"There are not many attractions in the entertainment field that possess the versatility that abounds in Eddie Durham and His All Star Girl orchestra. The greatest aggregation of musical girls, led by the talented Durham, to appear at the *Manhattan Casino* on Feb. 14, all can double on another instrument, sing and dance, give class to a band that critics throughout the nation have voiced praise to the extent of selecting it as one possessing musical adroitness." *Tampa Bay Times* (Feb. 13, 1944)[213]

"Note, however, that one specialty of Durham's band was that it had flash drummer *Kid Lips Hackett*. ...A collection of pulchritude, sixteen sweethearts on parade, the Durham Girl orchestra has plenty of zing when it comes to swing." *The Weekly Review* (Birmingham) (Feb. 26, 1944)[214]

"Three outstanding stage attractions will appear in the Apollo's show for the week beginning this coming Friday. They are: Eddie Durham's all girl band, Trummy Young and his new band and Sister Tharpe. Eddie Durham is the arranger and conductor for the all-girl band which is now in its third year of existence." *The New York Age*, April 1944.

"Eddie Durham's colored girls 'orchestra, which played at the Auditorium, Thursday evening, and repeats performance tonight on behalf of the Kiwanis club's welfare fund, is far removed from any preconception you have of what an all-girl orchestra might sound like. Since Leader Eddie Durham is responsible for most of the arrangements, their music leans heavily on typical Basie and Kansas City style riffs and powerhouse drive. Most of the solo work is given to Margaret Backstrom, tenor sax, and Jackie King, a capable pianist... Vocalist is Madeline Vernon and First Alto Margie Lusk with "Lips" Hackett...veteran vaudeville drummer who injects a lot of showmanship into the proceedings with his clowning, freak dancing and clever pantomime. **Net proceeds will be used to assist the club to equip a modern playground for children in a congested Winnipeg district.**" *The Winnipeg Tribune* May 19, 1944.

When *V-J Day* came (September 2, 1945) he was on a location job at *Sweets' Ballroom* in California.[1]

Eddie recalled: "Played one week… headed back to New York, giving each woman a week's pay and drawing on a $1,000 donation to take them all back to their homes… I took the bus to everybody's home… I carried 'em to Las Vegas, …Reno, Nevada… to see all the events, anything their hearts desired on the way in, and dropped everybody home on the way out. The money was flowin' like water. The All-Star band was in the money. Could draw and play. We played opposite Louis Jordan right there [in Oakland]. Hamp come one night. You couldn't wash those girls away, though. They knew all the novelties too. That was some band."

"…and those chicks could swing!… Eddie Durham wrote their arrangements and traveled with them… He was hell on guitar, and he stayed

---

[1] See "***Swingin' The Blues Series (Vol. 2) EDDIE DURHAM & THE LADIES OF JAZZ***" for full details.
176

with the Sweethearts a long time. They could blow, and he knew it."[215] *T-Bone Walker*, Guitarist (1910-1975)

"After Durham returned to New York, he trained singer Jean Parks to take over fronting the *All-Stars*, and within several months, the formidable women had been reassembled as *Jean Parks's All-Girl Band*. Durham continued to travel with the unit as manager and the band did theater tours with such stars as Fitzgerald, Moms Mabley, and Butterbeans and Susie. Unfortunately, it disbanded less than one year later, when Jean Parks became ill. This was the last female big-band Durham was involved with, and by the end of the forties, the era of the big bands, male and female, had started drawing to a close." [216]

"Eddie Durham worked with my combo in 1950 and we wrote "My Whole Life Through." This is why I had so much deep respect for Eddie Durham because he was one of the few top musicians and arrangers who was interested in the female musicians. He had a girls band called *The Eddie Durham All-Stars* which was a seventeen-piece band of great musicians. He did so much for the women.

When I went to *Fisk University* we were playing Durham's and Lunceford's stock arrangements. The musicians in our college band were from *Tennessee State, Vaharry Medical & Dental, Vanderbilt* and *Fisk Universities* and we had a heck of a band. We played all the local [high] saditty Country Clubs. The guys would always try to pick out the most difficult songs like "Body and Soul," "Sophisticated Lady" and of course we knew all of them. But the younger musicians, like Dizzy, Wynton Marsalis, and James Carter, were very appreciative. Carter recorded a live instrumental of "**My Whole Life Through**" in 2011 on his *At The Crossroads* CD.

But I never saw Eddie angry. Some of those musicians used to give him a fit, especially those girls like Heddy Smith and Ella Reese Thompson and Eddie would just smile and say," *That's not correct, play it over again.*" He would never raise his voice.

I knew about Eddie Durham from *The International Sweethearts of Rhythm* band. In that band was Tiny Davis, who eventually left and formed her own group called *The Hell Divers*. There was Vi Burnside, an outstanding saxophonist who also left and formed her own group. There was Jean Starr from Georgia, an outstanding trumpeter who I think studied to be a doctor. Jean Doody and Pauline Braddy were excellent drummers. On Alto tenor was Myrtle Young, and vocalist/bassist Margaret *Trump* Margo - fantastic performers. These were all friends of mine. Miss Jones was their chaperone. This was the glamour band - they were all light, fair-skinned.

Then, Roxy Lucas formed her band in Detroit. Little groups started showing up all over the place. Miss Jones was the chaperone of *The Sweethearts* and she was a very strict lady, like those proper ladies you see in the movies. *The Sweethearts* came out of *Piney Woods Orphanage*. In fact, *The Harlem Playgirls* members came into *The Eddie Durham All-Stars* band. Lela Julius led *The Harlem Playgirls*. She could sing and sight read, she played trombone, violin, and guitar. Alyse Wills had perfect international pitch, played over 20 instruments (she toured with Tommy Dorsey). She'd give the band a note from her voice and they would tune from that. Betty Roudybush, a pro pianist who could play like Mary Lou Williams. Marian Gange, guitarist. Betty Sattley, hot tenor saxophonist was part of our strong line-up."[217] ***Sarah McLawler***

Trio: Willie Mae Wong, Nova Lee McGee, Grace Bayron *Full personnel listing/Appendix "A"*

"I was just starting out, hanging around trying to meet musicians. Eddie invited me to the studio and right on the spot he wrote an arrangement for me of "That Ol' Rockin' Chair Got Me." Eddie was very quiet and we never knew where he lived. If you wanted Eddie you had to ask for him or run into him at a show. He always kept his family separate. I want everybody to say, '*Eddie Durham wrote it, or arranged it*' when they play his charts recorded by everybody else." ***Jean Davis***, trumpeter

In the 1940s when women were not always welcomed or seriously respected as musicians, Eddie Durham assisted women into the Music Unions across the United States. As musical director, composer and arranger, he mentored Mary Lou Williams, *The Sweethearts of Rhythm,* and also showcased, not one, but three of his all-women bands: *The Eddie Durham All-Stars, The Durhamettes,* and *The Darlings of Rhythm.* The importance of becoming a Union Member was because of the Union's national rule that when a traveling act came to town, two to three local Members *had* to be hired whether they performed or not. [2]

"Eddie Durham's colored girls' orchestra, which played at the Auditorium, Thursday evening, and repeats performance tonight on behalf of the Kiwanis club's welfare fund, is far removed from any preconception you have of what an all-girl orchestra might sound like. Since Leader Eddie Durham is responsible for most of the arrangements, their music leans heavily on typical Basie and Kansas City style riffs and powerhouse drive. Most of the solo work is given to Margaret Backstrom, tenor sax, and Jackie King, a capable pianist... Vocalist is Madeline Vernon and First Alto Margie Lusk with "Lips" Hackett...veteran vaudeville drummer who injects a lot of showmanship into the proceedings with his clowning, freak dancing and clever pantomime. Net proceeds will be used to assist the club to equip a modern playground for children in a congested Winnipeg district." *The Winnipeg Tribune* May 19, 1944[218]

---

[2] See "*Swingin' The Blues Series (Vol. 2) EDDIE DURHAM & THE LADIES OF JAZZ*" for full details.

"When he left the Sweethearts, he took some musicians with him and was also able to convince some members of another all-girl band from *Piney Woods*, the *Swinging Rays of Rhythm* (who were still with the school), to join his band. In turn, the *Darlings of Rhythm* core personnel consisted of musicians recruited out of Durham's band. In the summer of 1944, Gale launched a unique relationship with the *Prairie View Co-Eds.* [school]. When Durham gave up his band in November 1944, he continued to manage a group made of remaining members and fronted by Jean Parks. Traveling in private cars, the Co-Eds covered a great deal of segregated territory on a route that was often physically and emotionally grueling. ...It is no small matter that such bands as the *International Sweethearts of Rhythm, Anna Mae Winburn's Sweethearts of Rhythm, Eddie Durham's All-Star Girl Orchestra*, and the *Darlings of Rhythm* proved, well before Freedom Summer, that the holes in Jim Crow were big enough to drive a bus through. ...Many women got a chance to see parts of the world they would never otherwise have seen, to experience unprecedented popularity both as entertainers and as women, and to gather extraordinary adventures and memories beyond everyday Homefront life."[219]

Eddie Durham and Chuck Darwyn wrote "*Good Lookin' Fella*" sang by Mabel Scott in 1947 released by *Exclusive Records*.

180

Marriages/Children

Sometime during his tenure with the Blue Devils but before joining Bennie Moten, Eddie fathers his first child, Eddie, Jr., with Hattie Donaldson in December 1928, out of wedlock. They live in Washington, D.C. but Eddie is mostly on the road.

Eddie's first wedded marriage was on July 21, 1930 in Kansas City - a triple courthouse wedding with Willie "Mac" Washington and William Basie. His first daughter, Mabel Ruth, is born in 1935.

Eddie recalled: *"I married the prettiest girl in Kansas, and she stayed in the newspapers. We had our reception through the streets of Kansas City"*.

Eddie's second marriage was on April 23, 1939 in Indiana, to Earsie Bell Hiller. "Bell" played trombone in the *Eddie Durham All-Stars* and was with him during his tenure with Glenn Miller and on the USO Tours. His final marriage is to Lillian in 1961 in New York.

Eddie Durham, Sr.   Eddie Durham, Jr. with his mom & dad   Ed Durham, Jr. & Mabel Ruth with their dad Eddie Durham, Sr. (D.C. 1951)

Hattie Donaldson

"In the mid-1940s Eddie Durham came into my life when I must have been about 12 years old. At 2006 Amsterdam Avenue in Harlem, my family moved into Apartment #5 in October. Eddie moved into Apt. #6, probably December 1943. His wife was Earsie Bell Hiller, we called her Bell, she was a musician. Their daughter was Mabel Ruth. Mable grew to like all the roughness of the gangster life, bars and clubs all night, speakeasy's (speak low, keep the cops away) and after hour spots. The musicians were always so busy and I liked that movement of always going in and out. I was into Jazz and Swing Music because I danced. My whole family danced. Across the hall from Eddie, in Apt. #3 was Ray Hogan, from the Erskine Hawkins band. At 377 Edgecomb lived Sonny Rollins and in the neighborhood was J.C. Heard and Jimmy Crawford (who introduced me to Arnett Cobb & Johnny Griffin, who were related). I met Jimmy Shirley, who had a guitar & bass custom made all in one. Guitarist Lee Pope lived around the corner on Edgecomb." Drummer *"Rudi Sheriff Lawless"*

Eddie's mom Luella, died in 1945, having the joy of several grandchildren. His first mentor and eldest brother, Joe Jr. died in 1947. They saw Eddie reach his pinnacle of fame and fortune. Eddie returned to California where his cousins Allen and Clyde were, and he is not happy about what he has been hearing.

The Ink Spots

"Of historical significance - this is one of the songs that Bill Kenny and *The Ink Spots* recorded. In those days there were popular songs that became a part of everybody's life. This was before the advent of television, so radio played a large part in most people's lives, as people discussed current things today, people were talking about Bill Kenny and *The Ink Spots*. Both Al Grey and I performed "I Don't Want To Set The World On Fire" many times because we had a chance with Basie's band to perform with *The Ink Spots*." **Benny Powell**

Eddie recalled: "In 1948 I went to California where Allen [Durham] was playing. He had just left Allen Barry and Lionel Hampton's band and had a gig up in Chicago as a D.J. and I was out there with the Ink Spots."

END of *Volume One* of the *Swingin' The Blues Series.*

Swingin' The Blues Series:

Volume 2 - "Eddie Durham & The Ladies of Jazz" (1927-1987)

Volume 3 – "A Century of Secrets (1950-2013)"

Volume 4 – "Eddie Durham and The Harlem Blues & Jazz Band" (1980s)

Visit ***DurhamJazz.com*** for updates and links to all social media.

Please write about your reading experience on whichever site you purchased this Volume from.

To enhance this book, visit the *"Eddie Durham" youtube channel* for videos and Pictorial Discographies, featuring rare family photos (to the backdrop the song *"Fallin"*, written by Eric Durham, Sr.) among other live performances around the world.

Written during the COVID19 Pandemic (2019-2021).

APPENDIX A

Joseph Durham, Jr.

- Brass bass, trumpet, violin, cello, piano, arranger, musical director

President Theodore Roosevelt's Roughriders - ***Homecoming Band*** (Musical Director)

1922-29 *Durham Brothers (Jazzy) Orchestra; E.Battle's Dixie Ramblers* (M.D., arr., bb, violin)

1929 *Elmer Payne and his Ten Royal Americans*

1930 *Jasper "Jap" Allen* (tpt)

1931 *Blanche Calloway* (bb)

     Nathaniel "Nat King" Cole

-Recordings:

"*Blanche Calloway and Her Joy Boys*" (1931)

Personnel Blanche Calloway (vocals/Dir.), **Durham, Jr. (bb)**, Edgar Battle (ar), Joe Keyes, Clarence Smith (tpts); Cozy Cole (dr), Ben Webster (ts)

Alton Moore (tb), Booker Pitman (cl/as), Leroy Hardy (as), Clyde Hart (p), Andy Jackson (bj/g), Bill Massey (vocals)

Camden, New Jersey, March 27 – November 18, 1931 recordings:

March 27, 1931

"Just A Crazy Song (Hi Hi Hi)," "Sugar Blues," "I'm Gettin' Myself Ready For You," "Loveless Love"

-May 8, 1931

"Misery," "It's Right Here For You"

-June 11, 1931 (Herb Alvis - tb added)

"It Looks Like Susie," "Without That Gal!," "When I Can't Be With You",

"Make Me Know It (If You Mean What You Say!)," "Timely Tunes"? (as "Fred Armstrong and his Syncopators")

-November 18, 1931

"I Got What It Takes," "Growlin' Dan," "Concentratin' On You," "Last Dollar," "Blue Memories"

Earl Durham
- Bandleader, tenor/baritone sax

1916-1929 *Durham Brothers (Jazzy) Orchestra* (bandleader); *E. Battle's Dixie Ramblers*

1930s Minstrels; and lead a band in Hartford, Connecticut, where they called him the king of tenor and baritone saxophone, and clarinet.

1940's *The International Sweethearts of Rhythm* ten-week national radio run: "The Choice Hour".

Unable to locate any recordings of Earl Durham. Perhaps the radio broadcasts will surface one day.

Clyde Durham

- Brass bass

1916-1929 *Durham Brothers (Jazzy) Orchestra*; *E. Battle's Dixie Ramblers*

Armed Forces Radio Service transcription sessions, known as "Jubilee" programs recorded specifically for black servicemen in World War II.

Roosevelt Durham

- Fiddle/violin, piano, vocals

1916-1929 *Durham Brothers (Jazzy) Orchestra*; *E. Battle's Dixie Ramblers*

Unable to locate any recordings of Roosevelt Durham.

Herschel Evans

- Tenor sax, clarinet

1916-1929 *Durham Brothers (Jazzy) Orchestra*; *E. Battle's Dixie Ramblers*

Partial discography:

Troy Floyd's Shadowland Orch. *(Texas June 21, 1929-31 (w/Buddy Tate)* *(Scott Wenzel: https://mosaicrecords.tumblr.com/ Shadowland Orchestra, led by reedman Troy Floyd, recorded this rarity in San Antonio on June 21, 1929 for the Okeh label, and features what might be the first recorded solo by Herschel Evans.)*

Bennie Moten's Kansas City Orchestra (1933-35) – Evans never recorded with Moten.

Jones Chicago Cosmopolitans (Sept.1935) (rare but on YouTube)

Mildred Bailey (NYC June 1937 w/Buck Clayton)

Count Basie (1936-Dec.1939 **w/Eddie Durham** & Buck Clayton)

Harry James (NYC Dec.1937 & Jan.1938 **w/Eddie Durham** & Buck Clayton)

Teddy Wilson (NYC Oct.-Nov.1938 w/Harry James & Billie Holiday)

Lionel Hampton (NYC July/Jam Session Dec.1938) at The Paradise Cafe

Full discography by Jan Evansmo: http://www.jazzarcheology.com/artists/herschel_evans.pdf

Allen Durham

-Trombone

1916-1929 *Durham Brothers (Jazzy) Orchestra*; *E. Battle's Dixie Ramblers*

-**_Soundies_** (contributed by **_Mark Cantor_**):

Les Hite Orchestra (Soundtrack Feb. 23; Filming Feb. 25 & 26, 1942):

Mills Panoram Film Jukebox "That Old Ghost Train" - https://youtu.be/2CMLjdji6UA

Pudgy Boy - https://youtu.be/Q4cjOQolrLA

What To Do (*Savannah Churchill-voc)

The Devil Sat Down and Cried*

Film: Fools For Scandal 1938 - "There's A Boy In Harlem" - https://youtu.be/kiEgxIAueu0

-**Recordings**:

Andy Kirk and his Twelve Clouds of Joy (1929-31)

Personnel:

Andy Kirk (brass bass, bass sax), **Allen Durham (tb)**, Mary Lou Williams (arr, p), Edward McNeil (dr), John Harrington (cl/as), John Williams (as, bs), Lawrence Freeman (ts), William Dirvin (bj/g), Bill Massey (vo-*), Gene Prince, Harry Lawson (tpts); Lawson (vo**), Dick Roberts (vo***)

KMBC Radio, Kansas City Missouri, Nov. 7, 1929 recordings of:

KC591   "Mess-A-Stomp" (Williams)

KC592A   "Blue Clarinet Stomp" (Kirk)**

KC592B   "Blue Clarinet Stomp" **

KC593   "Cloudy" (Kirk)

November 8, 1929

KC596   "Casey Jones Special" (Kirk)

John Williams and his Memphis Stompers (same personnel)

KC600   "Somepin' Slow and Low" (Williams)

KC601   "Lotta Sax Appeal" (Williams)

Andy Kirk and his Twelve Clouds of Joy:

November 11, 1929

KC618   "Corky Stomp" (Kirk, Williams)

KC619   "Froggy Bottom" (Williams)

Chicago, April 29, 1930 **Edgar Battle (tpt)** replaces Prince

C4460A   "I Lost My Girl From Memphis"*

C4462A   "Loose Ankles" (Kirk, Williams)*

Chicago, April 30, 1930

C4470   "Snag It" (Oliver)

C4471   "Sweet And Hot" (Freeman)

C4472 "Mary's Idea" (Williams)

Chicago, May 1, 1930

C4480 "Once or Twice" (Cobb)

Mary Lou Williams, piano solos

C5724 "Night Life" (Williams)

C5725 "Drag 'Em" (M.L. Williams)

Seven Little Clouds of Joy: A. Durham, Lawson, Harington & rhythm section only:

Chicago, July 15, 1930

6017"Getting' Off A Mess" (Williams)

Andy Kirk and his Twelve Clouds of Joy (full band):

Chicago, October 9, 1930

C6430 "Dallas Blues" (Ward, Garatt)*

C6431 "Travelin' That Rocky Road" (Lovett, Smith)

C6432 "Honey, Just For You" (Freeman)*

C6433 "You Rascal, You" (Theard)*

New York, December 15, 1930

E35750 "Saturday" (Mitchell, Brooks)***

E3571 "Sophomore" (Hill, Causer)***

(1931)

Buck Clayton (1936)

T-Bone Walker and The Les Hite Orchestra

Recordings New York, June 1940:

Frank Pasley (g), T-Bone Walker (g/voc); **Allen Durham**, Britt Woodman (tb); Les Hite, Floyd Turnham (as); Quedellis Martyn, Roger Hurd (ts); Sol Moore (bs); Paul G. Campbell, Walter Williams, Forrest Powell (tpt); Nat Walker (p); Al Morgan (b); Oscar Bradley (d),

Varsity 8391, Blue Note 530, Elite X 10 (circa June 1940)

"Waiting For You" VAR 8396

"Board Meeting" VAR 8373

"T-Bone Blues" VAR 8391

"The World Is Waiting For The Sunrise"

"Board Meeting"

"That's the Lick"

"It Must Have Been A Dream"

"That's The Lick"

*Victor Bluebird March 6, 1941:

"Board Meetin'"

"That's the Lick"

Bluenote Records

"T-Bone Blues" (re-released)

Hit Records

c. January, or more likely June 1942 (Dizzy Gillespie, Allen Durham)

Les Hite (MD), Joe Wilder, Walter Williams, Dizzy Gillespie (tpt), **Allen Durham**, Leon Comegys, Al Cobbs (tb), John Brown, Floyd Turnham (as), Quedellis Martyn, Roger Herd (ts), Sol Moore (bs), Gerald Wiggins (p), Frank Pasley (g), Benny Booker (b), Oscar Bradley (d), Jimmy Anderson (*vo):

"I Remember You"

"Jersey Bounce"

"Idaho"

"One Dozen Roses"*

Eric Durham, Sr.

-Guitar

Funk band CAMEO LP's: "Cardiac Arrest" (1977)

"We All Know Who We Are" (1978),

"Ugly Ego" (1978) - All of the guitar work (electric, rhythm & lead).

Co-composer "Anything You Wanna Do" and "Stand Up".

Brooklyn Express/singles: "Spank-69" (1981), B side "Change Position-88" (guitar)

-arranger, composer

The Village People

Renato Zero (Italy)

Howard Kenny

Michael "Murch" Powers: *"Bluesiana Breeze"* CD: track "Istanbul" (Powers: guitars, Eric Durham: electronic orchestra, keyboards, bass).

Our dad used to always tell us *"I left you millions, but you're gonna have to dig for it."* So… I say'd that to say this: We are still digging, and things are still turning up! This is therefore not a definitive discography and hopefully it will be perfected someday, with the help of those reading this book.

Eddie Durham

- Guitar, slide & valve trombone, arranger, composer, choreographer:

1916-1929 *Durham Brothers (Jazzy) Orchestra*; *E. Battle's Dixie Ramblers*

-Soundies

Jimmie Lunceford and his Orchestra with *The Three Brown Jacks* and Myra Johnson "You Can't Pull The Wool Over My Eyes," "Rhythm Is Our Business*"* (1935 Vitaphone) **Durham** on tb, stage left/top/center. Directed by Joseph Henabery. (This DVD footage is an added feature on the film *Follow The Fleet* with Fred Astaire and Ginger Rogers-same year).

Born To Swing, (1972 BBC's 50m film documentary) focuses on surviving member of the Count Basie Band. Appearances include Count Basie, Buck Clayton, **Eddie Durham**, Papa Jo Jones, Snub Mosely, Joe Newman, Buddy Tate, Earle Warren with commentary by Gene Krupa, John Hammond, Andy Kirk.

Last Of The Blue Devils (1974 *Rhapsody Films*, 90m documentary) based on *The Oklahoma Blue Devils Orchestra* reunion at the *Musician's Union Hall* in Kansas City. Performances include Count Basie, Big Joe Turner, Jay McShann and **Eddie Durham**, focusing on Kansas City music more than any specific band. Produced by Bruce Ricker.

Eddie Durham Recordings:
Laura Henton

Kansas City, early November 1929

"Gospel Classics" 1927 - 1931 The Complete Recorded Works of Jessie May Hill, Laura Henton, Blind Willie Davis, Louisville Sanctified Singers and Unknowns. On "*Document Records*" #DOCD-5190. Total of 25 tracks on this CD with the tracks categorized "A-J" to distinguish Personnel. According to the liner notes, the four "i" - tracks 20-23 are ***Durham*** *on guitar* with Laura Henton (vocals, acc); Bennie Moten (p); Joe [or Vernon?] Page (tu):

"Just Can't Help From Crying"

"I Can Tell the World About Jesus"

"Plenty Good Room in my Father's Kingdom"

"Lord You Sure Been Good To Me".

Bennie Moten

Chicago Oct. 23/24, 1929

Bennie Moten (ldr), Ira "Buster" Moten (accordion), **Eddie Durham** (tb, g, arr), Count Basie (p), Leroy Berry (bjo), Thamon Hayes (tb), Harlan Leonard, Ed Lewis (sax), Vernon Page (bb), Woody Walder, Jack Washington (reeds), Booker Washington (clnt), Willie Mac Washington (dm).

"...heavy rhythm, slap-tonguing reeds, accordion, Rushing's vocal and Eddie Durham's solo guitar, and it sets the stage for good guitar performances. One can see Durham as an important pioneer on solo - and later electric guitar in jazz and popular music.

[On] "Band Box Shuffle" the descending 9th chords (dominant 7th with the 9th added) in the intro and coda are an early Durham arranging signature, as we will see repeatedly. The "pyramid" section uses a popular arranging device of the time in Eddie's style, again using 9th chords. **Dan Weinstein**[220]

Ten titles were recorded for Victor, seven have guitar soli:

57301-1 "Rumba Negro"	Solo 8 bars. (FM)
57303-1 "Band Box Shuffle"	Solo 16 bars. (FM)
57304-2 "Small Black"	Solo 8 bars. Coda. (FM)
57304-3 "Small Black"	As above (FM)
57305-2 "Every Day Blues"	Soli 16 and 6 bars (M)
57312-3 "Boot It"	Solo 4 bars. (M)
57315-1R "New Vine Street Blues"	As below (SM)
57315-2 "New Vine Street Blues"	Solo 24 bars. (SM)
57316-2 "Sweetheart Of Yesterday"	Solo 30 bars. (F)

Moten - Kansas City Oct. 27-31, 1930

Personnel as above plus Hot Lips Page (tp), Jimmie Rushing (vo). Eighteen titles were recorded for Victor, seven have guitar:

62910-1 "I Wish I Could Be Blue"	Intro 4 bars. (M)
62910-2 "I Wish I Could Be Blue"	As above. (M)
62912-1 "That Too Do"	Obbligato wth (acc) og (p) 24 bars. (M)
62912-2 "That Too Do"	As above. (M)
62914-1 "You Made Me Happy"	Solo 8 bars. (M)
62921-1 "Liza"	Obbligato 32 bars. (FM)
62921-2 "Liza"	As above. (FM)
62922-2 "Get' Goin'"	Soli 4 and 4 bars. (FM)
62923-1 "Professor Hot Stuff"	Solo 30 bars. (F)
62924-2 "When I'm Alone"	Soli 8 and 16 bars. (FM)

Moten, New York City April 15, 1931

Same. Two titles, one has guitar:
68900-2 "I Wanna Be Around My Baby"   Soli with orch 24 and 8 bars. (M)
Also on these sessions there are several original guitar soli. Certainly these sides show Eddie Durham to be the most under rated of guitar performers in jazz.

Moten, Summer 1929 - Camden, New Jersey Dec. 13, 1932

Hot Lips Page, Joe Keyes, Dee Stewart (tp), Dan Minor (tb), **Eddie Durham** (tb, g), Eddie Barefield (cl, as), Jack Washington (as, bar), Ben Webster (ts), Count Basie (p), Leroy Berry (g), Walter Page (b), Willie "Mac" Washington (dm), Jimmie Rushing, Josephine Garrison (vo), The Sterling Russell Trio (vo-group, Sterling Russell, Hamilton Stewart, Clifton Armstrong), Bennie Moten (ldr). Ten titles were recorded for Victor, five have guitar:

74846-1 "Toby"   Solo 8 bars. (F)

74847-1 "Moten Swing"   Solo 8 bars. (FM)

74849-1 "Imagination"   Intro 8 bars. Obbligato (vo-group)

"Imagination" features guitar all the way through, though most prominent in the first half, and he makes the most out of it. No longer is it only a 'vocal-group'- record, although of good quality, but a real guitar gasser!"

48 bars. Solo 4 bars. More obbl. (SM)

74851-1 "The Only Girl I Ever Loved" Brief break. (M)

74855-1 "Two Times"   In orch. (M)

Eddie Durham annotating full personnel:

The castanets in the song "Rumba Negro (Spanish Stomp)," could be likened to the tapping on his father, Joe, Sr.'s fiddle.

"Rumba Negro (Spanish Stomp)" (Basie/Moten)

Ed Lewis:	*first horn solo*
Eddie Durham:	*tb solo*
Woody Walder:	*cl*
Bennie Moten:	*p*
Vernon Page:	*tuba (could not play string bass)*
Buster Moten:	*Dir.*

"Jones Laws Blues" (take 3 & 2) - *Basie/Moten*

Eddie Durham:	*Arr., metal-bodied g., tb*
Take 3:	
Harlan Leonard:	*1st soloist after tpt intro*
Leroy (Buster) Berry:	*Banjo solo*
Take 2:	
Harlan Leonard	
Leroy (Buster) Barry:	*Banjo solo*
Eddie Durham:	*tb solo*
Bennie Moten:	*p*
Ed Lewis:	*(Intro and at the end)*
Buster Moten:	*Dir.*

"Band Box Shuffle" - *Basie/Moten*

Durham   Arr., metal-bodied g., tb
Ed Lewis: first horn solo
Eddie Durham: g. Solo
Buster Moten: Accordion
"I can't tell whose on p., could be Basie".

"Small Black" (Take 3 & 2) - Basie/Moten ED Arr.

Parallel 9th's again, before Basie's solo and before the next to last chorus. Dan Weinstein.
Edited Basie's p. solo out of take 3 and put it IN take 2. **Dan Weinstein**

Harlan "Mike" Leonard: 1st sax solo

Bill Basie: p.

Eddie Durham: Stella acoustic g. solo

Take 2

Bill Basie: p.

sounds like Ed Lewis 3 tpt solos:

Same tone sound like the solo... When other guys around too long, they pick up the same style.

Woody Walter: cl (both takes)

Buster Moten: accordion

Eddie Durham: resonator g. solos

"Everyday Blues (Yo-Yo Blues)" (Durham/Moten) R*esonator g.*

Durham: Arr., metal-bodied tb & resonator g. solo

Tenor spot in the middle of my solo…perhaps Jack Washington, 'cause he could play pretty high.
Willie didn't play that smooth, couldn't have been him.

October 24, 1929 – Victor Recordings:

Eddie Durham: Arr., metal-bodied g. & tb solo

"Boot It"

(The flip side of Every Day Blues): trombone solos (8 bars and 32 bars). The real revelations of this record, aside from Eddie's great arranging and harmonic devices, are his trombone solos. Thamon Hayes had been Moten's original trombonist, and his mostly middle range, down-home style is easily identifiable before this date. The style of the trombone solos here is quite different, requiring virtuoso technique and high range, along with a very modern (for the time) tonal conception. **Dan Weinstein**

"Mary Lee"

Some parallel 7th's early in the record, but also 9th's toward the end. **Dan Weinstein**

"Rit Dat Ray"

The descending 9th's in the intro are the same as "Squabblin," one of only two sides recorded by Walter Page's Blue Devils two months after this record. **Dan Weinstein**

"New Vine Street Blues" (Moten/Basie)

Eddie Durham   Arr., metal-bodied g. & tb

Durham guitar solo (24 bars). Durham's guitar solo stands out here, with his phrases in bar 14 and especially bar 16 being very "outside" the tonality... it certainly is wild. **Dan Weinstein**

"Sweethearts of Yesterday" (Moten/Hold/Sanders)

guitar solo (30 bars). Durham has a great guitar solo, his longest to this date. Hayes takes the trombone solo.

October 27, 1929 - Victor Recordings

"Won't You Be My Baby" (Moten/Rushing)

Kansas City - Victor Recordings

   October 28, 1930

Bennie Moten - Leader, Dir., **Eddie Durham (arr), (g) & (tb)**; Thamon Hayes (tb);

Buster Moten - pac, (p) Count Basie (p);

Oran "Hot Lips" Page?, Ed Lewis, Booker Washington - (tpt)

Harlan Leonard (clt), (ss), (as); Woody Walder - (clt), (ts);

Jack Washington** (clr), (as), (bs); Willie "Mac" Washington** (d);

Vernon Page (tuba); Leroy "Buster" Berry (b); Jimmy Rushing (v)

*Although all performers are listed (above), the discography focuses on composers and Eddie Durham's multiple roles, per song. (**cousins)*

"The Count" - Gordon

"I Wish I Could Be Blue" (Durham/Moten/Basie)

"That Too, Do" (**Durham**/Moten/Basie)

Guitar prominent under vocal. The two vocal choruses each became separate titles ("Good Morning Blues" and "Sent For You Yesterday") under Basie 7 years later. **Dan Weinstein**

"Oh, Eddie!" (**Durham**/Moten)

Trombone break (2 bars). Eddie Durham- the tb break toward the end. **Dan Weinstein**
...the last chorus sketches out ideas that later turned up in Moten Swing..." **Martin Williams**

"You Made Me Happy" (**Durham**/Moten)

Guitar solo (8 bars). Never released on 78rpm... A Durham composition/arrangement, not far behind "I Wish I Could Be Blue." Featuring mostly 4 beat tuba and a trombone solo, also an ascending chromatic parallel 9th's interlude, similar to 4½ years later for Lunceford's recording of Duke Ellington's "Bird of Paradise." **Dan Weinstein**

x

October 29, 1930 – *NOTE:* ***Dan Weinstein****

"Liza Lee" (Green/Stept)

Guitar accompaniment to Rushing vocal. 9th's in the second chorus and nice harmonic sequence in the modulation to the vocal. ***Dan Weinstein***

October 30, 1930

"Get Goin' (Get Ready)" (Seymour/Rich)

Guitar solo (4 bars + 4 bars). Block horn voicings and interesting modulation to the vocal. ***Dan Weinstein***

"Professor Hot Stuff" (**Durham**/Moten/Basie)

Guitar solo (30 bars). 20 bars of 9th's in the intro, followed by parallel augmented chords. The melody here is very similar to Moten Swing. ***Dan Weinstein***

"When I'm Alone" (Moten/Rushing)

Guitar solos (8 bars + 16 bars). The flip side of "I Wish I Could Be Blue," a spirited medium up-tempo romp ...helped immensely by Durham's great chart and Vernon Page's 4 beat tuba throughout. ***Dan Weinstein***

"When I'm Alone...shows the tempo at which the four-beat swing of the later band was worked out. Also, watch the hints of things to come in those crisp brass figures at the end." As we have seen in "I Wish I Could Be Blue," the Moten band also used 4 beat bass at this point on slower numbers, at least as fashioned by Eddie Durham. ***Martin Williams****:*

"New Moten Stomp" (Moten)

"As Long As I Love You" (Moten/Wood)

One bar chases between brass and saxes and a bridge similar to Moten Swing. ***Dan Weinstein***

October 31, 1930

"Somebody Stole My Gal" (Leo Wood) (Rushing-vo)

"Now That I Need You" (Moten/Basie/Smith)

Trombone solo (16 bars). Tight brass voicings and use of augmented chords. The speed, range and facility of the trombone solo are right out of Durham's toolkit. ***Dan Weinstein***

"Bouncin' Around" (Moten)

April 15, 1931

"Ya Got Love" (Goodhart/Nelson/Hoffman)

Rushing vocal, with faint Durham guitar backup. ***Dan Weinstein***

"I Wanna Be Around My Baby All The Time" (Young/Meyer)

-These [two] are the only 1931 recordings by Moten. Durham on "I Wanna Be Around...," plays a lot of obbligato guitar to the melody and to the vocal.[221] Durham is more audible on guitar in the first and last choruses.

Camden, NJ - Victor Recordings:

December 13, 1932

Bennie Moten - Leader, Dir.

Durham: (arr) (g) (tb)

Eddie Durham (ED) (g); Dan Minor (T. Hayes) & Durham (tbs);

Joe Keyes, Dee "Prince" Stewart, Oran "Hot Lips" Page (tpts); (E. Lewis & B. Washington); Eddie Barefield (cl, a-sax) (H. Leonard); Jack Washington - (as) (bs); Willie "Mac" Washington (d); Ben Webster (t-sax) (W. Walder);

Count Basie (p); Leroy "Buster" Berry (g,/banjo)

Walter Page (b) (V. Page/tuba); Jimmy Rushing - (v)

Sterling Russell, Hamilton Stewart, Clifton Armstrong (*The Sterling Russell Trio*) (v)

"Toby" (Buster Moten/Eddie Barefield), **Eddie Durham arr, g**

I arranged Blue Room, Toby and Milenberg Joys, maybe a little touch on Prince of Wales [Moten Swing and any of his own compositions]. Eddie Durham.

-g.solo (8 bars), tb solo (8 bars)

"Moten Swing" (Buster & Bennie Moten), arr, g & uncredited as composer

"The Blue Room" (Richard Rodgers/Lorenz Hart), arr

"Imagination" (Russell) , g

Guitar intro (8 bars), g. solo (5 bars) and prominent fills throughout. The recording balance brings Walter Page's bass and Durham's g. to the forefront. **Dan Weinstein**

"New Orleans" (Hoagy Carmichael, Sr.)

"The Only Girl I Ever Loved" (Basil Ziegler) arr, g

Durham g. solo (3 bars). Heard in sequence after "New Orleans," this sounds more modern, with ED's use of parallel 9th's, added 13th's in the intro and his patented tight brass voicing support. A Moten Swing referencing last 8 and a final modified pyramid. **Dan Weinstein**

"Milenberg Joys" (Roppolo-Mares-Morton-Melrose), arr

Jelly Roll Morton's Dixieland standard is restructured, reharmonized and cast in a brighter key, a whole step up from the original. The sax soli, similar to "Blue Room" is Durham's [arranging] authorship, as is the 4 bar chases between Barefield and Webster with brilliant brass backgrounds. Excitement with the faster tempo. **Dan Weinstein**

"Lafayette" (**Durham**/Basie), arr

"Prince of Wales" (Schoebel), ½ arr

The Savory Collection 1935-1940

WNEW remote broadcast, "Carnival of Swing" May 29, 1938

Personnel performing: **Eddie Durham: arr+, c*,** Henry "Buster" Smith: arr, Martin Block: announcer, Helen Humes, Jimmy Rushing: vocals

Buck Clayton, Harry Edison Ed Lewis: tpt

Earle Warren: as, Jack Washington: as, bari

Herschel Evans, Lester Young: cl, ts

Count Basie: p, Freddie Green: g, Jo Jones: d, Walter Page: b,

Eddie Durham, Dan Minor, Bennie Morton: trombones

"One O'Clock Jump+," "Every Tub+*," "Boogie Woogie," "Farewell Blues+," "Moten Swing+"

Willie Bryant

New York, January 4, 1935: "Chimes At The Meeting"- **Eddie Durham: arr**

Victor Recordings, New York, May-Aug.1935

Personnel:

Willie Bryant: leader/vo/talking; **Eddie Durham**, Alex Hill: arr

Robert "Mack" Horton, John "Shorty" Haughton: tb

Edgar Battle, Richard Clark, Benny Carter: tpt

Stanley Payne & Glyn Paque: cl, a-sax; Ben Webster & Johnny Russell: t-sax

Teddy Wilson: p; Arnold Adams: g; Louis Thompson: b; Cozy Cole: d

New York, May 8, 1935

"Rigamarole" (Harold Mooney) tb

"Long About Midnight" (Irving Mills, Alex Hill) tb

"The Sheik" (Ted Snyder) tb

"Jerry the Junker" (Clarence A. Stout, Clarence Williams) tb

August 1, 1935

"The Voice of Old Man River"

"Steak and Potatoes"

"Long Gone from Bowling Green"

"Liza"

Jimmie Lunceford

Jimmie Lunceford: Leader/Dir (as) on "Sleepy Time Gal"

Eddie Durham, Russell Bowles, Elmer Crumbley: tbs; Durham: a, c, g

Willie Smith: arr, as, bs, cl, vo

Eddie Tompkins, Sy Oliver, Paul Webster: trumpets (tpts); Oliver vo, arr

Laforet Dent & Dan Grissom: as; Grissom: cl, vo

Joe Thomas: ts, cl; Earl Carruthers: bars, as, cl; Edwin Wilcox: p, cel, arr

Al Norris: alternate g, vi; Moses Allen: b; Jimmy Crawford: d, vibes, glsp bells.

Vitaphone Soundtrack: Myra Johnson (vo) & Three Brown Jacks: Tap Dance.

For a complete *Lunceford* discography, purchase "The Jimmie Lunceford Legacy on Records" by Bertil Lyttkens, among others. Although all performers are listed, this discography focuses on composers (after the song title) and **Durham's** multiple roles (on trombone unless otherwise noted):

May 29, 1935 NYC (see retake September 23)

*Six titles were recorded for Decca, three have **Durham's guitar**:*

"Babs" (Ahlert/Young)

"Bird of Paradise" (Duke Ellington) **arr, g**

"Four or Five Times" 2 versions (Gay/Hellman) tb

"Rhapsody Jr." (Duke Ellington) **arr, g**

"Hittin' The Bottle" (Harold Arlen/Gorney/Harburg/Ted Koehler) (vocals-Sy Oliver; **g**, tb *Durham's historic seminal recording of amplified metal-bodied Dobro resophonic, non-electric **guitar**.*

"(If I had) Rhythm In My Nursery Rhymes" (Cahn/Ray/JL/Chaplin)

"Runnin' Wild" (Gibbs/Grey/Wood)

"Sleepy Time Gal" (Lorenzo/Whiting)

September 23, 1935

"Oh Boy" (**Eddie Durham**) c, arr, tb

"Swanee River" (Foster)

"Thunder" (Manners Lewis)

September 30, 1935 NYC

"Avalon" (Al Jolson) arr, g/intro 8 bars (4 bar tb solo-very end/compare "Boot It")

"Charmaine" (Erno Rapee/Lew Pollack)

"Hittin' The Bottle" (60016A Arlen/Gorney/Harburg/Koehler) (vo-SyO) arr, g

Historic seminal Recording of Amplified Guitar. Recorded with a metal-bodied Dobro resophonic, non-electric guitar: Solo 8 bars to obbligato to solo 4 bars.

"I'll Take the South" (60013A Palmer/Klages) g/obbligato (vo-group) 32 bars (F)

December 23, 1935

"I'm Nuts About Screwy Music" (Fred Rose, Jimmie Lunceford)

"My Blue Heaven" (Walter Donaldson/George Whiting) tb, g

"The Best Things In Life Are Free" (DeSylva, Brown, Henderson)

"The Melody Man" A & B versions (Hendricks/Sy Oliver)

August 31, 1936

"Organ Grinder's Swing" (Hudson, Mills) [A.Norris-guitar] tb

Eddie recalls: "Albert Norris did one little thing on Organ Grinder's Swing, and we had a hard time getting him to do that."

September 1, 1936

"On The Beach At Bali-Bali" (Sherman, Meskill, Silver)

"Me And The Moon" (Walter Hirsch, Lou Handman)

"Living From Day To Day" (Mary Schaeffer, Jerry Levinson)

"'Tain't Good (Like a Nickel)" (Hall, Whiting, Bernier)

October 14, 1936

"Harlem Shout" (**Eddie Durham**, Jimmie Lunceford) arr, tb

"Muddy Water" (deRose, Trent, Richman)

"I Can't Escape From You" (Robin, Whiting)

Vitaphone Film & Soundtrack

Directed by Joseph Henabery 1936 (Durham: tb, left, top, center)

(This DVD footage is an added feature on the 1936 film "Follow The Fleet" with Fred Astaire/Ginger Rogers) **Dan Weinstein***:*

"Vitaphone presents *Jimmie Lunceford and his Orchestra* with *The Three Brown Jacks* and Myra Johnson: *"Jazznocracy", "Rhythm Coming To Life Again", "Rhythm Is Our Business")", "You Can't Pull The Wool Over My Eyes", "Moonlight On The Ganges",*

October 26, 1936

"(This Is) My Last Affair" (Haven Johnson)

"Running A Temperature" (Fairchild, Pascal) arr, tb

January 18, 1937

Ed Brown (cl, as, ts) replaces Laforest

"Count Me Out" arr

"Honey Keep Your Mind On Me" *(61531A&B one unissued - Lunceford, Porter, Roberts) arr, g/intro 8 bars. Soli 2, 2 and 2 bars. (SM)*

"I'll See You In My Dreams" (Isham Jones, Gus Kahn)

     January 26, 1937 NYC

"He Ain't Got Rhythm" (61550A Irving Berlin) g/solo w/orch 22 bars. (M)

"Linger Awhile" (Rose, Owens)

"Honest and Truly" (Fred Rose)

"Slumming On Park Avenue" (Irving Berlin)

     June 15, 1937

"Coquette" (Lombardo, Green, Kahn)

"The Merry Go Round (two takes)" (Dave Franklin, Cliff Friend)

"Ragging The Scale" (Ed B. Claypoole)

"Hell's Bells" (Kassel)

"For Dancers Only" (Sy Oliver)

     July 8, 1937 NYC

"Posin'" (Sammy Cahn, Saul Chaplin)

"The First Time I Saw You" (Nathaniel Shilkret, Allie Wrubel)

"Honey Keep Your Mind On Me" (62346) arr, g *Won the "ALL AMERICAN POLL"*

"Put On Your Old Grey Bonnet" (Wenrich, Murphy)

     November 5, 1937

"Pigeon Walk" arr, tb, g (intro from Durham's "Time Out")

-The *Pittsburgh Courier,* Newspaper 11/12/38 reported: "Eddie arranged "What Do You Know About Love" for singer Alice Dixon in J. Lunceford's Orchestra".

     May 17, 1939

"Well, Alright Then" arr

     December 14, 1939

"Wham Rebop Boom Bam" (**Durham**, Taps Miller) c, arr

"Lunceford's Special" arr

"Uptown Blues"

     January 5, 1940

"Blues In The Groove" (**Durham**, Edgar Battle) c, arr

"It's Time To Jump And Shout" (**Durham**) c, arr

     May 9, 1940

"Swingin on C" (**Durham**) c, arr

"Strictly Instrumental" (Battle, Marcus, Sol Seiler, Benjamin) recorded June 26, 1942, E.Battle arr.

Count Basie

1937-March 26th Recordings - Count Basie Orchestra

Eddie Durham, tb/g/arr:

"Exactly Like You," "Boohoo," "The Glory of Love," "Boogie Woogie"

11/3/1937 Live Broadcast Recording at Meadowbrook Ballroom, Newark, NJ

"Good Morning Blues" - first time on record performing on an *electric* guitar

1937-1938 Recordings

Eddie Durham: tb, arr, c:

"John's Idea" (**Durham**, Basie) July 1937

"Time Out" (**Durham**, Battle) Aug.1937 - g

"Topsy" (**Durham**, Battle) Aug.1937

"Out The Window" (**Durham**, Basie) Oct.1937

1938-February

Eddie Durham: tb, g, arr, c:

"Sent For You Yesterday" (**Durham**, Basie, Rushing) Feb.1938*

"Swinging The Blues" (**Durham**, Basie)*

"Every Tub" (**Durham**, Basie)*

"Blues In The Groove" (**Durham**, Battle)

"It's Time To Jump And Shout" (**Durham**)

The Famous Door

Eddie Durham is not performing on these recordings, however his arrangements and compositions are used by the Count Basie Orchestra, as follows:

1. CBS remote broadcast, "Famous Door" August 18 - November 6, 1938:

"Shout And Feel It," "Blue and Sentimental," "I Never Knew"-arr;

"Good Morning Blues," "Harlem Shout"- **Eddie Durham arr/composer**;

2. "Columbia Dance Hour" program, CBS network - April 2 - May 19, 1938

"One O'Clock Jump";

"Every Tub," "Sent For You Yesterday," "Swinging The Blues"- **Durham arr/composer**

Harry James

(1937 & 1939)

Eddie Durham: tb, arr; Herschel Evans (ts);

Harry James, Buck Clayton: tpts

Earle Warren (as), Jack Washington (bs);

Jess Stacy (p), Walter Page (b), Jo Jones (d), Helen Humes (vo)

     Brunswick record label - December 1, 1937

"Jubilee" (Hoagy Carmichael, Adams)

"When We're Alone" (Penthouse Serenade) (Will Jason, Val Burton)

"(I Can Dream) Can't I?" (Kahal-Fain)

"Life Goes To A Party" - (Benny Goodman, Harry James)

"I left Harry an original, "Texas Chatter," which was recorded at a later time without me." "Texas Chatter" [and "One O'Clock Jump"] were recorded on Jan.5, 1938.

     January 3, 1939

"Georgiana" (McKenzie, Carle, Croom, Johnson) arr, tb, g

"Blues In The Dark" (Basie) arr, tb, g

Artie Shaw / **Billie Holiday** 1938

"Them There Eyes"

"My Blue Heaven" (RCA Victor album, air checks from the Hotel Pennsylvania broadcasts)

"On The Sunny Side Of The Street"

"I've Got The World On A String"

Eddie Durham / Base Four

- (KC5) Session

John Hammond, Sr. produced *The Kansas City Five* for the Brunswick Label (owned by *American Record Corp.*) on March 16-18, 1938

Personnel: Buck Clayton (trumpet), Freddie Green (rhythm guitar), Jo Jones (drums), Walter Page (bass) - **Eddie Durham leader, arranger, trombone, electric guitar**:

"Laughing at Life (Nick Kenny, Charles Kenny, Cornell Todd, Bobo Todd)

"Good Morning Blues" (**Durham**, Basie, Rushing-vo)

"I Know That You Know" (Anne Caldwell, Vincent Youmans)

"Love Me Or Leave Me" (Gus Kahn, Walter Donaldson) (1st issued 1976 Columbia CG33566)

Lester Young /KC 6 Session

Milt Gabler produced *The Kansas City Six* for the *Commodore* record label September 28, 1938

Personnel: **Eddie Durham & His Base Four (KC5);** *add* Lester Young (KC6th) (clarinet, ts):

"Way Down Yonder In New Orleans" (Henry Creamer, Turner Layton)

"Countless Blues" (Milt Gabler)

"Them There Eyes" (Maceo Pinkard, William Tracey, Doris Tauber) - F. Greene (voc).

"I Want A Little Girl" (Billy Moll, Murray Mencher)

"Pagin' The Devil" (Walter Page, Milt Gabler)

"Good Morning Blues" (**Durham**, Basie)

Benny Goodman

- (probably incomplete)

"The Hits of Benny" - *Capital Records* SM-1514 (LP):

"Jumpin' At The Woodside" (Basie) – (Columbia Records 35210, Los Angeles Aug. 10, 1939)

"Sent For You Yesterday and Here You Come Today" (**E. Durham**, B. Basie, J. Rushing) Victor Records 26170, recorded Feb. 1, 1939

"One O'Clock Jump" (Victor Records 25792, New York Feb. 16, 1938)

Glenn Miller

"In The Mood" (Joe Garland); Recorded 8/1/1939 - Bluebird 1939; **Arr. Eddie Durham**, Glenn Miller; **Recording personnel**: Clyde Hurley, Leigh Knowles, R.D. McMickle (t); Glenn Miller, Al Mastren, Paul Tanner (tb); Silver Schwartz (as, cl); Hal McIntyre (as); Harold Tennyson (as, bars, cl); Tex Beneke, Al Klink (tw); J.C. MacGregor; Richard Fisher (g); Rowland Bundock (b); Maurice Purtill (d).

"I Don't Want To Set The World On Fire" (Benjamin, Marcus, **Durham**, Seiler) Ray Eberle (vo) - "On The Air," *RCA Victor,* SF-7610 LP; LSP 2767; PPRS 5335.

Discography (by Ed Polic) of Songs, Arrangements by **E. Durham** for Glenn Miller:[222]

"Baby Me" - Archie Gottler, Lou Handman (cm); Harry Harris (lyr) 1939

Durham arrangement Score 275

"Careless (or Loveless) Love" - William Christopher (WC) Handy 1921

Eddie Durham arrangement 13Jul39 Score 277

"Durham" (Probably an untitled Durham original) - Score 274

"Glen Island Special" - Durham composer and arranger 1939

Score 278 Orchestration published

26Jul39 Recording 038140-1 Bluebird B-10388, etc.

6Sep39 NBC WFBR T-90, T-122, Soundcraft LP-1023, etc.

Durham arrangement 28Nov39

"I Want To Be Happy" (From the 1924 musical comedy "No No Nanette")

Vincent Youmans (cm); Irving Caesar (lyr)

Durham arrangement

1Aug39 Recording 038174-1 Bluebird B-10416, etc.

C-41, 10" acetate, 16" acetate, Soundcraft LP-1009, etc.

"Moten Swing" -Also called "Moten Stomp" and "Swing of Swings

Buster Moten, Bennie Moten 1933

Durham arrangement 26Jun39

"Royal Garden Blues" - Clarence Williams, Spencer Williams 1919

Durham arrangement 26Jun39 Score 259

"The Saint Louis Blues" - William Christopher (WC) Handy 1914

Durham arrangement 1939-1940 Orchestration published

5Jan40 Cafe Rouge T-122, C-40, 16" acetate, Black Jack LP 3018, etc.

"Shout"

[Correct title **"It's Time to Jump and Shout"** -- recorded by

Savitt and Lunceford; both recordings almost identical.]

Durham arrangement 26Jun39 Score 260

"Slip Horn Jive"- Durham composer and arranger Score 234

2Jun39 Recording 037182-1 Bluebird B-10317, etc.

2Jun39 Recording 037182-2 Bluebird AXM2-5512-2, etc.

"Tiger Rag" (Hold That Tiger!) - Tony Sbarbaro, Edwin Edwards, Henry Ragas, Larry Shields, D. James LaRocca (Original Dixieland Jazz Band) (cm); Harry DeCosta (lyr) 1917

Eddie Durham arrangement Score 314

5Jan40 Cafe Rouge C-41, 10" acetate, 16" acetate, Soundcraft LP-1009, etc.

6Nov40 Cafe Rouge 39-1, C-43, Soundcraft LP-1003, etc.

C-61 (12" acetate), WOR 4B, Soundcraft LP-1012, etc.

"The Weary Blues" - Durham arrangement - 6Jul39 Score 265

"Well Alright Then" (Tonight's the Night) - Frances Raye, Don "Raye" Macrae Wilhoite, Jr., Dan Howell 1939 Durham arrangement Score 262

"Wham (ReBop Boom Bam)" Eddie Durham, Taps Miller 1939 Score 268 Durham Arrangement - Orchestration published.

"White Star" Durham arrangement 6Jul1939.

"You Know That I Know (a/k/a "I Know") - Durham arrangement - Score 313.

Harlan Leonard

Bluebird Label Recordings

Eddie Durham, Jesse Stone (arr), Harlan Leonard (dir, cl, as, bar)

Edward Johnson, Williams H. Smith (t), James Ross (t, a, v), Myra Taylor, Ernie Williams-v

Fred Beckett, Richmond Henderson (tb), Darwin Jones-as-v, Henry Bridges-cl-ts, Jimmy Keith-ts, William Smith-p, Stan Morgan-g, Winston Williams-sb, Bill Hadnott-sb*, Jesse Price-d, Myra Taylor, Ernie Williams-v

March 11, 1940, New York

"I Don't Want To Set The World On Fire" (**Durham**, Benjamin, Seiler, Marcus)

July 15, 1940, Chicago - William (Billy) Hadnott replaced W.Williams on bass:

*"My Pop Gave Me A Nickel" (**Durham**, Seiler, Marcus)

Eddie Durham and His Band

"Kansas City Jazz LP" (originally an album of 78rpm's)

Dave Dexter – Producer, Decca 18125 (DL 8044) November 11, 1940

(4 tracks* currently available: MCA Records Inc. as Jazz Heritage Vol. 45 "**The Swinging Small Bands**" Vol. 2 (1940-1944) 510088D "*Eddie Durham And His Band*"). Compilations vary depending on which of this Dexter production or its reissue you own or obtain.

Durham (arr, tb, e-g)

Henry "Buster" Smith, Willard Brown (a-sax), Lemuel C. Johnson (t-sax); Joe Keyes (tpt), Conrad Frederick (p); Averill Pollard (b); and Arthur Herbert (d):

"Moten Swing" (B. Moten/I. Moten)

"I Want A Little Girl" (Murray Mencher/Billy Moll)

"Magic Carpet" (**E. Durham**)

"Fare Thee, Honey Fare Thee Well" (Mayo Williams, John Akers, Vol Stevens)

"South" (B. Moten/T. Hayes)

"Lafayette" (**Durham**/Basie)

"Boot It" (B. Moten)

Count Basie and His Orchestra:

Eddie Durham (arr), Earle Warren, Ronald Washington (a-sax), Walter Page (b), Jo Jones (d), Freddie Green (g), Basie (p), Herschel Evans, Lester Young (t-sax), Dan Minor, George Hunt, Eddie Durham (tb), Bobby Moore, Buck Clayton Ed Lewis (tpt), James Rushing (vo)

"Good Morning Blues" (**Durham**/Basie)

"Doggin Around" (Herschel Evans/Edgar Battle)

"Topsy" (**Durham**/Battle)

"Jumpin' At The Woodside"

"Countless Blues (Ad Lib Jump Blues)" (Milt Gabler)

Jan Savitt Orchestra

September 1940 - July 1941 arranged:

"Tuxedo Junction" arr (Jan. 14 and April 12, 1940 - Decca)

"Dear Old Southland"

"Turkey In The Straw"

Wrote and arranged:

"Blues In The Groove" arr (Feb. 3, 1940 - Decca)

"It's Time To Jump and Shout" arr (Feb. 3, 1940 - Decca) (Identical arr. for Jimmie Lunceford)

"Wham Rebop Boom Bam"

"Parade of the Wooden Soldiers" arr (Feb. 3, 1940 - Decca)

"W.P.A." arr (Apr. 29, 1940 - Decca)

"I Don't Want To Set The World On Fire" (Durham, *Marcus, Benjamin, Seiler 1938)*

Gerald L. Dupper a/k/a **Tommy Tucker** recorded it (Okeh Records) June 1941 - became his biggest hit, a Gold Record.

Harlan Leonard (clarinet) *& His Rockets, Myra Taylor* (v) recorded it March 11, 1940

Horace Heidt, Sr. and his Musical Knights recorded it (Columbia Records) (#1 on Billboard U.S. pop chart) 1941

Glenn Miller performed it on the Sunset Serenade Broadcast, November 12, 1941 with Ray Eberle, Marion Hutton, *The Four Modernaires* and Bobby Hackett.

The Ink Spots (Jerry Daniels, Orville Jones, Bill Kenny, Charlie Fuqua, Deek Watson) recorded it (Decca Records) (#4 on Billboard 1941) - R&R Hall of Fame

Featured in the Ad for the video game "**Fallout**", with millions of hits on youtube.

Frederick Brothers Music Corporation produced *Bon Bon & His Buddies* (July 23, 1941)

Bon Bon and His Buddies

- Decca recordings on July 23, 1941 (NYC):

"All That Meat and No Potatoes" (Ed Kirkeby, Fats Waller) - tb, g

"Sweet Mama (Papa's Getting Mad)" (Peter Frost, George Little, Fred Rose) - tb, g

"Blow, Gabriel, Blow" (Cole Porter) - tb, g

"I Don't Want To Set The World On Fire" (Bennie Benjamin, **Eddie Durham**, Sol Marcus, Eddie Seiler) - tb, g *(Note: This is the only recording of "Fire" which Durham <u>performs</u> on.)*

Durhamettes

For full details of Eddie's affiliations: "**Swingin' The Blues Series (Vol. 2)** – EDDIE DURHAM & THE LADIES *of Jazz*"

Personnel:

Singing Quartet: Alma Cortez, Lelia (aka Lela) Julius, Nova Lee McGee, and Elleragt Thomas

Rhythm: Frankie Eldridge – piano; Edith "Jersey" Farthing – bass; Marjorie "Trump, Gibson – drums

Trumpets: Thelma Lewis, Nova Lee McGee, Jean Starr

Trombones: Ersa Bell Hiller- Durham, Sammy Lee Jett, Jessie Turner and Lela Julius *(former leader of The Harlem Playgirls)*

Saxophones: Alma Cortez-baritone, Mildred Jones and Helen Scott-tenors, Ellarize Thompson and Selma Lee Williams-altos.

Frank Humphries Orchestra
"Pick-Up Label" (#1001) recordings (1945)

Personnel: Frank Humphries-tpt/vocals, **Eddie Durham-arr/tb**

Henry Boozier, "Brazil," Kenny Dorham-tpt, unknown-b & d

Eddie Durham, Jimmy Archey, George Stevenson Sr.-tb

Joe Bishop, Hildred Humphries-as, Teddy Humphries-p, Johnny Hicks and Don Warren-ts:

  - "After You've Gone" (Humphries)

  - "Lonesome Mood" (aka Lonesome Road)

"Eagle" (#1005 *circa 1952*-other personnel unknown:

Frank Humphries-vom, Eddie Durham-tb, Della Simpson-vof:

  - "Time & Time Again"[223]

George Williams
Hub Records circa 1945 Don Byas (leader), George Williams (vocals), **Eddie Durham (guitar/solo),** unknown (trumpet, bass, drums):[224]

"A Woman Gets Tired Of One Man All The Time" (Paul Carter, Charles H. Barker)

"Don't Care Blues" (Perry Bradford)

Some contemporary Male-sponsored Female Bands, after Eddie Durham:

Brides of Funkenstein and The Parlets – George Clinton

Emotions - Earth Wind & Fire

Fascinations – Curtis Mayfield

Funky Divas - James Brown

GTO's – Frank Zappa

Honey's – Brian Wilson

I Threes – Bob Marley

Ikettes – Ike Turner

Latin Fever – Larry Harlow

Love Unlimited - Barry White

Mary Jane Girls – Rick James

Motown – Gordy's

Raelettes – Ray Charles

Ronnettes and Crystals – Phil Spector

Vanity Six; *Appolonia Six* - Prince

Did You Know? **THE EDDIE DURHAM PARK & PAVILLION** *was designed with a guitar-shaped path, and has stationary playable instruments. It's located in his hometown on MLK, Jr. Blvd., San Marcos, 78666, U.S.A.*

INDEX

"It is not the critic that counts. Not the man who points out of how the strong man stumbles, or where the doer of deeds could've done them better. The credit belongs to the man who is actually in the arena...who strives valiantly. Who spends himself in a worthy cause; who at the best knows in the end the triumph of high achievement; who at the worse, if he fails, at least fails while daring greatly; so that his place shall never be with those cold and timid souls who neither know victory nor defeat."
*President **Theodore Roosevelt***

3

10

12

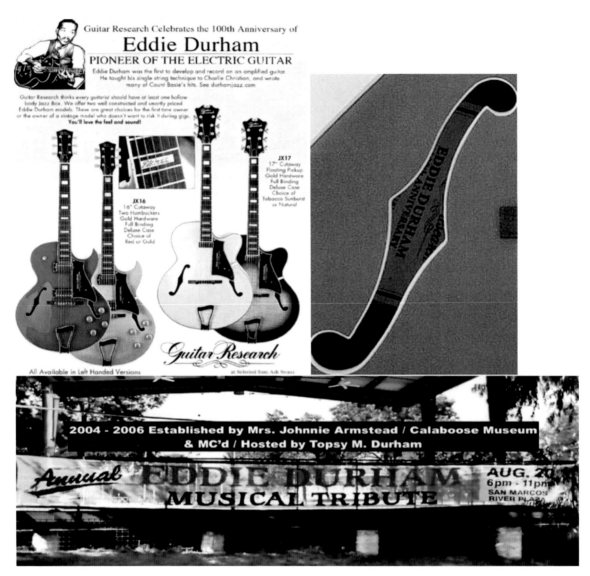

Did you know? *Sam Ash Music Stores* released 10,000 *Centennial Signature Guitars* in 2006. They are authenticated by plated signatures inside the *F*-Hole. New York's *"Dizzy's Coca-Cola Club* in the *Jazz At Lincoln Center"* building debuted the Eddie Durham guitar at a week-long musical tribute. *Sam Ash Music Stores in San Antonio* debuted them at the *Eddie Durham Centennial Tribute & Heritage Week*, San Marcos, Texas.

ENDNOTES

SPECIAL THANKS to *www.Newspapers.com* and www.*FindAGrave.com*

---

[1] *https://www.youtube.com/watch?v=oBx373pLD60*

[2] Film "Bolden" by Daniel Pritzker, 2019. Music by Wynton Marsalis, vocalist Catherine Russell, etc.

[3] The Beatles 2000, p. 36: (primary source); Clayson 2005, p. 40: (secondary source).

[4] Film "Sweet and Lowdown" by Woody Allen, 1999. Appearing Sean Penn, Nat Hentoff, Stanley Crouch, etc., and Sally Placksin mentioning Eddie Durham.

[5] The fifth step-brother, Sylvester, never performed or toured with them nor was he raised with them.

[6] Phil Schaap's interview with Eddie Durham, Birthday Broadcast August 1986 (live on WKCR -FM 89.9 Columbia University Radio NYC)

[7] Edward Burleson, William Lindsey, and Dr. Eli T. Merriman, in 1846, laid out the town of San Marcos (Stovall et al. 1986). In 1849 Colonel John L. Durham arrived in San Marcos. By 1850, the San Marcos community was established." (Molly F. Goodwin, 1998) Although it's not established whether John L. Durham is related to Berry Durham, Sr. (b.1810), in my opinion it would be neglectful not to strongly consider the military connection.

8 Hattie had a son, Sam, before she married Nunce. She was of Mexican/Cherokee descent and died circa 1911. Based on Marriage Certificates, Nunce remarried Elind Kerr on April 2, 1919, Hays County, TX and their son Willie Durham married Everleaner Malone on April 1, 1906. Willie had a sister Lilly, perhaps they were twins.

[9] Berry Martin Durham, Jr. (b. March 1830 d.15 Oct 1932; Berry "Nunce" Durham III (b.1850-d. ???); Berry Durham IV (b.21 Dec 1875- d.24 Jan 1951). The grave marker of Berry Durham, V says: "Berry Durham 21 Dec 1875 - 24 Jan 1951 Pvt. Sup Co 64 Pioneer Inf World War I".

[10] **Lampasas** is of Spanish etymology and signifies a level plain or tract of country." Other sources say it is a Mexican word meaning "water lilies," or an Indian word meaning "firefly." Galveston Daily News June 24, 1884

[11] Although Nunce was born "free," as a matter of Law children born to Native American mixed marriages were born free and therefore these mixed marriages were very common, and very much desired by African Americans. In my interview in 2020 with John, Melvin, and Carl Durham, they all relate personally knowing Nunce and said that he easily passed for Caucasian. Eddie Durham always related his heritage as Irish on the paternal side, with Mohawk and Cherokee on his maternal side.

12 Lou Ella's siblings were Dewitt, Mary and Earl Rabb. Earl was murdered August 1898 for dating a white woman, according to relatives who recorded as such in a family Bible.

13 Buried at Long Island National Cemetary, Pinelawn, New York

14 Since, among other factors, home births were not issued birth certificates, most birth years were documented from family records kept in a Bible, or passed down to a child by a family member. It is otherwise unclear why Eddie's and Roosevelt's birth years fluctuate from 1905-1910, but nevertheless, their dad Jose definitely lived past Roosevelt's birth. However, Joe Jr. provided the headcount for the 1910 census, where "Elwood" is listed as four years old but Roosevelt is not listed at all. We never knew my dad's name to be

"Elwood." There is also vague evidence that Eddie was instead born in 1905 and Roosevelt in 1906. The Eddie Durham Centennial Musical Tribute and Heritage Festival was held in San Marcos in 2006 since 1906 became the birth year most accepted.

[15] "Sharecropping" is a form of agriculture in which a landowner allows a tenant to use the land in return for a share of the crops produced on the land. Sharecropping has a long history and there are a wide range of different situations and types of agreements that have used a form of the system. Some are governed by tradition, and others by law. https://en.wikipedia.org/wiki/Sharecropping

[16] Smithsonian Oral History Series 1978 (IJS Rutgers University) interview by Helen Dance *https://rucore.libraries.rutgers.edu/rutgers-lib/52035/*

[17] Ibid. p61

18 Myrtle Durham had no children and both mother/daughter are buried together at Glendale Cemetary, Bloomfield, Essex County, New Jersey - Mayfair, Lot 1, Grave 1.

[19] Meeting The Blues -The Rise of the Texas Sound by Alan Govenar 1988 p35,36

20 Roosevel Durham served in World War II (Jan.1942-Oct.1945). In his adult years, he lived near Aunt Myrtle and their mother Lula, in New Jersey. Roosevelt died at the Veterans Memorial Hospital in New York and is buried in the National Cemetery, Farmingdale, New York (plot 3570 Sec. 2H).

[21]"One O'Clock Jump": The Unforgettable History of the Oklahoma City Blue Devils by Douglas H. Daniels 2006 p71 (Quotes from document on Burnett from Terrell Public Library, which cites G.T. Overstreet, "A Late Educator, William H. Burnett The Shadow of Burnett High School," Dallas *Star Post*, October 1, 1955, and E. P. Shaw, "Burnett High: Long Time Since Yesterday," Terrell *Tribune*, July 27, 1990; Durham quotes are from IJS interview Reel 1, p43)

[22] The World of Count Basie by Stanley Dance 1980 p61 (ED interviewed 1971)

[23] Swing City Newark Nightlife 1925-50 by Barbara J. Kukla 1991 p35 paperback

[24] Smithsonian Oral History Series 1978 (IJS Rutgers University) interview by Stanley & Helen Dance

[25] The World of Count Basie by Stanley Dance 1980 p61 (ED interviewed 1971)

[26] Swing City Newark Nightlife 1925-50 by Barbara J. Kukla 1991 p229 paperback

[27] The World of Count Basie by Stanley Dance 1980 p61 (ED interviewed 1971)

[28] Jazz The Rough Guide by Ian Carr, Digby Fairweather and Brian Priestley 1995 p202

[29] The 2010 Savory Collection booklet p24

[30] https://music.apple.com/us/artist/edgar-battle/31326167 and https://eugenechadbourne.com/dochistory

[31] Phil Schaap's interview with Eddie Durham, Birthday Broadcast, August 1986 (live on WKCR-FM 89.9 Columbia University Radio NYC)

[32] "Cowboy Circus and Cattle Round-Up During Wheat Show" *The Downs News and The Downs Times* (Downs, Kansas) - Thu, Oct 7, 1920 - p1

33 Phil Schaap's interview with Eddie Durham, Birthday Broadcast August 1986 (live on WKCR-FM 89.9 Columbia University Radio NYC)

[34] "Show Entirely From Ranch" The Kansas City Times (KC, Missouri) Tue, Dec 16, 1924 - Page 15

[35]"One O'Clock Jump": The Unforgettable History of the Oklahoma City Blue Devils by Douglas H. Daniels 2006 p75 with footnotes p245

[36] "Jazz and Blues Legends - Rough Guide to the Roots of Gospel." World Music Network/Riverboat Records 2020 Europe. https://worldmusic.net/products/rough-guide-to-the-roots-of-gospel

[37] From Traveling Show to Vaudeville - Theatrical Spectacle in America, 1830-1910 by The Johns Hopkins University Press 2003 p20 (edited by Robert M. Lewis)

[38] Meeting The Blues – The Rise of the Texas Sound by Alan Govenar 1988 p35

[39] Phil Schaap's interview with Eddie Durham, Birthday Broadcast August 1986 (live on WKCR -FM 89.9 Columbia University Radio NYC)

[40] Meeting The Blues – The Rise of the Texas Sound by Alan Govenar 1988 p6

[41] Swing City Newark Nightlife 1925-50 by Barbara J. Kukla 2002 p15 paperback

[42] Phil Schaap's interview with Eddie Durham, Birthday Broadcast August 1986 (live on WKCR -FM 89.9 Columbia University Radio NYC)

[43] "Eddie Durham And His All-Star Girl Band" The New York Age - Sat. Dec 18, 1943 p11

44 Stone also became arranger and musical director with: Terrence Holder/Clouds Of Joy; George E. Lee, recording with this band and its singer, Julia Lee (1929); Thamon Hayes' Kansas City Rockets (1931); and Harlan Leonard's Rockets (1934). Stone coached and rehearsed these bands. Among his best known compositions are 'Sorghum Switch', for Jimmy Dorsey, 'Smack Dab In The Middle', and 'Idaho', recorded by Benny Goodman and Guy Lombardo, the latter's version selling three million copies. Stone worked as arr/M.D. with the International Sweethearts Of Rhythm (early 1940's). He helped develop their stage presence, giving them the polish that became a byword of excellence. He married singer Evelyn McGee. Stone was hired in 1947 by Ahmet Ertegun for Atlantic Records as composer, arr, producer and A&R man. He recorded as aka Charlie (or Chuck) Calhound. Among songs composed with Atlantic were 'Money Honey', recorded by the Clyde McPhatter -fronted Drifters (number 1 in the R&B charts in 1953), and 'Soul On Fire', for LaVern Baker on which Stone played piano. He also arranged 'Big' Joe Turner's groundbreaking 1954 hit, 'Shake, Rattle And Roll'. www.oldies.com/artist-biography/Jesse-Stone.html

[45] Smithsonian Oral History Series 1978 (IJS Rutgers University) interview by Stanley Dance

[46]"One O'Clock Jump": The Unforgettable History of the Oklahoma City Blue Devils by Douglas H. Daniels 2006 p77 with footnotes p245

[47] Topsy M. Durham's interview with guitarist/bandleader Lawrence Lucie 2000 (videotaped by Joseph 'Nemo' Joly)

[48] Phil Schaap's interview with Eddie Durham, Birthday Broadcast August 1986 (live on WKCR -FM 89.9 Columbia University Radio NYC)

[49] Smithsonian Oral History Series 1978 (IJS Rutgers University) interview by Stanley Dance

[50] "Gospel Classics 1927-1931"Document Records DOCD-5190 (Austria), Liner Notes by Ken Romanowski, July 1993

[51] The NPR Curious Listener's Guide to Jazz by Loren Schoenberg 2002 p136 paperback

[52] *Downbeat Magazine* 6th Guitar Issue "Held Notes: Eddie Durham." By George Hoefer July 19, 1962 p54

[53] "One O'Clock Jump": The Unforgettable History of the Oklahoma City Blue Devils by Douglas H. Daniels 2006 p76 with footnotes p245 "Marc Rice, The Bennie Moten Orchestra; see also Gunther Schuller, Early Jazz: Its Roots and Musical Development (NY: Oxford University Press, 1986)

[54] Topsy M. Durham's interview with acoustic bassist Theodore Wilson, III 2000 (videotaped by Joseph "Nemo Joly & transcribed by Topsy M. Durham)

[55] The World of Count Basie by Stanley Dance 1980 p62 (ED interview 1971)

[56] *Downbeat Magazine* 6th Guitar Issue "Held Notes: Eddie Durham." By George Hoefer July 19, 1962 p54

[57] Kansas City Jazz From Ragtime to Bebop-A History by Frank Driggs and Chuck Haddix 2005 p112, 118-120 and footnotes

[58] Smithsonian Oral History Series 1978 (IJS Rutgers University) interview by Stanley Dance

[59] Before Motown: A History of Jazz in Detroit, 1920-60 by Lars Bjorn, Jim Gallert 2004 p45 and footnotes

[60] Smithsonian Oral History Series 1978 (IJS Rutgers University) interview by Stanley Dance

[61] Stomping The Blues by Albert Murray 1976 p158,170,174-176,222 paperback

[62] "Old Men With A Horn" Daily News (New York) Sun, Nov 7, 1976 p398 and The World of Count Basie by Stanley Dance 1980 p62, 64, 319,320

[63] *Downbeat Magazine* 6th Guitar Issue "Held Notes: Eddie Durham." By George Hoefer July 19, 1962 p57

[64] The Ghosts of Harlem-Sessions with Jazz Legends by Hank O'Neal 2009 p137

[65] Ibid. p138,139

[66] Smithsonian Oral History Series 1978 (IJS Rutgers University) interview by Stanley Dance

[67] Phil Schaap's interview with Eddie Durham, Birthday Broadcast August 1986 and "Remembering Freddie Green" Broadcast March 1, 1987 (live on WKCR -FM 89.9 Columbia University Radio NYC)

[68] Topsy M. Durham's interview with acoustic bassist Theodore Wilson, III 2000 (videotaped by Joseph "Nemo Joly & transcribed by Topsy M. Durham)

[69] The Ghosts of Harlem-Sessions with Jazz Legends by Hank O'Neal 2009 p174

[70] Phil Schaap's interview with Eddie Durham, Birthday Broadcast August 1986 (live on WKCR -FM 89.9 Columbia University Radio NYC)

[71] All Over the Map: True Heroes of Texas Music by Michael Corcoran (UNT Press, 2017)

[72] Topsy M. Durham's interview with pianist John Colianni, Jan 23, 2020

73 The World of Count Basie by Stanley Dance 1980 p68 (1971 interview)

[74] Phil Schaap's interview with Eddie Durham, live Birthday Broadcast August 1986 (live on WKCR -FM 89.9 Columbia University Radio NYC)

[75] Phil Schaap's interview with Eddie Durham, Birthday Broadcast August 1986 (live on WKCR-FM 89.9 Columbia University Radio NYC)

[76] *Downbeat Magazine* 6th Guitar Issue "Held Notes: Eddie Durham." By George Hoefer July 19, 1962 p54

[77] Smithsonian Oral History Series 1978 (IJS Rutgers University) interview by Stanley Dance

[78] "International Sweethearts of Rhythm–America's Hottest All-Girl Band" 1986 Documentary. Jezebel Productions & Rosetta Records, Greta Schiller, Andrea Weiss, Rosetta and Rebecca Reitz. Starring Anna Mae Winburn, Tiny Davis, Roz Cron, Helen Jones, Helen Saine, Evelyn McGee, and Jessie Stone, et.al..

[79] "Clayton, Buck Clayton's Jazz World" by Buck Clayton, assisted by Nancy M. Elliott 1989 p94-95

[80] Topsy M. Durham's interview with guitarist/bandleader Lawrence Lucie 2000 (videotaped by Joseph 'Nemo' Joly)

[81] Phil Schaap's interview with Eddie Durham, live Birthday Broadcast August 1986 (live on WKCR-FM 89.9 Columbia University Radio NYC)

[82] Rhythm Is Our Business: Jimmie Lunceford and the Harlem Express by Eddy Determeyer 2006 p99 and footnotes

[83] Phil Schaap's interview with Eddie Durham, live Birthday Broadcast August 1986 (live on WKCR-FM 89.9 Columbia University Radio NYC)

[84] Smithsonian Oral History Series 1978 (IJS Rutgers University) interview by Stanley Dance

[85] Phil Schaap's interview with Eddie Durham, "Remembering Freddie Green" Memorial Broadcast March 1, 1987 (live on WKCR-FM 89.9 Columbia University Radio NYC)

[86] Topsy M. Durham's interview with guitarist/bandleader Lawrence Lucie 2000 (videotaped by Joseph 'Nemo' Joly)

[87] Interview with Phil Schaap February 2010 (WKCR-FM Columbia University, New York City) by Deidre Lannon for Texas State University (VCYes Videographer)

[88] *Downbeat Magazine* 6th Guitar Issue "Held Notes: Eddie Durham." By George Hoefer July 19, 1962 p54

[89] "Jimmie Tour To Start Feb. 1" *The Pittsburgh Courier (Pittsburgh, Pennsylvania) - Sat, Jan 19, 1935 - Page 19*

[90] Phil Schaap's interview with Eddie Durham, live Birthday Broadcast August 1986 (live on WKCR-FM 89.9 Columbia University Radio NYC)

[91] The World of Count Basie by Stanley Dance 1980 p67 (ED interviewed 1971)

[92] Smithsonian Oral History Series 1978 (IJS Rutgers University) interview by Stanley Dance

[93] Stage & Screen, Music & Drama. "King of Sweden Hears Music" The Pittsburgh Courier (Pennsylvania) - Sat, Mar 20, 1937 p18

[94] "Lunceford Praised by Swedish Critics" Cumberland Evening Times (Maryland) Mon. May 10, 1937 p11

[95] Rhythm Is Our Business: Jimmie Lunceford and the Harlem Express by Eddy Determeyer 2006 p87 and footnotes

[96] Phil Schaap WKCR-FM 89.9 (Columbia University) "Out To Lunch" Monday, April, 2017 Broadcast

[97] Smithsonian Oral History Series 1978 (IJS Rutgers University) interview by Stanley Dance

98 The World of Count Basie by Stanley Dance 1980 p67 (1971 interview)

[99] The Ghosts of Harlem-Sessions with Jazz Legends by Hank O'Neal 2009 p141

[100] Topsy M. Durham's interview with Dan Weinstein 2018 (by telephone)

[101] Phil Schaap's interview with Eddie Durham, Birthday Broadcast August 1986 (live on WKCR -FM 89.9 Columbia University Radio NYC)

[102] Phil Schaap's interview with Eddie Durham, Birthday Broadcast August 1986 (live on WKCR -FM 89.9 Columbia University Radio NYC)

[103] Phil Schaap's interview with Eddie Durham, live Birthday Broadcast August 1986 (live on WKCR -FM 89.9 Columbia University Radio NYC)

[104] *Downbeat Magazine* 6th Guitar Issue "Held Notes: Eddie Durham." By George Hoefer July 19, 1962 p54

[105] Topsy M. Durham's interview with pianist John Colianni, Jan 23, 2020

[106] Phil Schaap's interview with Eddie Durham, Birthday Broadcast August 1986 (live on WKCR -FM 89.9 Columbia University Radio NYC)

[107] StLBlues.net by Peter "Cornbread" Cohen, CBP. Live Music Calendar *http://stlblues.net/pete_lockwood.htm*

[108] Morning Glory A Biography of Mary Lou Williams by Linda Dahl 1999 p101

[109] Smithsonian Oral History Series 1978 (IJS Rutgers University) interview by Stanley Dance

[110] Morning Glory A Biography of Mary Lou Williams by Linda Dahl 1999 p101

[111] Ibid.

[112] Ibid p98

[113] Ibid p99

[114] The Ghosts of Harlem-Sessions with Jazz Legends by Hank O'Neal 2009 p139,142,145

[115] Phil Schaap, WKCR.org/WKCR-FM 89.9 (HD1) (Columbia University) Musicians edition of Jazz Alternatives Monday, April, 2017 109th Birthday Broadcast and, "Jimmie Lunceford's Arrangers" https://media.music.txstate.edu/durham/interviews.html

[116] Ella Fitzgerald: A Biography of the First Lady of Jazz, Updated Edition by Stuart Nicholson 2014 p51 and footnotes

[117] Ibid p267

[118] The World of Count Basie by Stanley Dance 1980 p89 (Dicky Wells quote)

[119] Phil Schaap's interview with Eddie Durham, live Birthday Broadcast August 1986 (live on WKCR -FM 89.9 Columbia University Radio NYC)

[120] *Downbeat Magazine* 6th Guitar Issue "Held Notes: Eddie Durham." By George Hoefer July 19, 1962 p57

[121] The Ghosts of Harlem-Sessions with Jazz Legends by Hank O'Neal 2009 p268

[122] The World of Count Basie by Stanley Dance 1980 p68 (1971 interview)

[123] The 1976 Act also extended the term from 28 to 47 years for copyrights filed before 1978, which had not already entered public domain, giving a total new ownership term to authors of 75 years.[2]
The 1998 Act extended these terms to life of the author plus 70 years and for works of corporate authorship to 120 years after creation or 95 years after publication, whichever end is earlier.[3] Copyright protection for works published before January 1, 1978, was increased by 20 years to a total of 95 years from their

publication date. This law, also known as the **Sonny Bono Copyright Term Extension Act**, **Sonny Bono Act**, or (derisively) the **Mickey Mouse Protection Act**,[4] effectively "froze" the advancement date of the public domain in the United States for works covered by the older fixed term copyright rules. Under this Act, works made in 1923 or afterwards that were still protected by copyright in 1998 would not enter the public domain until January 1, 2019 or later.

https://en.wikipedia.org/wiki/Copyright_Term_Extension_Act#cite_note-1

[124] Topsy M. Durham's interview of trombonist Benny Powell June 1999 (videotaped by Joseph 'Nemo' Joly; transcribed by Topsy M. Durham)

[125] "And The Angels Swing - Jazz and Jesus at St. Peter's" By Charles W. Bell - Daily News (New York) Sun, Dec 22, 1985 p205

[126] Topsy M. Durham's interview of trombonist Al Grey June 1999 (videotaped by Joseph 'Nemo' Joly; transcribed by Topsy M. Durham)

[127] Music "LP gets back to Basie's basics" "Basie Beginnings - 1929-1932" (LP Record 9768-1-RB) by Les Zacheis, Gazette music columnist. *The Gazette (Cedar Rapids, Iowa) - Fri, Nov 10, 1969 - p41*

[128] Phil Schaap's interview with Eddie Durham, Birthday Broadcast August 1986 (live on WKCR -FM 89.9 Columbia University Radio NYC)

[129] The NPR Curious Listener's Guide to Jazz by Loren Schoenberg 2002 p195 paperback

[130] Lester Young, The "Kansas City" Sessions, GRP Records 1997 Loren Schoenberg (CD Liner)

[131] *Downbeat Magazine* "Caught In The Act - KC All Stars." By Stanley Dance May 15, 1969

[132] *Downbeat Magazine* 6th Guitar Issue "Held Notes: Eddie Durham." By George Hoefer July 19, 1962 p57

[133] The NPR Curious Listener's Guide to Jazz by Loren Schoenberg 2002 p216 paperback

[134] Freddie Green quote in The Los Angeles Times (California) - Tue, March 26, 1985 p67

[135] Guitar Music History Players by Richard Chapman 2000 p97

[136] "Bands swinging for decades" by Mary Campbell, The Latrobe Bulletin (Latrobe, Pennsylvania) Wed. Apr 16, 1986 p19

[137] "Sent For You Yesterday" Podcast article by Mike Zirpolo June 30, 2018

https://swingandbeyond.com/2018/06/30/sent-for-you-yesterday-live-1939-count-basie-with-jimmy-rushing/#bped-comments

[138] "Clayton, Buck Clayton's Jazz World" by Buck Clayton, assisted by Nancy M. Elliott 1989 p94-95

[139] Lester Leaps In-The Life and Times of Lester "Pres" Young by Douglas Henry Daniels 2002 p222-224

[140] "Clayton, Buck Clayton's Jazz World by Buck Clayton, Assisted by Nancy M. Elliott 1989 p94-95"

[141] "Ibid. p111

[142] The Tenor Sax of Herschel Evans, Jazz Solography Series v2. by Jan Evensmo, May 22, 2017

[143] Ibid.

[144] Ibid.

[145] Hamp by Lionel Hampton with James Haskins 1989 p77

[146] The World of Count Basie by Stanley Dance 1980 p63 (ED interviewed 1971)

[147] Meeting The Blues – The Rise of the Texas Sound by Alan Govenar 1988 p82

[148] The Ghosts of Harlem-Sessions with Jazz Legends by Hank O'Neal 2009 p141

[149] The World of Count Basie by Stanley Dance 1980 p66 (ED interviewed 1971)

[150] Smithsonian Oral History Series 1978 (IJS Rutgers University) interview by Stanley Dance

[151] Author's telephone interview with guitarist Chris Flory 2020

[152] Topsy M. Durham's interview of Benny Powell and Al Grey June 1999 (videotaped by Joseph 'Nemo' Joly)

[153] Phil Schaap's interview with Eddie Durham, Birthday Broadcast August 1986 (live on WKCR -FM 89.9 Columbia University Radio NYC)

[154] Phil Schaap's interview with Eddie Durham, Birthday Broadcast August 1986 (live on WKCR -FM 89.9 Columbia University Radio NYC)

[155] The World of Count Basie by Stanley Dance 1980 p63 (ED interviewed 1971)

[156] Glenn D. Mittler interviews Eddie Durham 1981 (telephone interview)

[157] Interview with Phil Schaap February 2010 (WKCR-FM Columbia University, New York City) by Deidre Lannon for Texas State University (VCYes Videographer)

[158] Smithsonian Oral History Series 1978 (IJS Rutgers University) interview by Stanley & Helen Dance

[159] *Downbeat Magazine* 6th Guitar Issue "Held Notes: Eddie Durham." By George Hoefer July 19, 1962 p57

[160] Phil Schaap's interview with Eddie Durham, Birthday Broadcast August 1986 (live on WKCR -FM 89.9 Columbia University Radio NYC)

[161] Phil Schaap's interview with Eddie Durham, live Birthday Broadcast August 1986 (live on WKCR -FM 89.9 Columbia University Radio NYC)

[162] "Artie Shaw, Self-Exiled Swing Artist, Returns to His Trade" Elizabethton Star (Elizabethton, Tennessee) 13 Jun 1940 Thu p1

[163] 10th Anniversary of Jazz Appreciation Month (forum) "Women & Jazz-Transforming a Nation" at The National Museum of American History. International Sweethearts of Rhythm. Moderators: Sally Placksin, & Kathy Hughes; quoting panelist Rosalind "Roz" Cron.

[164] Phil Schaap's interview with Eddie Durham, Birthday Broadcast August 1986 (live on WKCR -FM 89.9 Columbia University Radio NYC)

[165] Glenn Miller Archive - University of Colorado Boulder, "A Portrait of Glenn Miller" Produced by Dennis M. Spragg, p11 Updated April 2018

[166] A Heretical View of a Phenomenon 'Glenn Miller Never Turned ME On'. *Leonard Feather, Los Angeles Times Service* - The Miami Herald (Florida) Sun, Aug 18, 1974 p142

[167] Glenn Miller Archive - University of Colorado Boulder, "A Portrait of Glenn Miller" Produced by Dennis M. Spragg, p14 Updated April 2018

[168] Glenn D. Mittler interviews Eddie Durham 1981 (telephone interview)

[169] "All Girl Band To Be Here Thursday - Eddie Durham Orchestra to Play for Dance at Victory Lodge Hall." The Bristol Herald Courier (Tennessee), Sun. Oct. 24, 1943 p17

[170] Republican and Herald Newspaper (Pottsville, Pennsylvania) - Fri, May 14, 1943 Page 8

[171] "Music Matters" Edmonton Journal (Alberta, Canada) - Sat, May 6, 1944 - p18

[172] The Detroit Tribune (Detroit, Michigan) – Sat, Oct 16, 1943 – p14

[173] "Coming To The Cavern" Star-Phoenix (Saskatoon, Saskatchewan, Canada) - 19 May 1944 – p4

[174] The World of Count Basie by Stanley Dance 1980 p69 (1971 interview)

[175] Glenn Miller Archive - University of Colorado Boulder, "A Portrait of Glenn Miller" Produced by Dennis M. Spragg, p16 Updated April 2018

[176] Kansas City Jazz From Ragtime to Bebop-A History by Frank Driggs and Chuck Haddix 2005 p193, 195-196

[177] Listening In with Ben Gross, Daily News (New York, New York) - Thu, Jun 6, 1940 - last para, Page 128

[178] Broadway by Danton Walker "Cabarabian Nites" Daily News (New York, New York) - Wed, June 19, 1940 - para 3, Page 440

[179] Jazz Cavalcade: The Inside Story Of Jazz by Dave Dexter, Jr. 2011 De Capo Press, NY

[180] Jazz Cavalcade: The Inside Story Of Jazz by Dave Dexter, Jr. 2011 De Capo Press, NY

[181] Kansas City Jazz From Ragtime to Bebop-A History by Frank Driggs and Chuck Haddix 2005 p199-200 and footnotes

[182] Downbeat Magazine 6th Guitar Issue "Held Notes: Eddie Durham." By George Hoefer July 19, 1962 p57

[183] The World of Count Basie by Stanley Dance 1980 p68 (1971 interview)

[184] Smithsonian Oral History Series 1978 (IJS Rutgers University) interview by Stanley Dance

[185] "Mixed Team Composes Hit Tune" The Pittsburgh Courier, Sat. Aug 23, 1941 p21

[186] Phil Schaap with Eddie Durham, Birthday Broadcast August 1986 (live interview-WKCR -FM 89.9 Columbia University Radio NYC)

[187] Hamp by Lionel Hampton with James Haskins 1989 p.45-46,55

[188] Morning Glory A Biography of Mary Lou Williams by Linda Dahl 1999 p90-101

[189] Kansas City Jazz From Ragtime to Bebop-A History by Frank Driggs and Chuck Haddix 2005 p197

[190] "Swing band players have been swinging for decades" The Bayton Sun Newspaper Article (Baytown, Texas) 16 Apr 1986 interview by Mary Campbell p25

[191] "Stompin' At The Savoy" by Frank Butler. The Vancouver Sun (British Columbia, Canada) Thu, Aug 28, 1969 - p.79

[192] Phil Schaap's interview with Eddie Durham, Birthday Broadcast August 1986 (live on WKCR -FM 89.9 Columbia University Radio NYC)

[193] Ibid.

[194] Facebook post October 6, 2017 Emir Pekmez

[195] (source: Wikipedia) http://www.recordingpioneers.com/RP_NEWMAN2.html. Notes: These (Esoteric 548) titles were also released on Charlie Christian-Dizzy Gillespie 1941 Historical Performances (Vogue 600135)."

[196] Topsy M. Durham's interview with acoustic bassist Theodore Wilson, III 2000 (videotaped by Joseph "Nemo Joly & transcribed by Topsy M. Durham)

[197] Jazz Mavericks of the Lone Star State, by Dave Oliphant 2007 p177

[198] C.J. Hazevoet's "Don Byas Discography 1938-1946"

[199] "Musicians: It's Important for Kids to Discover Jazz" Petoskey News-Review (Michican) Tue, Apr 24, 1984 p8

[200] Topsy M. Durham's interview with organist/pianist/bandleader Sarah McLawler 2003 (videotaped by Joseph 'Nemo' Joly)

[201] Ibid. Trumpeter Ms. Jean Davis

[202] "The World of Count Basie" by Stanley Dance 1980 p68 (1971 interview)

[203] "Jazz - Eddie Durham And The Ladies" by Nels Nelson, Jazz Columnist, Philadelphia Daily News (Pennsylvania) - Fri, Mar 27, 1987 p68

[204] "Paradise to Give Children's Party" Detroit Free Press (Detroit, Michigan) Tue, Dec 22, 1942 - Page 17

[205] "Private Bus Ban Heavy Blow To Many Bands" The Pittsburgh Courier (Pennsylvania) Sat, Mar 13, 1943 by Billy Howe (Theatrical Editor)

[206] The Bijou Blog hosted by Debbie Reynolds, August 24, 2009
http://matineeatthebijou.blogspot.com/2009/08/all-girl-bands-international.html

[207] "The sweethearts of jazz" by Valerie Colyer. The Age (Melbourne, Victoria, Australia) , Friday 8, August 1986 p 14

[208] "Eddie Durham Revue Direct From Broadway" Barksdale's Bark (Barksdale Field, Louisiana)-Sat, Aug 7, 1943 p1

[209] "Ella Fitzgerald, 4 Keys, Eddie Durham Featured At Apollo" The New York Age Newspaper, June 19, 1943 p10 and "Ella Fitzgerald on Apollo Revue With Eddie Durham" Oct 16, 1943 p10

[210] "I've Been Around" by Ted Yates (Publications) "The Weekly Review (Birmingham, Alabama) - Sat, Feb 19, 1944 - Page 7

[211] Topsy M. Durham's interview with organist/pianist/bandleader Sarah McLawler 2003 (videotaped by Joseph 'Nemo' Joly)

[212] Swing Shift "All-Girl" Bands of the 1940's by Sherrie Tucker 2000 p41, 71, 106

[213] "Eddie Durham and Girl Orchestra Here on Monday" Tampa Bay Times (St. Petersburg, Florida) Sun. Feb. 13, 1944 p28

[214] "Brings All-Girl Band To Birmingham" The Weekly Review (Alabama) Sat, Feb 26, 1944 p3

[215] "The T-Bone Walker Story Stormy Monday," by Helen Oakley Dance, Forward by B.B. King 1978 p46

[216] "American Women In Jazz 1900 to the Present, Their Words, Lives, and Music" by Sally Placksin 1982 p.150-151 (paperback)

24

[217] Topsy M. Durham's interview with organist/pianist/bandleader Sarah McLawler 2003 (videotaped by Joseph 'Nemo' Joly)

[218] "Eddie Durham and the quartet, the Durhamettes" The Winnipeg Tribune (Manitoba, Canada) Sat. May 13, 1944 and "Colored Girls' Band Challenges Male Swingsters In Own Field" ibid Fri, May 19, 1944 p11.

[219] Swing Shift "All-Girl" Bands of the 1940's by Sherrie Tucker 2000 p118, 153, 162, 229

[220] Citations belong to Dan Weinstein, Martin Williams (liner notes to RCA Vintage LP (LPV 514) "Count Basie in Kansas City 1930-32," Gunther Schuller (the books "Early Jazz" and "The Swing Era") and Ross Russell (the book "Jazz Style in Kansas City and the Southwest" Berkeley, Univ. CA Press, 1971 rpt. 1983).

[221] Phil Schaap's interview with Eddie Durham, Birthday Broadcast August 1986 (live on WKCR -FM 89.9 Columbia University Radio NYC)

[222] Discography provided by Ed Polic

[223] A study entitled: Mister "After You've Gone," a forgotten trumpeter, Frank "Fat Man" Humphries (tp, voc) 1913-1978 and record label scans, by Mario Schneeberger, 2001 and 2016, www.JazzDocumentation.ch (and photos)

[224] C.J. Hazevoet's "Don Byas Discography 1938-1946"

Made in the USA
Middletown, DE
11 October 2023

40640795R00139